UNDISC

SLO

To my mother, Betty Alexander, for all her love, help and support, and to my dear and greatly missed late father, Alex Alexander.

Tania Alexander was born in London in 1964. She started skiing when she was seven years old and has skied in a great many European resorts ranging from glitzy and fashionable places such as St Moritz to the lesser-known places that are reviewed in this book. She began her journalist career with *Time Out* magazine in 1985 where she worked for three years writing about sport and fitness and acting as their ski editor. She has contributed to several other national publications and writes a regular page for the *Mail on Sunday*'s 'You' magazine.

UNDISCOVERED
SLOPES

Tania Alexander

Macdonald
Queen Anne Press

A *Queen Anne Press* BOOK

© Tania Alexander 1989

First published in Great Britain in 1989 by
Queen Anne Press, a division of
Macdonald & Co (Publishers) Ltd
Headway House
66–73 Shoe Lane
London EC4P 4AB

A member of Maxwell Pergamon Publishing Corporation plc

Design and illustrations by Judith Clark
Maps by Hard Lines

British Library Cataloguing in Publication Data
Alexander, Tania
    Undiscovered slopes.
    1. Europe. Skiing resorts—Visitors' guides
    I. Title
    914'.04558
    ISBN 0-356-17933-8

PHOTOGRAPHS: All pictures, including the front cover, by Tim Barnett, except pages 1Top Hirschegg Tourist Office, 4Bottom Le Grand Bornand Tourist Office, 6B Les Sept Laux Tourist Office, 8T Les Gets Tourist Office, 8B Wildhaus Tourist Office, 9 ZEFA, 10–11 Zauchensee Tourist Office, 12T Greg Evans, 12B Denis Mitchell, 13T Felix Oppenheimer, 15T Club Turkey, 15B Flims Tourist Office.

Typeset by SB Datagraphics Ltd, Colchester
Printed and bound in Great Britain by
Richard Clay Ltd, Bungay, Suffolk

Contents

ACKNOWLEDGEMENTS

Additional research for this book was done by:

Ian Watson; Arnie Wilson; Charles Halifax; Conrad Brunner; Jill Crawshaw; Eva Faber; Jim and Helen Clenell; Willy Campbell; Don Perretta; Betty Alexander; Karin Silverstein.

Finally, I would like to thank the following organisations without whom this book would not have been possible:

Air Europe, Air France, Austrian Airlines, Dan Air, Swiss Air, Pegasus Skybus, Avis Car Hire, Ski Miquel, White Roc, Ski Total, Dynastar, The Ski Club of Great Britain, Douglas Cox Tyrie, and Executive Health Centres; Ellis Brigham; Sandie Barker; Ski La.

The Resorts

The resorts have been arranged alphabetically, under their country headings. Prices given are in local currency. These can only be a rough estimate, as they obviously fluctuate from season to season. Although you should not find hordes of British tourists at any of these resorts, some of them do get busy at peak times, such as Christmas/New Year and Easter. Unless you are taking your own children, I would advise avoiding the continental school holidays (usually February). The dates of the holidays vary from year to year and country to country, so it is best to check with the local tourist office before you book. I have listed the British companies that go to the resorts for addresses and phone numbers see page 197). This often changes from season to season so if you have a problem finding a company, please check with the local tourist office. All details are correct at time of writing, but remember that prices, hotels, restaurants etc are all susceptible to change.

OFF-PISTE WARNING!

The best way to get off the beaten track is to ski off-piste. However good a skier you are, the mountains are still potentially dangerous, so *please* never ski off-piste alone or without a qualified local guide.

MAPS

The piste maps in this book are intended as a general guide only. Skiers are advised to contact the resort tourist office upon arrival for a more detailed plan.

Introduction

When I first started skiing, I thought there were only a handful of European resorts worth visiting. Everyone seemed to rave about the same places (St Anton, Courchevel, Zermatt, Avoriaz etc), endorsed by conservative ski companies, books and magazines. The British skier has always tended to go where his or her friends ski. So Henry and Caroline head off for Verbier, Meribel or Val d'Isère, whilst Trevor and Sharon join their friends in Soll, Mayrhofen or Sauze d'Oulx. Personally, I don't know which is worse—dodging the Sloanes in their Barbour jackets whooping it up on Verbier's slopes, or counting how many times the empty lager cans roll across the coach floor on the way to Mayrhofen. If you're the sort of person who enjoys the camaraderie of such 'here-we-go' holidays, this book is not for you. You'll find plenty of information about these mainstream resorts in other books—or ask your friends.

This book is for anyone who, like myself, hates being herded together with hundreds of other British holidaymakers. Firstly, I must apologise to Mr Dick Yates-Smith, who no doubt hates this book. For this entrepreneur made his money by opening the famous Dick's T-Bar in Val d'Isère, which is almost entirely populated by Brits. You're practically guaranteed to bump into someone you know from back home. But for me, skiing is all about escapism. I go to the mountains to get away from everything—the last thing I want is to meet my accountant or next-door neighbour on my way down the pistes. This book is for the adventurous spirits who want to find their own private haven in the snow. It's for anyone who wants to try something slightly different, be it skiing in the midnight sun in Scandinavia or touring the tiny Austro-Italian villages in the South Tirol.

With the help of the tourist boards, friends in the industry, a dedicated team of researchers and other skiers' recommendations, I've found over 30 superb resorts

9

that are not packed with Brits. This is not to say that the occasional discerning British skier will not have already been there, but the mass market has not cottoned on to them yet. One of the moral difficulties when writing about anything that's 'undiscovered' is that you risk spoiling the place. But there's more than enough skiing in Europe to accommodate us all and as many of the resorts I mention don't have an enormous bed capacity, I don't foresee any of them ever becoming a Benidorm of the Alps.

I've grouped the resorts in countries. As you've probably all been skiing at least once or twice, you'll know how each country has its own characteristics— eg the Austrian resorts make up in atmosphere what they lose in height; the French resorts are usually purpose-built for convenience. But it would be unfair to generalise about any of the resorts I've covered. They are all special in their own way and distinctive in character—Andermatt, a striking Swiss military town; Uludag, Turkey's premier ski resort on Mount Olympus; Le Grand Bornand, a pretty French market town; and many more. They vary in size and facilities—I can't say which is best. It's up to you to choose which you find most appealing.

I wouldn't be so bold as to boast that all the resorts will offer skiing as challenging or extensive as well-known areas such as Les Trois Vallées. But unless you're in training for the next Olympics, you should find plenty to keep you occupied. You may in fact find you ski more in some of these smaller resorts, as there is often less queueing. What's the point of going to Verbier, if you spend half the day in the lift queue? As some of these resorts are less built-up, there is also often more scope for off-piste. Most British skiers only have one, or if they are lucky, two weeks skiing a year. Unless you're up at dawn and out skiing all day there is a limit to how many runs you can do. If you *are* a kilometre-freak, I've included a couple of resorts linked into big well-known circuits—Les Gets in the Portes du Soleil, and Stuben in the Arlberg and St Anton circuit. Or you may like to try the Italian Dolomites which comprise 1,050 km of pistes, and nearly 500 lifts, all under one lift pass. That should keep you busy. I have also included a chapter on 'exotic' ski destinations such as Argentina, Chile, India and Japan.

One of the problems that once-a-year skiers have is getting off that 'intermediate plateau'. You spend the first few days getting your ski legs back, start to enjoy yourself by the middle of the week, and only begin to improve when it's time to go home. I've spoken to various experts such as Ali Ross and Sarah Ferguson who give advice on how to get off this plateau.

Finally there's a chapter for all those, akin to my own heart, who like doing things just for the thrill of it. A winter sports holiday does not need to be limited to traditional downhill. Why not join the piste poseurs and learn to mono-ski, snow-surf, hang-glide or paraglide. For an unforgettable experience, I'd recommend heli-skiing. In true James Bond style, you're dumped off by helicopter at the top of a mountain. From here you can descend slopes that would otherwise be unaccessible to mankind. It is an amazing feeling to carve the first tracks down a field of virgin snow. Europe is full of undiscovered slopes. Hopefully, this book will bring them a little closer to you.

Austria

Austria is the best-known skiing country for the British. Thousands of beginners take their first tentative steps on skis on Austrian snow. The ski brochures are full of little Austrian villages, some such as Mayrhofen which are overspilling with Brits. But there are still some very good resorts which have not been overrun by British package tour operators.

It is easy to understand why people love skiing in Austria. Most of the ski resorts are in small farming communities—authentic rustic villages rather than soulless purpose-built resorts. New developments have been carefully put together in traditional wooden style—you are very unlikely to see any architectural eyesores in Austria. Instead, you will find pretty picture-postcard villages, usually dominated by an onion-domed church, clustered round by snow-topped buildings with wooden balconies and painted stucco. It is the atmosphere that makes Austria such an attractive holiday location. *Gemütlichkeit* is the special word used to describe that inviting blend of cosiness, warmth and friendliness. The locals are very welcoming and seem to have much more time for you than most other ski nations. Skiing in Austria is more leisurely than in other countries. In France, there is a tendency to fight until the death to get on the lifts. The surly lift-men let everyone get on with it. In Austria, the lifts slow down for you get on and there is often a little man who wipes the snow off the seat first.

Austria is an excellent place to learn to ski. Their famous national ski schools may be rather old-fashioned, but they do teach with an admirable amount of patience and precision. Classes are usually for a full rather than a half-day. They really are determined to teach you to ski. Aggressive, experienced skiers may find many Austrian resorts too limiting, although St Anton and its neighbouring Arlberg villages have some of the most challenging slopes in the world. Areas

11

such as Salzburgerland have also spent a lot of money in expanding their lift connections so there are now 'ski circuses', such as Saalbach/Hinterglemm, where you can ski a circuit of the valley. There are other big ski areas, such as Zauchensee (100 km) which are not well-known by the Brits.

Most Austrian resorts are at low altitude but this does not necessarily mean that they are a bad bet for snow. In the disastrous 1988/89 season, Austrian resorts fared better than anywhere else. However, if you are the sort of person who likes to put your skis on in the hotel and slide straight on to the slopes, you should check which resort you are going to. Most of the skiing in Austria is above the villages, so you may have to walk, catch a bus, or take several lifts to get up there.

When most people talk about skiing in Austria, they think of the Tirol, the area around Innsbruck. Although this is a charming province, most of it is now commercialised. Salzburgerland is one of the smallest and most beautiful of the Austrian provinces and still has some excellent undiscovered resorts such as Altenmarkt/Zauchensee, Dorfgastein and Neukirchen. Karnten (Carinthia) is not such a well-known province apart from being the home of Franz Klammer. The skiing here is split into two main regions, the Tauern mountains in the north and the Karawanken range in the south. This southern region borders onto Yugoslavia and Italy. The Voralberg is in the western-tip of Austria, bordered by Switzerland, Liechtenstein, Italy and West Germany. It includes Austria's most challenging network of Lech and Zürs which are linked to the Arlberg resorts of St Anton, Stuben and St Christoph.

A holiday in Austria is about more than just skiing. Most villages have plenty of other activities such as ice-skating, curling, sleigh-rides and cleared paths for walking. The hotels often have fitness facilities such as swimming pools, saunas and weight-rooms. Many of the resorts are close to the airports so transfer times are short and you can often have a day's excursion to the enchanting cities of Salzburg or Innsbruck. If you have a car, it is also very scenic to drive over the Brenner Pass into the South Tirol and do some duty-free shopping (leather and liquor are particularly good buys).

The après-ski in Austria is a major attraction. There are usually plenty of little rustic *hüttes* on the slopes where you can stop off for a quick schnapps in between skiing. This national firewater is guaranteed to warm you up on the coldest of days, and there are also several delicious hot drinks such as *jägatee* (tea with schnapps), *grög* (tea with rum) or the famous *glühwein* (hot wine with water, cinnamon, cloves and sugar). In the Arlberg there are ice bars outside in the snow where they play oom-pah-pah music. Austria is a land of sounds. Wherever you go, be it the ski lifts, tea houses, bars or restaurants, you are likely to hear their jolly national tunes. The Austrians love to sing, play instruments and dance. Their famous tea dances range from stomping about in ski boots in a little *hütte* to smart, full-scale hotel functions. Austrian tea rooms are enough to tempt the staunchest dieter with *apfelstrudel* (flaky pastry containing thinly sliced apples, raisins and cinnamon) and *sachertorte* (chocolate cake with a layer of apricot jam). In the evening, many of the bars have a dance floor—unlike in France there is no entry fee. In the less-commercialised villages, these are good places to meet the locals and watch them dance cheek-to-cheek in old-fashioned waltz-style.

Austrian cuisine is meat-based with lots of *schwinefleisch* (pork) and *kalbfleisch* (veal). Alpine specialities include *leberknödelsuppe* (liver dumpling soup), *kartoffelsuppe* (potato soup with sour cream and caraway), *schinkenplatte* (cured ham with gherkins and pickled onions) *käsespätzle* (little dumplings with cheese) and *germeknödl* (sweet steamed dumplings filled with plum jam and served with hot butter and poppy seeds).

Accommodation is of a very high standard. Their apartments are much, much larger and of better quality than you will find in France. A *pension haus* is a family house where you can get bed and breakfast. A *gasthaus* is like an inn with a restaurant. Most of their hotels are family-run and very clean and comfortable. Wherever you stay, whether it is a little pension haus or a plush hotel, you are guaranteed to feel at home.

Exchange rate (June 1989): £1 = 21 S

FURTHER INFORMATION:

Austrian National Tourist Office, 30 St George Street, London W1R OAL (Tel: 01 629 0461).

DORFGASTEIN

- **HEIGHT OF RESORT**
  830 m.

- **HIGHEST LIFT**
  2027 m.

- **WHY GO THERE?**
  Good skiing for intermediates and advanced.
  Reasonable prices.
  Little queueing.

- **WHO GOES THERE?**
  Germans.
  Austrians, particularly the Viennese.

- **COMPANIES THAT GO THERE**
  None.

Dorfgastein is one of three traditional resorts in the long and awe-inspiring Gastein valley in Salzburgerland. This valley used to be a favourite sojourn of the Hapsburgs (the former Austrian Royal Family). The best-known of the resorts is Badgastein, a spa resort that was in its hey-day about 20 years ago. There are still some grand buildings, but it is certainly not a trendy resort and does not attract a young clientele. Bad Hofgastein is smaller, also with thermal baths. Dorfgastein is the quietest and cheapest of these three resorts. It is a simple, unspoilt village, typically Austrian in layout with a square and church in the centre. There are not many shops. It is more informal and friendly than the other resorts, although it does suffer from a lack of sun as it is stacked up high on the eastern hillside of the valley. I must have seen it at its worst in January, when it was cold and dark. Most of the tourists are German or Austrian, looking for a quiet, reasonably-priced place to stay with the kudos of grandiose Badgastein only 15 minutes away by car. The ski lift departure is above the village, about 5-10 minutes' walk. There is a free ski bus. A car would be an advantage, especially if you want to go into Badgastein or Bad Hofgastein at night. There are also some hotels next to the Dorfgastein lift station.

THE SKIING

This is a superb area for skiing, particularly for intermediates and experts. The runs in this area tend to be long and offer lots of variety in both the types of piste and scenery. Dorfgastein is a good base as it tends to be overlooked by the more affluent skiers who ski further up the valley. Snow permitting, you can ski back down to the village at the end of the day. There are 80 km of pistes (250 km in the Gastein Valley). In Dorfgastein, the majority of these are red, but there are also five blues and one black. They are all north-facing which helps keep the snow, as long as you can bear the cold. It is for this reason that it is not a good family resort. The nursery area is low down, at the bottom of the chair-lifts. Snow is guaranteed through the use of canons, but the lower slopes can be very cold and icy at the beginning of the season. Dorfgastein has a compact efficient lift system (21 in total). It is possible to do a ski safari over Fulseck to Grossarl. This can be done by using only three lifts and the inexperienced intermediate can accomplish it by using a blue and a red run. There is plenty of opportunity for off-piste, particularly in the Kreuzkogel area. The slopes here benefit from getting the sun early in the day and there are some excellent bump runs. Good skiers who have travelled by car would benefit from buying the Gastein Super Ski Card which gives them access to 54 lifts and 250 km of pistes. This also gives free use of the valley's interconnecting buses and trains. The nearest access to the rest of the skiing in this valley is at Bad Hofgastein where there is a funicular railway connecting with a cable car to the main Schlossalm (2,050 m) ski area. Bad Hofgastein is about 10 minutes away by car.

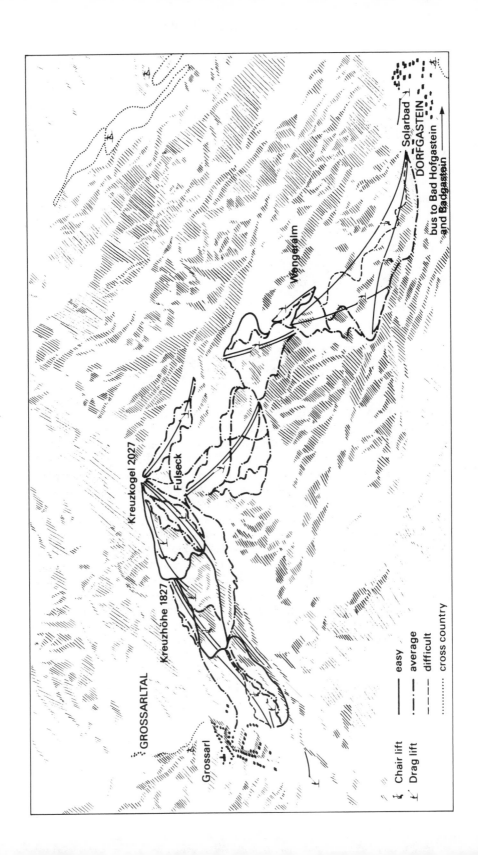

GROSSARLTAL

Grossarl

Kreuzhöhe 1827

Kreuzkogel 2027

Fulseck

Wengeralm

Solarbad
DORFGASTEIN

bus to Bad Hofgastein
and Badgastein

Chair lift   easy
Drag lift   average
              difficult
              cross country

CROSS-COUNTRY

Limited. 30 km of prepared tracks on the valley floor.

SKI SCHOOL

(Tel: 064 33 538 or 447).
Group lessons start on Mondays, 950S for six days (4 hours per day). 1,440S private lessons (4 hours). They offer ski safaris to all the other areas included in the Gastein lift pass; also cross-country lessons. Ski kindergarten (3-15 years old).

LIFT PASSES

Schischaukel-Dorfgastein. 80 km, 22 lifts. 1,050S (550S kids). Children under six ski free. Gastein Super Ski Card. 250 km, 54 lifts. 1,400S (850S kids). Lifts are free for children under six.

WHERE TO EAT, DRINK & BOOGIE

There are lots of rustic *hüttes* to stop off for a quick schnapps or snack when you are skiing. Several of these also offer meals and accommodation. There are more restaurants on the Grossarl side of the mountain. There are also a couple of good restaurants near the Dorfgastein lift station. I would recommend Pension Schihäusl which does wonderful local food such as cheese soup and special dumplings. There are 10 restaurants in the village, including one pizzeria, and several bars. The cuisine tends to be traditional Gastein food rather than international. The most expensive hotels in the village, Kirchenwirt and Römerhof, both serve typical Austrian cuisine. Cafe St Rupert makes excellent home-made pizza, and wonderful ice-creams. They have a nine-pin bowling alley—scoring a strike is an excellent excuse for another few schnapps. Nightlife is quiet—the highlight of the week is the Ski disco (floodlight skiing to music) which happens every Wednesday 6 pm-10 pm. There are also two proper discos, Kuh-Bar and K-Keller. The Kuh-Bar is popular for golden oldies every Thursday. Don't expect Acid House. If you want something livelier, go to Badgastein where they have everything from tea dancing to a casino. Bad Hofgastein also has a good selection of bars and discos. But swimming in Badgastein's or Bad Hofgastein's thermal baths is much more popular than boogying all night, and much kinder on those aching limbs.

WHAT ELSE TO DO THERE

Hang-gliding and parascending—international meeting every January.
Floodlit tobogganing every Wednesday.
Solarbad—outdoor heated swimming pool at bottom of lift station with sauna, massage and solarium.
Automatic bowling alley.
Thermal baths in Bad Hofgastein and Badgastein.

WHERE TO STAY

There are no big plush hotels in Dorfgastein. Most of the accommodation is in gasthaus, pension haus or apartments. They do have a good selection of mid-range hotels. At the top end of the range are the Hotel Kirchenwirt (Tel: 064 33 251) 550-580S half board, and the Hotel-Restaurant Römerhof (Tel: 064 33 209) 420-650S half board. Gasthof Pension Schihäusl (Tel: 064 33 248) is next to the slopes. 440S-465S half board.

IN CASE OF EMERGENCY

Doctor in the resort: One.
Nearest Chemist: Bad Hofgastein.
Nearest Dentist: Bad Hofgastein.
Nearest Hospital: Schwarzach St Veit (15 km) or Zell am See (35 km).
Helicopter Rescue: Yes.

HOW TO GET THERE

Nearest Airport: Salzburg.
Transfer time: $1\frac{1}{2}$ hours.
Train connection: Dorfgastein.

FURTHER INFORMATION

Tourist Office A-5632 Dorfgastein, Salzburgerland (Tel: 064 33 277).

HINTERSTODER

- **HEIGHT OF RESORT**
  600 m.

- **HIGHEST LIFT**
  2,050 m.

- **WHY GO THERE?**
  Good snow record.
  Value for money.
  Confidence-building skiing for beginners/intermediates.

- **WHO GOES THERE?**
  Austrian families.
  Germans and the Dutch.

- **COMPANIES THAT GO THERE**
  Ski Miguel.

Hinterstoder is the epitome of *gemütlichkeit*—the Austrian word for friendliness and cosy charm. It is a quiet little resort in Upper Austria, about 75 km from Linz. It is not the prettiest of villages as it is spread out along one main road. But it has a certain laid-back charm—the perfect place for non-aggressive skiers to escape for a few days. The village comprises about seven hotels, several guest houses, apartments and chalets, an onion-domed church, a supermarket, a couple of tea rooms, and a few bars and restaurants. It is certainly not a sophisticated resort—if you're looking for a glitzy nightlife don't come here. This is a place for someone who wants a simple unpretentious holiday, cheaper than the better-known Austrian resorts. Hinterstoder is very traditional—the ski shop I went to was staffed by an old Austrian man who was dressed in breeches and braces, like an old-fashioned toymaker. He spent a long time choosing me the best equipment—it seemed that nothing in the world could have hurried him.

Most of the hotels and restaurants are staffed by pretty local girls in traditional costume. In the discos (yes, there are two in Hinterstoder) the youngsters hold hands and dance waltz-style to the latest chart sounds. But there is more going on than at first meets the eye. The drinking and merriment in the bars goes on until well into the early hours of the morning, although outside in the street it is so quiet you can hear every footstep.

The locals are very friendly. On the first day, I was walking down the street to the tourist office when a sprightly grey-haired man bounded across the road and asked me if I needed any help. I later discovered that he was Helmut Mayr, the director of the ski school, who makes a point of getting to know all the tourists. Last season, Hinterstoder had some of the best snow in Europe. Other resorts were trying to bus skiers in but the police closed off the village whenever it got too crowded.

THE SKIING

The skiing in and around Hinterstoder is more extensive than it looks. A new six-seater gondola takes you up to Huttererböden (1,400 m) from where most of Hinterstoder's pistes are visible. As the area is so compact, it is very safe for families. There are two baby lifts and a small nursery slope for beginners. The next stage is a drag-lift (*schullift*) up to a short but fairly steep blue run. One rather nervous beginner I spoke to said she found the skiing too hard, although in perfect snow conditions I don't think there would be a problem.

Second-year skiers should find the skiing ideal. Ambitious intermediates and expert skiers would probably be bored after a day or two. The pistes are all below the treeline so visiblity is always good and it is very picturesque. As all the runs radiate down to a central area, it is easy to see if there are any queues. Usually queueing is not a problem—I was there in February when all the schools were on holiday and at a time when skiers were being bussed in from other resorts. Even then, I never waited more than 15 minutes. From the Huttererböden there is a long chair-lift (12 minutes) up to Hutterer Höss (1,858 m). This gives access to a long easy blue run or a choice of reds. The red run nearest to the drag lift is very narrow and moguly.

Between the drag-lift and the chair-lift there are also two unpisted and challenging red runs. From Hutterer Höss expert skiers can take a steep moguly black run which can be very difficult if the conditions are not good. The black turns into a red run at the bottom. Another chair-lift will take you up to the top again with a choice of the long easy blue or another black. At the end of the day there is a long winding blue run towards the village. Alternatively you can ski down from the middle station to the village on an invigorating red run. There is plenty of opportunity for off-piste in the trees between the pistes. There are also ski touring possibilities. Bärenalmbahn (660 m-1,150 m) is 10 minutes away by ski bus and has five runs including a World Cup downhill. Spital is about 30 minutes' bus-ride from Hinterstoder and is included in the same lift pass. The skiing here is easier than at Hinterstoder, perfect for families and beginners. The ski area is reached by a little train that plays Austrian yodelling music. Although they do not have as many lifts, the runs are long and interesting. I particularly enjoyed the wide flat blue run from Gammeringsattel (1,605 m) down to the bottom—perfect cruising at the end of the day.

Snowboarding is very popular in Hinterstoder. The daughter of the owner of the Stoderhof Hotel was the Women's World Champion and her brother is champion of Austria. There is a half-pipe at the middle station and some excellent steep off-piste for snowboarding. The resort can also arrange special

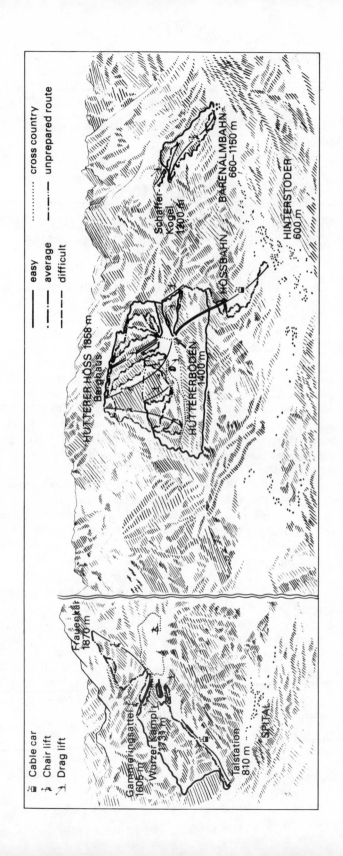

'Fun' weeks which comprise three days' snowboard tuition and three days' paragliding.

CROSS-COUNTRY

28 km of marked cross-country runs in the valley as well as a peak run on the Huttererböden.

SKI SCHOOL

(Tel: 075 64 50 50).

The ski school is run by the friendly Helmut Mayr. His instructors (15 full time, 35 in high season) are an intelligent bunch, many of whom are also studying academic subjects. Reports from guests in the Stoderhof Hotel were very favourable. One English group had a private instructor called Manfred for the week, who was so excellent that they immediately booked him up for the following season. The ski school uses video analysis and tries to introduce skiers to powder and demanding terrain as soon as possible. At the end of the week there is an ability test and a race. Cross-country instruction is available. They also teach snowboarding. The ski school operates from the middle station. Five days (four hours per day) 850S. Snowboarding 480S for three half-days. Cross-country 480S for three half-days. There is a ski kindergarten for three years and older. 1,080S for five days, including lunch and day care. Children's ski lessons (four years and older) 850S for five days.

LIFT PASSES

930S for six days. Covers Hinterstoder, Höss, Bärenalm and Wurzeralmbahne, Spritrigl and Wurbauerkogellifte, Spital. Free ski bus.

WHERE TO EAT, DRINK & BOOGIE

There are five places to eat on the Hinterstoder slopes. Most people congregate at the middle station where there are a couple of uninspiring-looking places serving sausages and chips. If, like me, you are not a great sausage fan, I would give these places a miss, particularly in high season when there is a lot of queueing. Provided you don't mind walking uphill a bit, the best place for lunch is the Berghotel which does both Austrian specialities and international cuisine. Their spaghetti with mussel sauce was delicious. In Spital, I would recommend the friendly little rustic eating house, the Linzerhaus.

Après-ski in Hinterstoder starts as soon as you've clomped down the metal stairs at the bottom lift station. Everyone congregates at the tiny Bosner Hütte, a wooden kiosk where they play jolly Austrian music. There are no seats, but skiers are happy to stand around outside chatting and drinking jägatee or the house speciality *Schneekanone* (a hot creamy alcoholic drink). If you have a sweet tooth you can have tea at Cafe Annemarie or Cafe-Konditorei Gollner. Most of the eating is in hotels. I can well recommend the Stoderhof, where Herr

Fruhmann, the owner, is also the chef. We had some delicious meals there and my vegetarian friend was particularly impressed by the special dishes prepared for her.

Poppengut (Tel: 075 64 52 68) is a smart hotel just outside of the village. This has an excellent restaurant where you can eat pepper steaks, and a rustic pizzeria in the basement, popular with the young locals. As it is a long walk to go on spec, it is advisable to book.

There are not many bars in Hinterstoder, so it does not take long to get to know everyone staying in the village. My favourite was the Siglu Pub which looks like a goldfish bowl turned upside down. This small glass bar is open until the early hours of the morning. The Post Bar gets busy after midnight. This is a basement bar/disco—you have to bang on the door to be let in. It is all very seventies—fluorescent lights and out-of-date music, but this does not seem to stop the Austrian swingers enjoying themselves. Finally, you should pay a visit to Tanz-Café Stockerberg in Vorderstoder, about 10 minutes by car from Hinterstoder. This is a lively restaurant/disco which has special 'bone-eating' nights twice a week, when for about 100S you can have a drink and eat as many barbecued ribs as you like. They also do *raclette* evenings. Although the drinks are not expensive, it is easy to spend a lot of money here as they have a special drinking game. This involves trying to hammer nails into a large tree trunk. The more hammered you get, the harder this is! If yours is the last nail in, you buy the round—traditionally some lethal concoction of brandy and coke. As most people leave the Stockerberg legless, there is a free taxi service back to Hinterstoder.

WHAT ELSE TO DO THERE

Ice skating (on a frozen swimming pool). Curling.
Sleigh rides.
Tobogganing.
Paragliding.
Hang-gliding.
Fitness centre.
Swimming at Hotel Stoderhof or Berghotel (only if you are staying there).
30 km of prepared walks.

WHERE TO STAY

Hotel Stoderhof (Tel: 075 64 52 66) is a good family-run hotel only a couple of minutes' walk from the lifts. It is a large modern chalet-style building with an attractive pine interior, a stylish bar and clean and comfortable rooms. They also have a small indoor swimming pool made of aluminium (rather like swimming in a washing-up sink!), a well-equipped gymnasium and a sauna. It is very much a family set-up: father does the cooking, mother runs the hotel, the son is a champion snowboarder and teaches in the ski school when he is not racing. The daughter runs an excellent massage and beauty business in the hotel. The massage and facial I had there were superb. From 550S–690S half board per night. The Berghotel (Tel: 075 64 54 21) is a large luxurious chalet-style hotel, 10 km from the village. It is accessible by car but snow chains are advisable. Although it is very convenient for skiing as it is near the middle station (1,400 m), the hotel is rather cut off in the evening. It is a comfortable hotel with an excellent restaurant and pampering facilities such as an indoor swimming pool with underwater massage jets, solarium, sauna, masseur and children's playroom. It is owned by Dr Sedlak who has a medical practice in the hotel. From 510S per night half board. Hinterstoder also has plenty of guest houses, chalets and apartments. Full details from the Tourist Office (see below).

IN CASE OF EMERGENCY

Doctor in the resort: One.
Chemist in the resort: One.
Nearest Dentist: Windischgarten (15 km).
Nearest Hospital: Kirchdorf (20 km).
Helicopter Rescue: Yes.

HOW TO GET THERE

Nearest Airport: Linz or Salzburg.
Transfer time: One hour by train from Linz. $2\frac{1}{2}$ hours by train from Salzburg. $1\frac{3}{4}$ hours by coach from Salzburg.
Train connection: Direct from Linz to Hinterstoder station, then 15 minutes by bus. From Salzburg via Linz.

FURTHER INFORMATION

Tourist Office Hinterstoder, A-4573 (Tel: 075 64 52 63).

KLEINWALSERTAL

Politically and economically, Kleinwalsertal is rather unusual. Territorially it is in Austria, but the only approach is through Germany. Local currency is the Deutschmark, and even the beer (and very good it is too) is Bavarian. The

23

- **HEIGHT OF RESORT**
  1,100 m.

- **HIGHEST LIFT**
  2,100 m.

- **WHY GO THERE?**
  Politically and economically interesting region.
  A busy, sophisticated area with plenty of opportunity for shopping and entertainment.
  Lack of British tourists.
  A second-generation resort that has not become too commercial.

- **WHO GOES THERE?**
  Serious skiers and mountaineers (Mittelberg).
  Jet set (Riezlern).
  Local weekenders.
  Independent travellers who want to avoid being packaged.
  90 per cent West German, 5 per cent Dutch, the rest Belgian, American and English.

- **COMPANIES THAT GO THERE**
  None.

atmosphere, however, is Austro-Swiss. Taxes are paid to Vienna in Austria but VAT refunds are sent from Bonn in Germany. In order to send a postcard home, you will need an Austrian stamp, but will pay for it in Deutschmarks. To confuse things even further, the local dialect shows signs of Swiss origins.

The Kleinwalsertal is a mountain valley in the Voralberg, 1,100 m to 1,250 m above sea level. There are three picture-postcard villages spread out along the valley—Riezlern, Hirschegg and Mittelberg. The valley was first inhabited seven centuries ago by people from Wallis who brought with them a tradition of wooden houses built into the hillsides. They called it the 'Valley of the Breitach' after the foaming stream that gushes through the valley.

Riezlern attracts the Rhineland jet set and snow bunnies and has its own casino. There is also an old part of Riezlern, dominated by the ancient parish church with its murals and ceiling paintings by the Munich artist Martin von Feuerstein. Hirschegg is the place to stay if you are in search of an authentic village. This is set on the sunny side of the valley, with sturdy rustic houses. Hirschegg also has the Walserhaus, a rustically built festival centre where many events are held. This centre houses the tourist office, ski-pass office, library, festival hall, conference rooms, restaurants and kids rooms and holds pottery, wood-carving and painting courses. There is even a peasant theatre. The whole valley and its mountains used to be known as the Mittelberg. Today, it is only the highest village 'in the midst of the mountains' which bears this name.

Mittelberg is quiet and attracts families and sportspeople. There is one other hamlet called Baad, which is rather dead now that the Kuhstalli disco is rarely in operation, and is best appreciated by real sporty hearties. Mittelberg and Baad are at the far end of the valley, where the massive cliff faces close off the Kleinwalsertal from its Austrian homeland.

Exchange rate (June 1989): £1 = 3 DM

THE SKIING

The skiing in Kleinwalsertal is best for beginners and intermediates but there is something to suit every skier with 80 km of pistes. Most of the runs are blue (40). There are also 12 reds and one black. All the villages have their own nursery slopes. The Kleinwalsertal is spread out, but there is an excellent free ski bus service—one of the few in the Alps which runs regularly, reliably and early and late enough to be of real use to skiers. I never used the car once to go skiing in this area.

Kleinwalsertal has a superb snow record—it is quite normal to find up to two metres of snow in early April. The most beautiful time to ski there is in springtime when the late snow in the mountains contrasts with the valley blossoming below.

There are three main areas—Kanzelwand, Walmendingerhorn and Ifen 2,000. Kanzelwand is accessible from Riezlern via a rather antiquated gondola. This area is an intermediate's paradise with a wonderful 2.5 km red (more like pink) run from the top to the bottom. Intermediates could easily ski just in this area for two days without getting bored as the Kanzelwand links into the Fellhorn area of Germany.

Ifen 2,000 is just outside Hirschegg and is linked to the village by the ski bus. This area actually goes up to 2,100 m. At the end of their first week, most beginners should easily be able to ski the 7 km Gleitweg from the summit of the lifts back to the bottom station. (NB: Do not be tempted to stop off for refreshments at the Aven Hütte restaurant at the bottom as, despite its rustic wooden ski lodge appearance, it is a nasty expensive self-service place with surly staff.)

Walmendingerhorn, above Baad and Mittelberg, is often called 'Humdinger-horn' as, although it only has a few lifts, there is unlimited off-piste. The Walmendingerhorn gives access to some very steep off-piste over to Schwarzwassertal. This should only be attempted by experts, and *never* without a guide. There is also some good powder on Gehrenhang, an off-piste route between the top of Kanzelwand and the village of Riezlern.

Queueing can be a problem at weekends on the access lifts. I soon discovered that the trick is to get there before 9.30 am as this is when the ski buses arrive and queues build up. The ski schools start at 10 am. At weekends, the locals, who refuse to queue, head off to the tiny Heuberg area behind Walserhaus and then ski Gleitweg, Heuberg, Mittelberg and Hirschegg, which are linked by a *gleitweg* (transit piste).

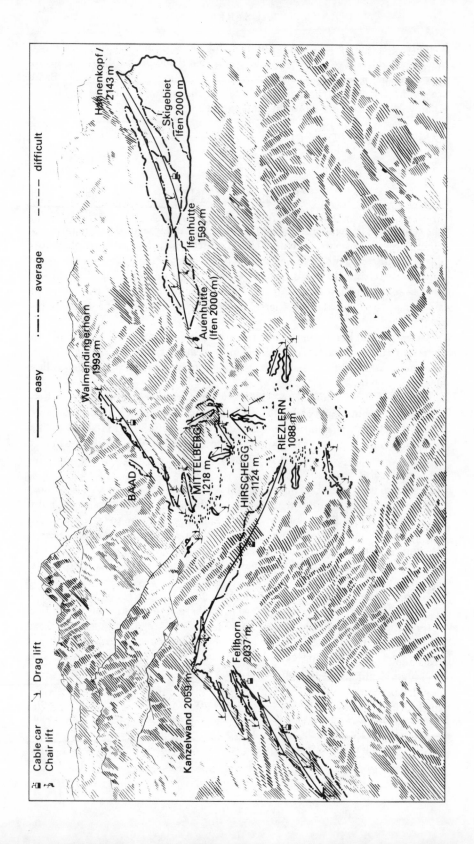

Cable car
Chair lift

Drag lift

easy
average
difficult

Kanzelwand 2059 m

Walmendingerhorn 1993 m

BAAD

MITTELBERG 1218 m

Felthorn 2037 m

HIRSCHEGG 1124 m

RIEZLERN 1088 m

Auenhütte (Ifen 2000 m)

Ifenhütte 1592 m

Skigebiet Ifen 2000 m

Hahnenkopf / 2143 m

There is a lot of alternative skiing in Kleinwalsertal including mono-ski, snowboard, and freestyle. There are also special snowboarding weeks, glacier and touring weeks, or even skiing and tennis weeks.

CROSS-COUNTRY

44 km of cross-country skiing tracks including high-altitude 3 km ring 'loipe' at Ifen 2,000.

SKI SCHOOL

There are eight ski schools with approximately 350 ski instructors. Toni Brewer's School in Riezlern has the highest proportion of English-speaking instructors. There are also two children's ski schools, ski-bob school, cross-country ski school and a school for ski touring and ski mountaineering.125DM for five days (115DM kids). Private lessons 180DM per day.

LIFT PASSES

About 162-177DM for six days (119-129DM kids). Includes ski bus and all three Oberstdorf areas.

WHERE TO EAT, DRINK & BOOGIE

There are plenty of restaurants and huts on the slopes. In Kanzelwand, the Adlerhorst is a wooden hut with a large sun terrace, sheltered from the wind, where everyone strips off. I even saw a couple of women sunbathing topless! There are ice bars at the top and middle stations on Ifen. The Ifenhütte, at the middle station, is a good place for lunch. In Walmendinger, the Bühlalpe is a hotel in the middle of the run down to the valley. Watch out you don't make my mistake of drinking too much of their Obstler (Lake Constance Schnapps). The Kleinwalsertal is a lively place after skiing with lots of restaurants, cafes and bars. The most sophisticated nightlife is in Riezlern where there are bars and nightclubs playing good live music and a casino with roulette, black jack, slot-machines and baccarat. There is dancing to live music from 4 pm at the Cafe Amely.

There are about 60 restaurants in the valley serving everything from Bavarian and Austrian to Italian, Chinese and French cuisine. Dinner *à deux* costs about 60DM-100DM. A glühwein is about 4.50DM, a pint of Bavarian beer about 3.30DM. The Bistro in Hirschegg is run by Andi and Jimmi and is a popular bar with the locals. There is a pizzeria next door. The Kreuzkeller is a rustic drinking house. In Mittelberg *the* place is Charivari—a loud and cheerful 'pub' where there are crude mottos on the walls and they play rustic games like *naglen* (hammering nails into a tree-trunk—last one in buys the round, see page 22). The Zwolfer Pils Bar is popular with the local ski instructors. One of them warned me to beware of the 'bum-biting postman'—very strange. If you are looking for something with a little more class, go to S Bodmer, a smooth piano bar in the Steinbeck Hotel. The Almhoff Rupp is a restaurant in Reizlern that has won many awards. It is expensive. The Hallers Kegel Stube does some of the best steaks in town and is very reasonable: about 45DM for two including drinks. This restaurant is particularly welcoming to children before 7 pm. In Hirschegg I would recommend eating at the pizzeria next to the Bistro Gallena in the Walserhaus, the Gasthof Hirsch or the Ifen Hotel. If you like trout, you should go to Sonnwinkel in Mittelberg.

WHAT ELSE TO DO THERE

Lots!
Swimming pools. Saunas, solaria.
Ice-skating and curling rinks.
Tobogganing run and toboggan lift.
30 km of cleared paths for winter walks.
Bowling alleys.
Ski-bob tracks and school.
Floodlit skiing.
Pool-billiards.
Ski jump.
Riding stables.
Horse-drawn sledges.
Three covered tennis courts—can do special skiing and tennis combinations.
Peasant theatre.
Museum of 'ski history' in the Walserhaus.

WHERE TO STAY

There is a good choice of accommodation including apartments, pensions and hotels. I would recommend the four-star Ifen Hotel in Hirschegg where Gunter Sachs, Boris Becker and Natassia Kinski have all stayed (Tel: 055 17 5071). 140DM-214DM per night half board. Hotel Wildental (Tel: 055 17 6544) in Mittelberg charges 94DM-140DM half board. The Gasthof-Hotel Steinbock (Tel: 055 17 5033) in Mittelberg charges 85DM-117DM half board. The Hotel Post (Tel: 055 17 5215) in Riezlern, 86DM-125DM per night half board.

IN CASE OF EMERGENCY

Doctors: Three.
Chemist: One.
Dentist: One.

Nearest Hospital: Oberstdorf, West Germany (10 km).
Helicopter Rescue: Yes.

HOW TO GET THERE

Nearest Airport: Munich-Riem.
Transfer time: 2 hours by car, 3 hours by bus.
Train connection: Oberstdorf-Munich—$2\frac{1}{2}$ hours.

FURTHER INFORMATION

Tourist Office Kleinwalsertal Walserhaus, A-6992 Hirschegg (Tel: 055 17 5114).

NEUKIRCHEN

- **HEIGHT OF RESORT**
  '856' m.

- **HIGHEST LIFT**
  2,150 m.

- **WHY GO THERE?**
  Excellent place to learn to ski.
  Gentle, flattering pistes.
  Good for cross-country.
  Prepared walks.

- **WHO GOES THERE?**
  Lots of young Germans.
  Families.

- **COMPANIES THAT GO THERE**
  Adventure Express.

It's hard to find a pretty, traditional Austrian village which has not been discovered by the British market. Neukirchen is one such gem. It is a charming unsophisticated little village in the Oberpinzgau region of Salzburg, half way between the better-known resorts of Zell am See and Gerlos. It is set in spectacular scenery amongst the fir trees of the Hohe Tauern National Park and dominated by the mighty Großvenediger mountain, which is the third highest in Austria. The village itself is quite compact with a traditional church in the centre, a small square and a long main street set on a slight incline. Considering there are only 2,400 inhabitants, they have a good selection of shops selling traditional crafts, sportswear, food, clothes, even quality jewellery and crystal stones. The architecture is an attractive blend of old rustic buildings and modern houses. It is not a sophisticated resort but it is quite bustling particularly at peak après-ski times between 3 pm and 6 pm or after 9 pm.

Neukirchen is a friendly and family-orientated resort. There is an excellent kindergarten which organises fun events such as sleigh rides and tobogganing. This must be one of the nicest places in the Alps to learn to ski.

THE SKIING

Neukirchen has a small ski area that is perfect for beginners as well as for intermediates who want to polish up their technique in a safe environment. There is nothing to intimidate you in Neukirchen with lots of flattering easy runs as well a couple of more testing reds. There are some beginners' slopes in the centre of town and another baby lift at the top of the mountain. There are only seven main lifts on the mountain. Queueing (up to 30 minutes) can be a problem in peak season, both in the morning and at the end of the day when the only way down the mountain is in the gondola. But the ski area is deceptive. You can't actually see the main Wildkogel ski area from the village.

The first time I arrived at the top, I was amazed how much skiing there was. Each lift offers at least two different descents and the longest run is over $1\frac{1}{2}$ km. The pistes are well marked and prepared and because the skiing area forms a bowl, at a good height, the snow conditions are reliable. It is a very safe area with no chance of getting lost. All the runs are nice and wide, so they don't get worn so quickly and are perfect for building confidence. I particularly enjoyed the easy wide descent from Frühmesser (2,235 m). There are no black runs in Neukirchen but the red run from the top of the Pfeifferkopf lift will challenge the more adventurous intermediate. This run normally includes two or three mogul fields. There is another red run from the top of the Wildkogel down to the middle station. A few runs down this piste at the end of the day should satisfy any intermediate skier.

Speed freaks should take the long scenic blue/green run which winds its way through the trees from the middle station to the Stockenbaum restaurant. There is a short 10-minute walk at the bottom of the run to the restaurant. Here you can sit and have a few glühweins before catching the bus back to the village. This is certainly more relaxing than having to queue for the gondola down to the village.

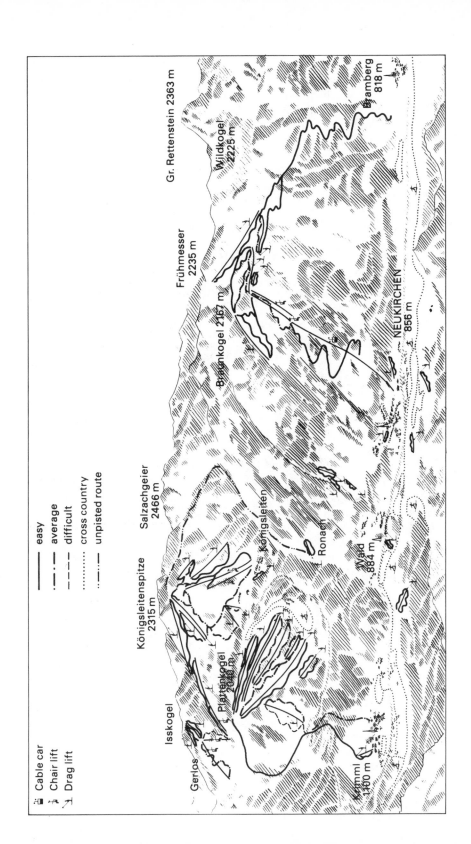

Cable car
Chair lift
Drag lift

easy
average
difficult
cross country
unpisted route

Gr. Rettenstein 2363 m

Wildkogel 2225 m

Bramberg 818 m

Frühmesser 2235 m

Bruckkogel 2167 m

NEUKIRCHEN 856 m

Salzachgeier 2466 m

Königsleitenspitze 2315 m

Königsleiten

Ronach

Wald 884 m

Isskogel

Plattenkogel 2041 m

Gerlos

Krimml 1100 m

Neukirchen is a good resort for learning off-piste—there is some gentle powder between the pistes and some harder off-piste down the front of the mountain. The ski school organises special powder weeks.

There is more skiing nearby at at Hochkrimml and Königsleiten (60 km in total). If Neukirchen had a more innovative management, it would be possible to link it to Kitzbuhel with just three more lifts.

CROSS-COUNTRY

This is a super resort for cross-country, with 47 km of trails, which start close to the village. Most of these are very flat and easy. It links in to the Pinzga Loipe. Can also ski over to Mittersill and Kaprun. Ski school (Tel: 065 65 63 33).

SKI SCHOOL

(Tel: 065 65 63 33 33).
English spoken. 950S six days (group lessons usually start on Mondays). Private lessons 1,520S four hours. Good kindergarten for $2\frac{1}{2}$-4yr olds. 1,400S for six days (9.30 am-4 pm) with lunch, sleigh rides, tobogganing etc.

LIFT PASSES

940S-1,038S six days (642-990S kids).

WHERE TO EAT, DRINK & BOOGIE

There are several good places to eat on the slopes. There is a rustic mountain hut near the middle station, which does self-service food and has a panoramic view over the Hohe Tauern National Park. The Stockenbaum is a bit off the beaten track (you will need to catch the bus back to the village) but it serves excellent traditional food, such as goulash soup or roast beef with fried onions and potatoes. As the nursery slopes are in the village, many of the beginners eat in the hotels and restaurants.

Most of the tourists are Germans who are on half board and eat in their hotels in the evenings. Consequently the resort is rather quiet at dinner time but perks up again after 9 pm. Prices are reasonable—a large beer costs approximately 23S. There are several bars and cafes to drink in. The Kanne is a lively bar at the bottom of the chair-lift in the village. The Salett'l is a popular drinking house for the local ski school. Rudi's Pub is a modern bar at the bottom of the chair-lift. Most of the eating is in hotel restaurants. There is also one pizzeria and a few cafes. Local specialities include cheese noodles and dumplings. For traditional food I would recommend eating at the Hotel Kammerlander, Hotel Gassner or Gasthof Hotel Unterbrunn. There is a good disco, next to Rudi's Pub.

WHAT ELSE TO DO THERE

Paragliding is very popular.
Natural ice rink (skates are for hire in Mittersill, not at the rink).
Curling.
Bowling.
Swimming in hotels open to the public. Steam bath in Hotel Kammerlander.
Floodlit tobogganing.
Cinemas (German speaking only).
Sleigh rides.
Folk museum in nearby Brambers.
Over 50 km of prepared walking tracks.
Local train to Zell am See.
The frozen Krimmler Waterfalls.

WHERE TO STAY

Neukirchen has an excellent choice of accommodation, most of it in small hotels and guest houses. There are apartments for self-caterers. I would recommend the Kammerlander Hotel (Tel: 065 65 62 31) which is well-located in the centre of town. This is an old-fashioned building, which has been tastefully refurbished. It is a good place to pamper yourself as they have a super relaxation/leisure area with steam bath, swimming pool, sauna, solarium and rest room. 365S-510S. The Gassner (Tel: 065 65 62 32) is at the top end of the village—a nice place to stay if you have a car. 360S half board. There are some good gasthofs such as Unterbrunn (Tel: 065 65 62 26). This is a lovely old building in the centre of town. It has a rustic dining room and is attached to the Salett'l bar-a popular place with the locals. 370S-400S half board with bathroom. The Steiger (Tel: 065 65 63 59) is further away from the centre, and more basic, but the host is very friendly and it is reasonably priced. 330S-370S half board with bathroom. There are also many pension haus where for 200S you should find bed and breakfast (room with private facilities). Some hotels such as the Kammerlander and Gassner, offer excellent discounts, up to 50 per cent off for children. There is also a good selection of apartments.

IN CASE OF EMERGENCY

Doctor in resort: One.
Chemist in resort: One.
Dentist in resort: One.
Nearest Hospital: Mittersill.
Helicopter Rescue: Yes.

HOW TO GET THERE

Nearest Airport: Innsbruck or Salzburg.
Transfer time: $1\frac{1}{2}$-2 hours.
Train connection: Train to Zell am See and then local train.

FURTHER INFORMATION

Tourist Office A-5741 Neukirchen am Großvenediger (Tel: 065 65 62 56).

STUBEN

- **HEIGHT OF RESORT**
  1,400 m.

- **HIGHEST LIFT**
  2,800 m.

- **WHY GO THERE?**
  Quiet, unspoilt, Austrian village, linked to the famous St Anton/ Arlberg ski circuit.
  Excellent off-piste.
  Good snow record.

- **WHO GOES THERE?**
  Serious skiers.
  Laid-back Germans, Austrians and Swiss.

- **COMPANIES THAT GO THERE**
  Ski Total.

Stuben offers you the best of both worlds—an unsophisticated, traditional village with access to the world-famous St Anton ski circuit in the Arlberg. The atmosphere in Stuben is quiet and cosy—it does not take long to get to know everybody as the place is so tiny. There is one 'main street' comprising a few old traditional hotels, a box-room of a post office, and a grocery which also acts as newsagent, toyshop, chemist, general store and ski shop. The village is 'run' by a couple of influential figures. The first is Nikki Fritz, who owns the oldest hotel in the village—the Post. As the name suggests, this used to be a posting house for travellers coming over the Arlberg Pass. It has been in the Fritz family for over 500 years and has some wonderful old Austrian furniture, big log fires and a gastronomic restaurant. Nikki is also the tourist director of the resort (the 'tourist office' is in the Hotel Post) and is an ardent environmentalist who is anxious to keep the village small and unspoilt.

The other well-known character in the village is Willie Mathies, an ex-racer and ski hero of the Arlberg. He runs the ski school and also has a bar which is always packed and the centre of village gossip. On my second evening, it was snowing very heavily, and we were glad to be in the warmth of Willie's stübli, drinking schnapps with chunks of peach in, and playing cards. Then a lady burst in to warn everybody that 'the road' would be closed in 10 minutes. Stuben is surrounded by imposing mountains and vulnerably located for avalanches. In heavy snowfalls the lifts and road are closed and the village is cut off, sometimes for days. The young Dutch couple at the bar were most concerned as they had to catch a plane early the following morning. A middle-aged lady from Texas was getting very panicky, saying how it would 'never happen in the States' and that she was scared to go out in case she got 'swallowed up in all that snow'.

The following day all the lifts were closed and Willie, who is responsible for the avalanche control, was in and out of his bar with a walkie-talkie. There was nothing to do but eat and drink and get to know the locals and the other tourists. I was quite happy to spend a leisurely day, until I had a rather frightening experience, walking back to the chalet. It was only 3 pm and still light but snowing heavily. The thick snow-drifts made it difficult to negotiate the narrow path up the hill—if I had slipped off, I would have ended up to my neck in snow. I was slowly making tracks when a young ski instructor leaned out of a chalet window and shouted something at me in German. I could not understand what he said, but from the frantic way he was waving his arms, it was quite clear that he was not just asking me in for a jägatee. Then in broken English he bellowed 'Quick! Avalanche! To your house! Run!' I ran. Although it must have been a funny sight as the hill was very steep and I was sliding all over the place, I was terrified, convinced my time had come and that I would drown in snow. I later discovered that it was only a tiny avalanche and that there was no way it would have reached the village. The instructor had been put on 'avalanche patrol' and had probably been over-cautious. But as somebody was killed a couple of years ago, Stuben is understandably strict in its monitoring of avalanches.

THE SKIING

Although there are a couple of good nursery slopes on the sunny side of the village, I would not recommend Stuben for beginners (unless they are very brave). Most of the runs are very hard and graded lower than they would be elsewhere. But for intermediates and advanced skiers, Stuben is the queue-free backdoor into the 200 km of exhilarating pistes in the Arlberg (St Anton and St Christoph) and the Voralberg (Lech and Zürs). There is only one chair-lift out of Stuben, but there is hardly any queuing, probably because it is so long and can be cold and windy. This chair takes you to the Albona middle station (1,840 m) where there is a blue (more like red) run down to Rauz. There is also a very steep black run back down to Stuben. The chair-lift continues up to Albonagrat (2,400 m) which is renowned for its off-piste skiing and challenging pistes. From here you can ski off-piste down to Langan (with a guide), stay overnight in the Kaltenberg Hütte and get a bus back in the morning.

There is also an opportunity to ski on or off the pistes down to St Christoph or St Anton. From St Anton you can take a cable car up to Vallugagrat (2,650 m). The lift-men won't let you continue up to Valluga (2,811 m) unless you are accompanied by a guide. From here it is possible to ski off-piste to Zürs and do the 'White Circle'—if you are not a good enough skier or the conditions are not right you should take a bus (30S) to Zürs. The White Circle is a pleasant half-day circuit, suitable for intermediates. From Zürs you ski across a frozen lake and through the trees to the pretty little village of Zug. Here there is a new chair-lift up to Palmenalpe (2,100 m). There is a nice restaurant at Palmenalpe but it does get very crowded—it is best to ski on to Oberlech for lunch.

In Oberlech there are some easy and intermediate motorway pistes as well as some more challenging black runs from Kriegerhorn (2,178 m). There are several blue runs down to Lech. From here, you cross the village and take a long cable car up to Rükikopf. You can ski on or off the pistes down to Zürs and catch the bus back home. If you stay in Stuben you should not miss the opportunity of skiing the 10 km intermediate run from Valluga to Stuben. Mogul lovers should also try the black Mattunjoch run, which is particularly exhilarating in spring 'fern' snow.

CROSS-COUNTRY

Stuben is not a cross-country resort. There are only a token 5 km of paths, and 60 km in the Arlberg.

SKI SCHOOL

(Tel: 055 82217).

Stuben was the birthplace of Hannes Schneider who founded the famous Arlberg ski school at the beginning of the century. Stuben's ski school is now run by ex-racer Willie Mathies who is the modern hero of the Arlberg. He also runs a popular stübli bar where all his trophies and competition photos are displayed and where most of his 20 loyal instructors can be found out of working hours. Willie is an informal sort of chap, who goes out of his way to get to know all the ski school clients. As it is such a small village everyone goes to his bar, and this enables him to ask how they are getting on with their lessons. It is a very personal service—they even send Christmas cards to their private students. 1,150S for six full days. Private lesson 1,500S per day.

LIFT PASSES

1,570S for six-day pass to whole area. Children 900S.

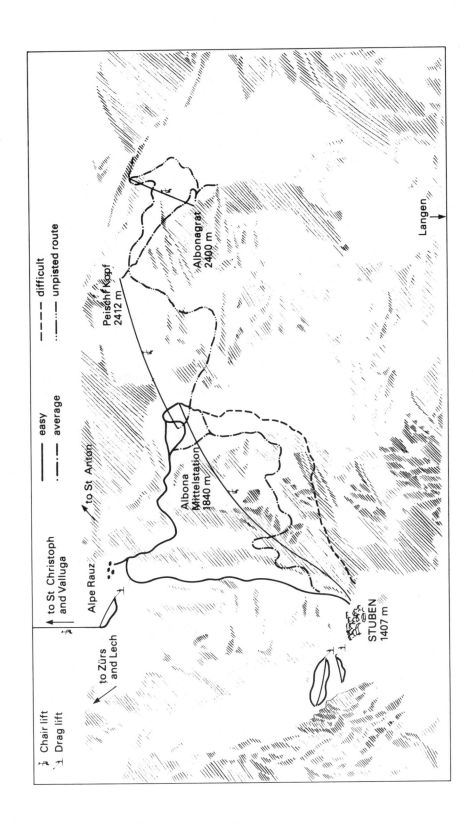

WHERE TO EAT, DRINK & BOOGIE

There are 24 alpine restaurants in the Arlberg—some of these (in the St Anton area) are 'ice bars' where the drinks are kept naturally cold outside, and they play thigh-slapping ooom-pah-pah music. One of the most famous bars in St Anton is the Krazy Kangeroo. This is particularly popular between 3 pm and 6 pm, and as it is at the bottom of the pistes, is within easy slithering distance of the road where you can catch a bus home. If you are feeling adventurous you can ski over to Ulmerhütte, stay the night, watch a spectacular sunrise and then ski down. The Gasthof Berghaus in Stuben is a popular place for lunch, après-ski, and dinner, serving traditional Austrian fare such as *Tirolerknödelsuppe* (dumpling soup). The S'Murmele has a big new bar where you can eat goulash soup, and is popular with skiers from 3 pm onwards.

Après-ski in Stuben is very laid-back—although no-one throws wild parties many people stay up very late just chatting to friends in the bars and restaurants. Willie's Pils Stübli is always busy and a good place to meet people. The Sport Café is a casual place to eat—there is a a pizza cellar downstairs. People come from far afield to eat at the sophisticated Mondschein Hotel which has a superb restaurant—I savoured their wonderfully tender *filet de boeuf*. The owner and the chef, Werner Walch, enjoys showing connoisseurs the treasures in his wine cellar. I don't think he was very impressed when I asked for water with my meal. The Post Hotel also has a gastronomic restaurant. There is only one disco in Stuben—the Tenne in the Hotel Albona. This is a quiet, laid-back place, more like a bar than a nightclub. There is no entry fee and a beer is no more expensive than elsewhere (about 30S for half a litre).

WHAT ELSE TO DO THERE

Not much.
The Mondschein Hotel has a small swimming pool but this can only be used by guests.

WHERE TO STAY

Although it is only a tiny place, there are two excellent four-star hotels in Stuben. Hotel Gasthof Mondschein (Tel: 055 82 511) is an elegant old chalet-style building which dates back to 1739. They have a a wonderful collection of antique furniture and oil paintings. The rooms are fully modernised and there is a cosy wood-panelled lounge and bar with a log fire. The hotel has a small indoor swimming pool, sauna and solarium. From 750S-880S half board, with bathroom.

The Hotel Post (Tel: 055 82 761) has been owned by the Fritz family for over

500 years, and used to be the last stop on the tiring and sometimes dangerous pass over the Arlberg. It is now a very attractive and comfortable hotel. I particularly liked their single rooms as they have the original painted wooden cot-style beds. Downstairs the rooms have wonderful wooden-panelled ceilings and big log fires. From 725S-825S half board, with bathroom. There are five other hotels in the village as well as several guesthouses. Ski Total are the only English company in Stuben. They have a large chalet where the staff live in.

IN CASE OF EMERGENCY

There are no Medical Facilities in Stuben.
Nearest Doctor: St Anton.
Nearest Chemist: Zürs.
Nearest Dentist: St Anton.
Nearest Hospital: St Anton or Lech.
Helicopter Rescue: Yes.

HOW TO GET THERE

Nearest Airport: Innsbruck or Zurich.
Train connection: Zurich to Langan (3 hours) then bus (10 minutes).

FURTHER INFORMATION

Tourist Office Verkehrsverein Stuben, A-6762 Stuben/Arlberg (Tel: 055 82 761).

ZAUCHENSEE

Zauchensee is one of the very few purpose-built resorts in Austria, and is linked in to a three-valley lift system with 100 km of pistes. It is a compact little resort which was tastefully built about 20 years ago in traditional rustic Austrian style. It is a quiet place that attracts serious skiers rather than all-night party-goers—nightlife is virtually non-existent unless you take a taxi to the more humming resort of Altenmarkt, 10 km away. Austria is not known for 'doorstep' skiing, but Zauchensee offers convenience skiing at its best. The 'resort' is just a clustering of half a dozen comfortable hotels, all within a couple of minutes' walking distance from the lifts, as well as a selection of mountain huts/cafes on both sides of the road. At the end of the day you can ski straight to the bars or hotels.

Zauchensee (1,350 m) is a very high resort by Austrian standards and usually boasts good snow from early December through to the end of April. Although there are very few British, it attracts a mixed clientele–mainly Austrians and Germans but also Dutch, Italians, Yugoslavians, French, Swiss, Danes and Swedes.

Most people stay further down the mountain at Altenmarkt (850 m). Although it is not so convenient for the skiing, they can take a picturesque 20-minute bus ride up to the lifts at Zauchensee every morning. Altenmarkt is an old traditional Austrian village, very accessible by road as it is just off the motorway. In the main street there are several hotels, shops, banks and après-ski bars. The rest of the village is rather spread out—instead of being in the centre, the church and village square are unusually located at the far end of the main street.

- **HEIGHT OF RESORT**
  1,350 m.

- **HIGHEST LIFT**
  2,188 m.

- **WHY GO THERE?**
  Tasteful Austrian purpose-built resort with French-style doorstep skiing.
  Three valleys with interconnected lift system.
  Reliable snow conditions, long season and little queueing.
  Very friendly.

- **WHO GOES THERE?**
  International selection of serious skiers.
  Austrians and Germans who are keener on skiing than après-ski.
  Party poopers.

- **COMPANIES THAT GO THERE**
  Mogul Ski—most of their accommodation is in the nearby village of Altenmarkt.

THE SKIING

Zauchensee is linked to Flachauwinkl and Kleinarl and offers direct access to 100 km of pistes. The skiing is best suited to intermediates and above. Because the resort is so high (1,350 m) they have a long season (beginning of December to May) and the snow conditions are usually excellent. It is a skier's paradise as there are miles and miles of well-kept pistes and little, if any, queueing.

Zauchensee has been designed so you have direct access to the pistes and never have to walk for more than a couple of minutes. The bus from Altenmarkt costs about 20S. If you have your own car, you can park about 10 minutes' walk from the lifts (there is a free shuttle bus service). Altenmarkt has its own beginners' slopes but these tend to get bare quite easily. The snow is much better up in Zauchensee where there are some good sunny nursery slopes on one side of the village. Timid beginners may find the progression to the main slopes too radical—it is a resort which is best appreciated by second-year skiers onwards. There are lifts on both sides of Zauchensee. There is a gentle blue run, Tauern Karsch, over the back of the Rauchkopf mountain (1,890 m) and a long easy descent right into the village. There is also a superb long black run back down to the village.

The most challenging of all the runs is the permanently unpisted east-facing descent from Gamskogel, aptly named 'Extrem'. Most of the skiing is through the trees, but up on Gamskogel there are wide open spaces above the treeline. You can ski over to Flachauwinkl and cross over to more lifts and pistes on the 'Zauchi'. This is a dinky little train, which plays traditional Austrian music and is towed along by a tractor. There are some challenging red runs from Mooskopf (1,980 m) to Kleinarl (1,014 m). Powder freaks can ski off-piste over three valleys all the way from Zauchensee to Flachauwinkl and Kleinarl. Very keen skiers may want to buy the Salzburger Sportwelt Amadé pass which gives access to 120 lifts and 320 km, although you would definitely need a car to make this feasible. Most skiers will find the three valleys more than adequate.

CROSS-COUNTRY

Altenmarkt is the best base for cross-country as it links into the Tauern Loipe with 50 km of tracks. The connecting track from Zauchensee is very difficult and not advisable for beginners. Club Nordic 2,000, A-5441 Altenmarkt (Tel: 064 52 511) organises all sorts of courses in cross-country, telemarking, ski touring, and even cross-country with yoga.

SKI SCHOOL

Skischule Altenmarkt Zauchensee, A-5541 Altenmarkt (Tel: 064 52 60 70). There is a good ski school based in both Altenmarkt and Zauchensee. The instructors speak English and their director, Otto Hanselmann, has worked in New Zealand and Australia. They also organise ski guiding and courses in cross-country, telemarking, monoski, snow-surf. 930S for five days. They take children from 4 years old. 5 days with lunch 1,430S. The Tourist Office can arrange a baby-sitting service—70S per hour, 350S per day.

LIFT PASSES

1,160S (710S children) covering Zauchensee, Flachauwinkl and Kleinarl.

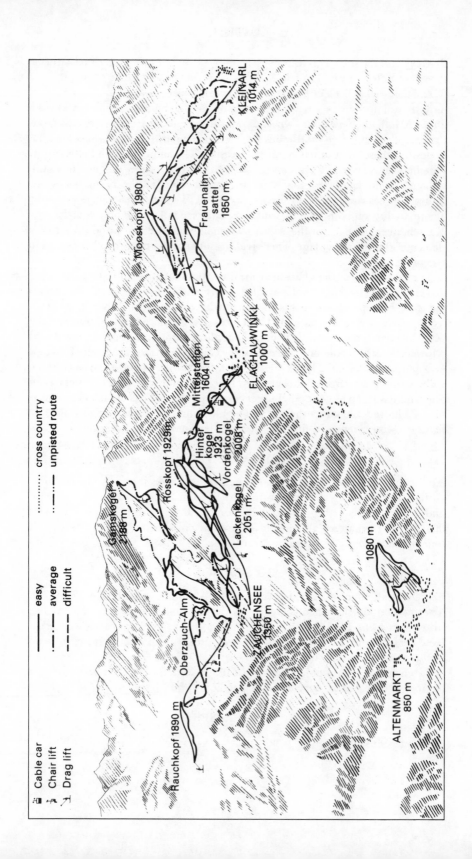

Cable car

Chair lift

Drag lift

easy

average

difficult

cross country

unpisted route

Rauchkopf 1890 m

Oberzauch-Alm

ZAUCHENSEE 1350 m

Gamskogel 2188 m

Rosskopf 1929 m

Hinter kogel 1923 m

Vordenkogel 2008 m

Mittelstation 1604 m

Lackenkogel 2051 m

FLACHAUWINKL 1000 m

Mooskopf 1980 m

Frauenalm sattel 1850 m

KLEINARL 1014 m

1080 m

ALTENMARKT 850 m

WHERE TO EAT, DRINK & BOOGIE

This must be one of the best areas for alpine restaurants—there seems to be one at the top of every lift. Most of these are steamy rustic *hüttes*, where everyone crams in for schnapps and beer. The Glömeralm, just above the Flachauwinkl gondola station, is excellent for sunbathing. The restaurant at the top of the 'Blue 13' run in Zauchensee is supposed to serve the best *Kaiserschmarren* (an Austrian-style sweet pancake with sultanas and icing sugar, served with fruit compôte) in Austria.

Après-ski in Zauchensee is *very* quiet. The idea is that you will have done so much skiing, you will just want to curl up with a good book and fall asleep. Skiers tend to congregate in the Umbrella bar at the Hotel Zauchenseehof. There are a couple of very traditional wooden rustic restaurants in the middle of the village which have a limited selection of food but an excellent atmosphere. The best one, for lunch or dinner, is the Felserhütte where they serve excellent hot and cold snacks from 30S upwards. A goulash soup costs about 35S, mixed ham and cheese platter 60S. You should be able to eat a three-course meal in Zauchensee for about 120-160S. There is one disco in the Zauchenseehof hotel. But those in search of the bright (well, brighter!) lights will have to take a taxi to Altenmarkt, where there is more going on in the way of bars and discos. The Arche Noah is a pizzeria/disco that is very popular with youngsters and the locals. The Tauernstübe is more sophisticated and also has a restaurant. There is also a super cafe opposite the church which does wonderful cakes, glühweins etc. Most of the restaurants are in hotels. You can watch the chef making the pizzas at the Arche Noah. The Lugs-ins-Land hotel has a friendly restaurant where you can have an excellent meal for about 120-160S per head.

WHAT ELSE TO DO THERE

Ice skating on natural lake in Zauchensee.
Hotels have saunas, fitness rooms, table tennis.
Sleigh rides.
Swimming pool in Altenmarkt.
Bowling in Altenmarkt.
Indoor tennis in Altenmarkt.
Folk museum in Altenmarkt.
Excursions to Salzburg—quick motorway connection.

WHERE TO STAY

The hotels in Zauchensee are modern, chalet-style buildings. As the resort has few other facilities, hotels are well-equipped with their own saunas, solaria, fitness rooms, table tennis etc. All the rooms have private facilities. The resort is only 20 years old so there are no rooms without facilities. Hotel Zauchenseehof (Tel: 064 52 82 12) is an excellent four-star hotel in the centre of the village, right next to the slopes and lifts. This has big spacious rooms (some with three beds) and its own nightclub and bar, sauna, solarium, fitness room and table tennis. 480S-570S half board. Cheaper accommodation is available in Altenmarkt, from about 200S per night bed and breakfast.

IN CASE OF EMERGENCY

Nearest Doctor: Altenmarkt.
Nearest Chemist: Altenmarkt.
Nearest Dentist: Altenmarkt.
Nearest Hospital: Altenmarkt.
Helicopter Rescue: Yes.

HOW TO GET THERE

Nearest Airport: Salzburg.
Transfer time: 1 hour.
Train connection: Express to Radstadt (3 km away).

FURTHER INFORMATION

Tourist Office Altenmarkt/Zauchensee Hauptplatz 81, A-5541 Alten-markt (064 52 511).

France

Serious skiers go to France. There is no denying that our closest continental neighbour has some of the best skiing in the world. France is a lazy skiers' paradise. Their forté is the purpose-built resort where you can literally step out the door of your hotel/apartment on to the pistes. These resorts are full of ardent kilometre freaks whose sole aim is to pack in as much skiing as possible in a week. There are some massive ski areas in France, such as the Trois Valleés, where it is possible for a holiday skier never to ski the same run twice. Traditional mountain resorts, such as Chamonix and Argentière, have some of the most challenging skiing in Europe. Their impressive mountains are popular both in the winter for skiing and in the summer for mountaineering.

The French are probably the most adventurous skiing nation. They are always inventing new methods of teaching. Some resorts such as Les Arcs are pioneers of alternative types of skiing such as mono, snowboard and parapente (paragliding). Even in the small resorts, you will see young sportifs on their snowboards wearing brightly coloured clothes and fluorescent sun block. French purpose-built resorts vary in style and atmosphere. Some of the older ones such as Flaine, which was built in the sixties, have about as much panache as a shopping mall on the snow. Apart from doorstep skiing, they have little to offer. Some of the more recent resorts are built in a more attractive rustic style. But French resorts are not all purpose-built. There are plenty of traditional villages with their own slopes or that are linked into big ski areas. These vary in atmosphere from simple farming communities to more jetsetty environments.

French skiing is mainly based in the Alps and the Pyrenees. Most of the skiing is in the old duchy of Savoy in the Alps which has been split into Haute-Savoie (north) and Savoie (south). Resorts are easily reached by the Autoroute Blanche from Geneva airport. Le Grand Bornand, for example, is a charming market town/ski resort, only 45 minutes' drive from the airport—ideal for weekend skiing. There are still many resorts in this region which have not been discovered by the British. The Portes du Soleil is one of the best linked areas in Europe, comprising eight French resorts and seven Swiss resorts. Most of the English stay in the French resorts of Avoriaz or Morzine. Les Gets is a lively resort with attractive chalet-style buildings. Although it is very popular with the French, it is relatively unknown by the British.

One of my favourite French resorts is the old historical town of Samoëns which is linked to the Grand Massif and that architectural monstrosity—Flaine. The Dauphiné region is within easy access of Grenoble and Lyon airport. This has some excellent uncrowded resorts, such as Villard-de-Lans, which has been strangely overlooked by the British.

The French Pyrenees are on the border of Spain. Spa resorts such as Barèges are now well-known to the British ski market. Although the snow record is much better in the Pyrenees than many people make out, the climate is milder than in the Alps because it is nearer the Atlantic, so it can quickly thaw out. Font Romeu is one of the few Pyreneean resorts that has still not been discovered by the British. The people in the Pyrenees have a reputation for their hospitality and friendliness, and as the skiing is generally less challenging than in the Alps, the resorts tend to attract a less fanatical crowd of skiers. Prices are also cheaper.

The French are very keen on self-catering. This enables families and groups to spend a budget week in an otherwise expensive area. But if you have never stayed in a French rented apartment, be warned. They are usually *very* cramped. A studio for two, by Austrian standards, will sleep at least six in France, with beds concealed in all sorts of strange places, such as under tables or inside cupboards! Most French resorts have some sort of hotel accommodation which tends to be modern and functional rather than full of character. French hotels are not usually such good value for money as Swiss or Austrian.

Purpose-built resorts are ideal for children. Many of them are traffic-free. The complexes are usually compact so there is nowhere for the kids to get lost. Most of the resorts have kindergartens (*jardins de neige*) for the toddlers and some even have Baby Clubs. Unfortunately, many of the French do not or do not like to speak English. It helps if you make an effort even if it is just the occasional *Bonjour* and *Merci*.

Not all French purpose-built resorts have been cleverly designed. Some of the earlier ones have not allowed for the growth of tourism and have had to spread out across the mountain. Satellite villages have sprung up in places such as Isola 2,000, which means a *navette* (shuttle bus) has to be used—something no self-respecting purpose-built resort should ever have to do.

French après-ski tends to centre round bars, cafés and restaurants. The food is usually excellent although expensive. You may pay more for a meal in a French ski resort than you would in one of the glamourous Côte d'Azur towns, such as Cannes. The alpine restaurants on the pistes are often self-service but usually serve good full-course meals or filling country dishes such as *jambon cru* (mountain ham), *charcuterie* (coarse salamis and hams), thick soups with French bread or rich herb omelettes with a fresh green salad. The village restaurants offer more haute cuisine, such as *escargots* (snails in garlic butter) and flambéed steak. There are also local French Alpine specialities such as *fondue savoyarde* (a rich cheese fondue) and *gratin dauphinois* (slices of potato baked in cream, cheese and nutmeg). If you are self-catering, it is always worth stocking up with local wines from the supermarket—these are usually excellent value. Beer in France is more expensive than wine. Most of the resorts have discothèques where young French trendies demonstrate their dancing skills. Most of them do Ceroc, which is a very stylish French version of rock and roll. The clubs charge about 80F entry fee which includes one drink. Drinks in these places are very expensive.

France is such a big country that you could fill several volumes with details of its marvellous ski resorts—I have only been able to pick out a few. There are other regions such as the Maurienne Valley in Savoie and the Alpes Maritimes in the South of France where there is also plenty to discover. France offers such variety that there should be something to suit everybody.

Exchange rate (June 1989): £1 = 10 F.

FURTHER INFORMATION

The French Government Tourist Office 178 Piccadilly, London W1V 0AL (Tel 01 491 7622 or 499 6911 for recorded information).

CHAMROUSSE

Chamrousse came to fame in 1968 when it hosted the Winter Olympics. These downhill courses are now open to the public, and it certainly boosts piste credibility to say you have skied them. Chamrousse, in the Dauphiné, is the archetypal French purpose-built resort, designed to be functional rather than pretty. It is however, a very pretty place to ski as the resort is surrounded by lots of trees and forested land. The resort is split into two parts, Recoin and Roche Béranger, about 3 km apart by road, but linked by ski area.

Chamrousse is so close to Grenoble (30-40 minutes' drive) that you can see the bright lights of the city from the pistes. It is a very popular local resort with the Grenoblois. Lots of the students/workers use it for day-skiing but a well-devised lift-system ensures that there is no queueing.

It is an exceptionally good resort for children. Les Marmots (Tel: 76 89 96 14) has a crèche for children from 3 months to 6 years old and another centre for 3-12 year olds. The ski school has the *Club des Oursons* (Bear Club) which takes children from 3 years old. The best facilities are at the Roche Béranger end of town where there is a heated indoor swimming pool, mini-motorised buggy course and kindergarten. There is a café right next door to the baby pistes and a toboggan area for little kids.

- **HEIGHT OF RESORT**
  1,650-1,750 m.

- **HIGHEST LIFT**
  2,255 m.

- **WHY GO THERE?**
  Convenience skiing.
  Excellent facilities for children.
  Good roads and easy transfers.
  Brag factor—ski the Olympics 1968 Downhill Courses.

- **WHO GOES THERE?**
  Locals from Grenoble.
  Students from Grenoble University.
  French families.
  Parisian weekenders.
  Lots of dogs.

- **COMPANIES THAT GO THERE**
  Ski Tonic.
  Air France.

THE SKIING

This is convenience skiing at its best with the pistes leading directly off the street. There are 70 km in all, catering for all standards, but particularly good for beginners and intermediates. The easiest slopes are at the Roche Béranger end. The two areas are well-linked and integrated. The Recoin slopes are steeper and include the Men and Women's Olympic downhill courses. Many of the runs are lined with fir trees although some of the higher runs are rather exposed and suffer from the wind blowing away the snow. Most of the off-piste is in between existing pistes rather than in inaccessible areas. As there are so many trees there is very little risk of avalanche. The lift system has been well-devised with no bottlenecks. Even on a Wednesday afternoon when the resort was full with school kids, I never had to wait longer than five minutes.

Chamrousse is a popular resort for *nouvelles sensations* such as monoski and snowboarding.

CROSS-COUNTRY

Plateau de l'Arselle is an excellent cross-country area, about 1 km down the road from Roche Béranger (also linked by chair-lift). This high plateau (1,700 m) offers 55 km of tree-lined trails with spectacular views on every side. As it is so high, snow conditions are usually good from December to May.

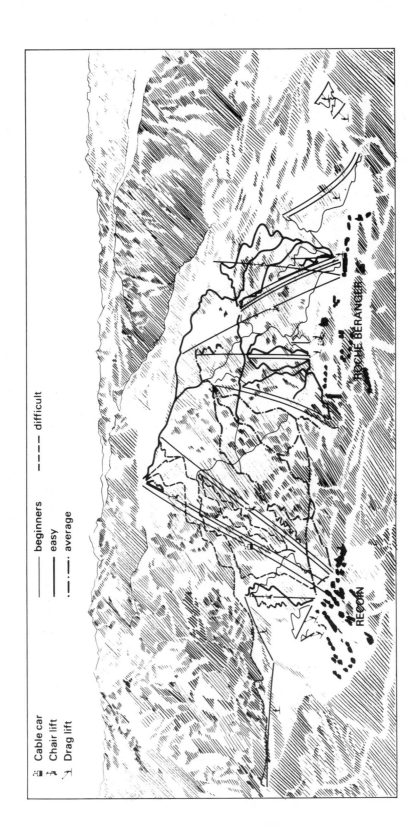

Cable car
Chair lift
Drag lift

beginners ——— difficult
easy
average

ROCHE BÉRANGER

REGOIN

SKI SCHOOL

Recoin (Tel: 76 89 90 30), Roche Béranger (Tel: 76 89 94 25).There are 80 Ecole de Ski Français instructors in Chamrousse. It is no problem finding English instruction. Twenty of them speak English, and another 20 are busy learning two nights a week in Grenoble! Five half-days ($2\frac{1}{2}$ hours per day) 299F (282F under 12s). Private lessons in skiing, snowboarding, mono-skiing or cross-country, 120F per hour. 3-6yr olds (Club des Oursons, Les Marmots) 305F for 5 half-days.

LIFT PASSES

440F for six days. Covers all the skiing. No reduction for children.

WHERE TO EAT, DRINK & BOOGIE

If you are the sort of person who likes to find little rustic hideaways dotted across the mountain for regular pit-stops, you will not like Chamrousse. On the first day, I was most alarmed that I could not see anywhere to eat on the pistes. There are actually only two mountain restaurants. Le Bar Restaurant is at the top of the cable car, and has magnificent views and good *vin chaud*. Le Snack Bar is underneath the Lacs Achard chair-lift, accessible by blue runs. This is a friendly place that does hearty skiing lunches such as a hamburger and chips for 30F, or crêpes, omelettes etc.

There are plenty of bars and cafés in both parts of Chamrousse. Prices are reasonable, about 10F for a beer, 10F-12F for a vin chaud. Dîner-à-deux costs 80F-150F per head plus wine. I would recommend eating at Ecureuil (Tel 76 89 90 13) or L'Igloo (Tel 76 89 90 69) in Recoin, and O'cho (Tel 76 89 96 48) or Petit Christiana (Tel 76 89 94 51) in Roche Béranger. A slap-up four-course meal at the Hotel Bérangère will cost about 150F per head without wine. Although it is predominantly a family resort, Chamrousse is quite lively at night in high season. There are two nightclubs, Le Club in the Hotel Bèrangère and La Bamba in Recoin.

WHAT ELSE TO DO THERE

Paragliding (Tel: 76 89 98 47) from one flight to weekend courses.
Ski-doos are James Bond style scooters on the snow (Tel: 76 89 92 69).
Snow and ice-driving course.
Ice-skating.
Swimming pool.
The ski school arranges guided walks in snow shoes.
Hotel Bérangère has a solarium, sauna and gym.

Chamrousse has one cinema and the honour of holding the International Comedy Film Festival every March.

WHERE TO STAY

Most of the accommodation is self-catering. Hotel Bérangère at Roche Béranger (Tel: 76 89 91 11) is a three-star hotel with its own gym, sauna and night club. 290F-400F per night half board. Le Virage at Recoin (Tel: 76 89 90 63) is a two-star hotel. 170F-210F per night half board.

IN CASE OF EMERGENCY

Doctor in resort: Two. Ambulance service (Tel: 76 89 94 68).
Chemist in resort: One in Roche Béranger.
Nearest dentist: Uriage (18 km).
Nearest Hospital: Three in Grenoble (30 minutes by road, 10 minutes by helicopter).
Helicopter Rescue: Yes.

HOW TO GET THERE

Nearest Airport: Grenoble (via charter) or Lyon (via scheduled Air France).
Transfer time: 30-40 minutes (Grenoble), $1\frac{1}{2}$ hours (Lyon).
Train connection: Paris to Grenoble, via TGV, 3 hours.

FURTHER INFORMATION

Tourist Office 38410 Chamrousse. Le Recoin (Tel: 76 89 92 65), Roche Béranger (Tel: 76 89 94 88).

FONT-ROMEU

Font-Romeu (pronounced *Fon Romeur*) is a small unpretentious French town on the eastern side of the Pyrenees, just 15 km from Spain. Purpose-built in 1920, the granite architecture is unspectacular but harmonious—at least there are no hideous modern tower blocks. One of the most attractive features of this

- **HEIGHT OF RESORT**
  1,800 m.

- **HIGHEST LIFT**
  2,200 m

- **WHY GO THERE?**
  The cheap prices of the Pyrenees minus the 'here-we-go' British
  atmosphere of the better-known Andorra resorts.
  Sun, sun, sun.
  Guaranteed skiing—sophisticated artificial snow-making facilities.
  Excellent environment for kids and beginners.
  Extensive sports facilities.

- **WHO GOES THERE?**
  Young sportifs for altitude-training.
  French families.
  Weekenders from Perpignan and Toulouse.

- **COMPANIES THAT GO THERE**
  No British companies. Dan Air run regular schedule flights to
  Perpignan and Toulouse. Apex prices (14 days in advance) from £127
  (Perpignan), £116 (Toulouse).

resort is that it is set deep amongst the pine forests, which gives it a gentle charm that you will not find in the Alps.

Font-Romeu is a perfect skiing environment as both sun and snow are guaranteed: the former because it is so far south, on the same latitude as Rome, the latter due to a very sophisticated artificial snow-making service. The quality of this artificial snow is extremely good and when carefully groomed by the pisteurs, it forms a firm base free of ice and rocks. The system, the biggest snow-making facility in Europe, cost the resort three million francs, but this is not reflected in the price of the lift passes (see below). Other ski resorts in the Pyrenees are beginning to install these systems in an effort to attract visitors from the Alps, but nowhere else is the process as highly developed as here. A word of warning about the sun: up in the mountains it is much stronger than it looks, so do not forget bring suncream and a good pair of glasses. Your holiday could be ruined if you do not take these simple precautions, especially in the spring.

Skiing in the Pyrenees is often associated with Andorra, and coach-loads of British 'here-we-go' lager louts. Font-Romeu is not this sort of place. So far it has been undiscovered by the British package tour operators and remains a delightful, sunny south-facing resort with a wonderful view across the wide Capcir valley and the big peaks of France and Spain.

Font-Romeu has a large Sports Academy which during term-time acts as a local school. This has exceptionally good facilities and attracts the cream of French sporting talent who go there for serious altitude training. In Font-Romeu, the locals make you very aware that you are not in France or Spain but in the unofficial Catalan nation. We were serenaded by a guitarist who sang a Catalan version of the Beatles, as well as other nationalistic songs. There were lots of poignant references to the terrible Spanish oppression under Franco. This old dictator forbade the Spanish Catalans to speak their language—an incomprehensible mixture of French and Spanish. You will hear Catalan in Font-Romeu—for local good-will it's as well to know the common greeting *Bon dia*. The locals all speak French.

THE SKIING

Font-Romeu is a small ski resort by alpine standards, but it has plenty of skiing to keep the average skier satisfied. There are 39 pistes and 23 lifts. There are two connecting areas, Calme and Col del Pam. The south side has long green and blue runs which provide the perfect environment for children and beginners. As it is also milder than in the Alps, learning is that much more enjoyable. Although the skiing is high (2,204 m), the warmer climate means that the tree-line reaches right up to the top of the mountain, so there is plenty of opportunity for skiing through the woods. Most of the runs are short, wide and lined with pine trees. The perfectly-prepared pistes and the plentiful sunshine are ideal for anyone who might be daunted by a more imposing and craggy environment. On the other side of the hill there are two roller-coaster black runs which I enjoyed a lot, although by usual standards they would probably be graded red as they are rather short. There is no artificial snow on Calme, but if the natural conditions are good, there are several reds and one long black which winds right down to Les Aveillans. Font-Romeu's skiing also connects with Pyrénées 2,000, adding some pleasant but short runs through the trees. Although I didn't have time to explore it, according to my enthusiastic instructor there is a lot of off-piste potential without the peril of too many rocks. I didn't experience any queues, but between 10 am and 12 pm you may see a lot of the local schoolkids in training.

CROSS-COUNTRY

Font-Romeu is very popular for cross-country skiing with 45 km of trails, and 190 km in the region. I also saw a lot of telemarking, but this is about as 'alternative' as you can get in this resort.

SKI SCHOOL

Two-hour classes 58F (48F kids). Private lesson 115F per hour

LIFT PASSES

Six days: high season 550F (390F kids), low season 490F (390F kids).

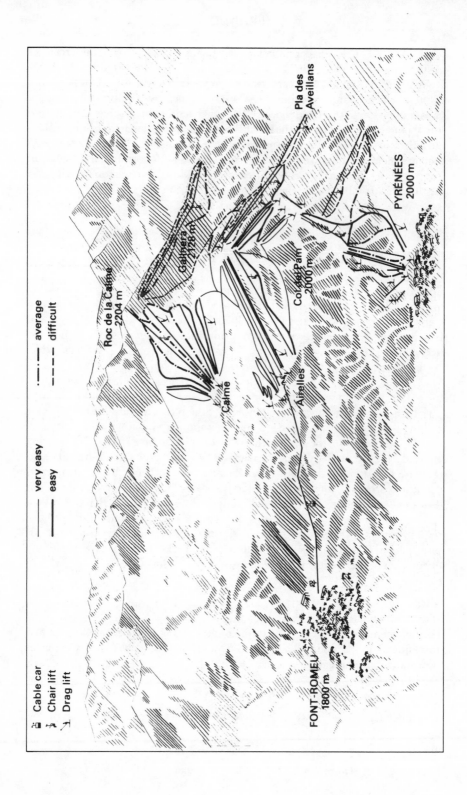

Cable car
Chair lift
Drag lift

very easy
easy
average
difficult

Roc de la Calme
2204 m

Galinera
128 m

Pla des
Aveillans

Col del Pam
2000 m

PYRÉNÉES
2000 m

Calme

Airelles

FONT-ROMEU
1800 m

WHERE TO EAT, DRINK & BOOGIE

Après-ski in Font-Romeu is French in atmosphere but not in price. Eating out in the Pyrenees costs considerably less than its equivalent in the Alps. For example an excellent dîner-à-deux at the Hotel Carlit costs about 150F-200F. This is the only three-star hotel/restaurant in Font-Romeu and is conveniently located in the middle of town. The manager's passion for the local foods is reflected in the menu: the standard French courses are complimented by the dry meats, sweet cakes and excellent local wines such as Fitou and Corbière. There are another six restaurants, as well as plenty of bars. Drinks are much cheaper than in other French ski resorts. Here, a beer costs 10F rather than the 16F you would expect to pay in a more glitzy resort such as Meribel. I took to the local drink called Mauré which is a potent brew similar to port. There are two alpine restaurants—one on Calme and another on Col del Pam. I was not impressed by the latter. It's the sort of featureless and functional eating-place you'd expect to find in an Eastern Block country such as Bulgaria. The pâtisserie shop in town is very ornate and sells lots of sweet nutty cakes.

For a small resort, there is no shortage of nightlife. There are four night clubs. We were taken to Le Pyrénées where the French impressed us with their Ceroc (the French equivalent to rock 'n' roll dancing). We also went to Le Casino, a larger club with all the usual Travolta trappings of a seventies disco - lit-up dance floor, stroboscopes, and several dark corners for canoodling. Le Casino, appropriately, also has a room upstairs for roulette and black jack where a 100F win gave a little boost to my holiday.

WHAT ELSE TO DO THERE

The pride and joy of Font-Romeu is the Sports Academy. This 'pre-Olympic' centre was built in 1968, just outside the town. In term-time it is used as a school for budding athletes and asthmatic children. In the holidays it's the home of many French sporting heroes. The facilities are very impressive: an Olympic-sized heated swimming pool, indoor tennis and squash courts, ice-skating (not always available to the public due to regular ice-hockey matches). There is also a stables which has some world-class horses and an indoor riding hall. The use of the latter is also restricted, but nice to look at all the same. One of the school's most famous ex-pupils is Freddy Burton, the recently retired British World Cup downhiller. He was a team-mate of Konrad Bartelski and Martin Bell, and won the British Championship in 1985. He now teaches in Font-Romeu's ski school and trains the local youth ski team.

WHERE TO STAY

There are plenty of places to stay in Font-Romeu–about 25 hotels. For example, the three-star Hotel Carlit (Tel: 068 30 07 45) charges from 260F per night half board. Full details from the Tourist Office.

IN CASE OF EMERGENCY

Doctors in resort: Fifteen.
Chemists in resort: Two.
Dentists in resort: Three.
Nearest Hospital: Prades (40 km).
Helicopter Rescue: Yes.

HOW TO GET THERE

Nearest Airport: Perpignan.
Transfer Time: $1\frac{1}{2}$ hours.
Train connection: Puig Cerda.

FURTHER INFORMATION

Tourist Office Avenue Emmanuel-Brousse 66120 Font-Romeu (Tel: 068 30 02 74).

LES ANGLES

Les Angles is a 20-minute drive down the valley from Font-Romeu. There is a navette shuttle service between these two resorts although they are not covered by the same lift pass. Les Angles (1,600 m) is a modern purpose-built resort, smaller than Font-Romeu but more spread out along the side of the mountain. There is a small old section with a rather beautiful church, set amidst a disorganised mess of modern buildings. The high street does not have much character, which is a shame as the village is well-located at the foot of the ski slopes and overlooks the Capcir Valley. The ski slopes do not have as many snow canons as in Font-Romeu (70 rather than 250) but snow is ensured on the nursery area, a fair blue run and a red run of genuinely high quality. The latter is called 'Le Mur' (the wall) and runs from the top of the main chair-lift down to the resort, a drop of nearly 400 m. It has been used as the bottom leg of an official FIS downhill and gets its name from a particularly hairy drop-off in the middle. There is plenty of potential for off-piste. The nursery area is at the top of the main gondola. The highest lift is 2,400 m.

The après-ski is not as lively as in Font-Romeu. There is only one night club - the best bet for evening entertainment is the sports complex. This was built in 1988 in the middle of town. If you have a lift pass, you are entitled to use all its facilities. There is a large ice-skating rink, a full-sized bowling alley, a large indoor swimming pool with separate kiddies' pool, a keep-fit room, saunas and a spacious bar/restaurant. You can also rent 'Kitty Kats', small snow-mobiles, at the top of the mountain.

FURTHER INFORMATION

Tourist Office Réservation Centrale, 66210 Les Angles (Tel: 68 04 32 76).

LA GRAVE

- **HEIGHT OF RESORT**
  1,481 m.

- **HIGHEST LIFT**
  3,564 m.

- **WHY GO THERE?**
  A couple of days of off-piste thrills and spills.
  Unpretentious French mountaineering resort.
  Views of extraordinary grandeur.

- **WHO GOES THERE?**
  Serious skiers.
  Powder hounds.
  Climbers.

- **COMPANIES THAT GO THERE**
  None.

La Grave is a climbing resort near the Italian border, on the Grenoble to Briançon road. The main attraction for skiers is the off-piste. A main cable car takes you to the top of the mountain and offers several wild unpisted routes back down to the village. Up until recently it has been almost untouched by commercialism, attracting a loyal following of climbers and the more adventurous and experienced skiers who want to get away from the pistes. Unfortunately, La Grave is no longer such a purist off-piste resort, as in the 1988/89 season it was linked across the Glacier de la Girase with the well-known resort of Les Deux Alpes. This will probably mean that it will start to attract hordes of French and British skiers anxious to prove their off-piste credibility on La Grave's stunningly beautiful terrain. If you like off-piste, I suggest you try and visit this resort as soon as possible before it gets totally swamped with day-trippers from Les Deux Alpes.

The village itself is small and rustic, delightfully higgledy-piggledy with a picturesque church and chapel. It is reached from the dramatic-looking pass between Les Deux Alpes and Serre Chevalier. At a height of 1,481 m, it is set against a backdrop of outstandingly beautiful mountains, dominated by La Meije (3,983 m).

THE SKIING

La Grave is a resort for experienced skiers and powder hounds. It is not the sort of place you would want to go for a week, but is perfect for a couple of days' powder skiing. There are no British companies, as yet, in La Grave, although most of the big operators go to Les Deux Alpes. The unpisted runs are reached by a two-stage cable car which leaves the centre of the village. There are various routes down to the village, some in powder or loose snow, while others (on the left as you descend) are often deeply mogulled. There are no signposts or avalanche warnings. As with any off-piste, this should never be attempted without a guide.

The skiing in La Grave is all off-piste apart from the new area right at the top where two drag-lifts have just been built to provide skiing in both summer and winter. This glacier ski area is between Dome de la Lauze (3,564 m) and Point Trifide at Col des Ruillans (3,200 m). Col des Ruillans provides the link with Les Deux Alpes. Intermediates should enjoy this new ski area (one red, four blue runs) and the chance to ski over to Les Deux Alpes, but should not attempt the unpisted routes down to the village without a guide who feels they have enough ability.

There never used to be any queues in La Grave, although the new link with Les Deux Alpes may create a problem.

CROSS-COUNTRY

12 km in La Grave, 18 km in nearby Villar d'Arène.

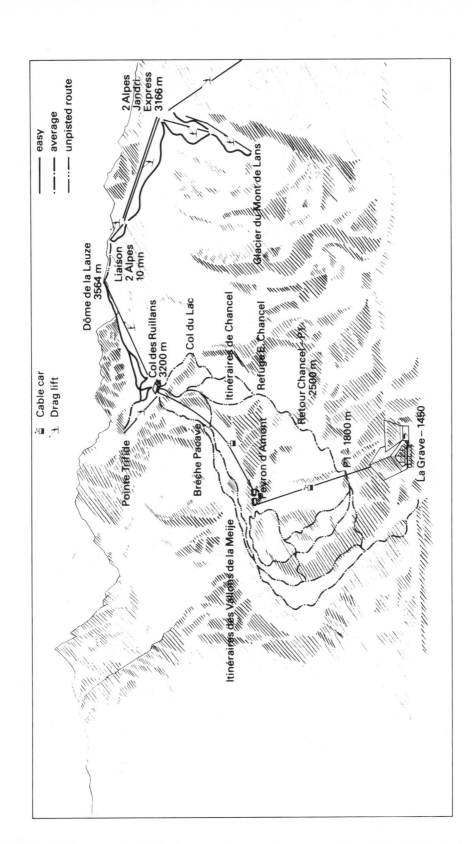

easy
average
unpisted route

:: Cable car
⅂ Drag lift

2 Alpes
Jandri
Express
3166 m

Liaison
2 Alpes
10 mn

Dôme de la Lauze
3564 m

Glacier du Mont de Lans

Col des Ruillans
3200 m

Col du Lac

Itinéraires de Chancel

Refuge Chancel

Pointe Trifide

Brèche Pacave

Peyron d'Amont

Retour Chancel
2500 m

P¹ = 1800 m

Itinéraires des Vallons de la Meije

La Grave – 1450

SKI SCHOOL

There is no ski school in La Grave itself but lessons are available on the glacier. Ecole de Ski Francais (Tel 76 79 92 86).

LIFT PASSES

110F per day (Monday to Friday), 130F per day (weekends and Bank Holidays).

WHERE TO EAT, DRINK & BOOGIE

There are a few places to eat on the mountain. Refuge Chancel is an old rustic restaurant. There are also two new restaurants at Peyrou D'Amont (halfway stage of the cable-car) and Col des Ruillans (at the top of the gondola).

La Grave is quiet after dark but there is a handful of bars and all the hotels have restaurants. There is also a crêperie. The area is known for its excellent mountain cheeses and pasta.

WHAT ELSE TO DO THERE

Exhibitions of handicrafts and regional cooking in Villar d'Arène (next village). Shrine and panorama in Le Chazelet (nearby village).
Visit Briançon, the highest town in Europe (28 km).

WHERE TO STAY

There are 500 beds in La Grave with plenty of cheap accommodation. Expect to pay about 120F-200F per night half board, or 150F-250F per night full board.

IN CASE OF EMERGENCY

Doctor in resort: One.
Nearest chemist: Bourg d'Oisans (28 km).
Nearest dentist: Bourg d'Oisans (28 km).
Nearest hospital: Briançon (28 km).
Helicopter rescue service: Yes. From Les Deux Alpes (18 km).

HOW TO GET THERE

Nearest Airport: Grenoble. Also accessible from Lyon or Turin.
Transfer time: About 1½ hours from Grenoble.
Train connection: Paris to Grenoble (3 hours) then coach.

FURTHER INFORMATION

Tourist Office La Grave (Tel: 76 79 90 05).

LES GETS

- **HEIGHT OF RESORT**
  1172 m.

- **HIGHEST LIFT**
  1850 m.

- **WHY GO THERE?**
  Access to 650 km of pistes in the Portes du Soleil—without the coach-loads of British.
  Excellent facilities for children.
  French ambiance.

- **WHO GOES THERE?**
  Trendy young French skiers.
  French ski bunnies who'd rather sun themselves on the terrraces than exert themselves on the pistes.
  Families.
  85 per cent French and a cosmopolitan mix of Belgians, Dutch, Germans, Italians, Swiss, Danes and British.

- **COMPANIES THAT GO THERE**
  There are a handful of English companies in Les Gets, but these are mainly chalet-based, with a small bed capacity:
  Ski Total.
  Supersport Travel.
  Red Fox.
  Ski MM.
  Ski West.

The Portes du Soleil is a massive ski area, linking a dozen French and Swiss resorts via 220 lifts and 650 km of pistes. It is certainly not 'undiscovered', but most of the British congregate in Avoriaz or Morzine. Les Gets is only 6 km down the road from Morzine, yet it is distinctly French in style and clientele. There is one main street, chock-a-block with smart chalet-style hotels, bars and restaurants. Another street runs parallel—together they form a humming centre that is almost as busy in the daytime as it is after the lifts have shut. Every Thursday they have a market. Many of the hotels have large sun terraces, looking on to the Chavannes ski slopes. These terraces are often packed with chic young people sunning themselves in deckchairs. Les Gets is a place to pose. It is also a ski-shopaholics' paradise (and their partners' idea of financial hell!) as there are 22 ski shops, all trying to sell the most outrageous, and expensive, clothes and equipment. Les Gets is the sort of resort where you will see couples in 'his 'n' her' designer ski suits, and babies wrapped up in fur blankets and beaver bonnets. I once read an English review which accused Les Gets of lacking atmosphere. Although it does not have the *gemütlichkeit* of an Austrian resort, it has that certain French 'je ne sais quoi'. It is a stylish resort where most of the socialising takes place in bars and cafés. Bring your Ray-Bans.

One problem is traffic. There is a covered car park and the main square has been turned into a rather ugly parking lot—which sadly rather spoils the charm of the town centre. There is also a very busy one-way system (do keep your wits about you when crossing the roads). This is a shame, because otherwise it is a fantastic resort for small children. There is a baby club for little ones from 3 months to 3 years old (Tel 50 79 84 84), supervised by a nurse. The ESF (French ski school) take children from 2 to 5 years. They play with them, teach them to ski, and also have provisions for their rest and lunch. The rival ski school, Ski Espace, takes children from 3 years old. The under-5s get a free ski pass. Les Gets is also very French in its alternative approach to skiing. There is hang-gliding, paragliding, snowboarding and mono-skiing. You can also learn to ride trike or quad (a three or four-wheeled motorbike) or cruise round the pistes James-Bond style on a skidoo (snow bike). It is a place to ski and be seen.

THE SKIING

Les Gets has the charm of a traditional town, combined with the skiing convenience of a modern purpose-built resort. Many of the hotels are right next to the lifts. There are two main ski areas—Chavannes (links Les Gets to the Morzine and the Portes du Soleil) and Mont Chéry. Mont Chéry has more challenging skiing than Chavannes, and is usually less crowded as it is not linked to the rest of the Portes du Soleil. From the middle station, you have a spectacular view of Mont Blanc. Mont Chéry has four black runs including a couple of steep ones through the trees. If you have had too many vin chauds and don't want to risk the black run back down to the village, you can take the gondola or a red run. Chavannes is a more popular ski area and is reached by road, gondola, or a new four-seater chair-lift. Here there are several restaurants with sun terraces and one hotel—Croix Blanche (Tel 50 79 73 78). From this side of Les Gets it is possible to ski over to Morzine. A bus, or a walk across town and a cable car, takes you on into Avoriaz and the rest of the Portes du Soleil.

This well-known area provides good skiing for all standards and does not really need an introduction to the British skier. Les Gets has some very good nursery slopes in Chavannes and right next to the village, but I heard one of the more nervous novices complain that the progression to the main slopes is too radical and 'intimidating'.

CROSS-COUNTRY

Cross-country skiing is quite popular in Les Gets. They have 25 km of prepared tracks.

SKI SCHOOL

There are three ski schools and 120 instructors in Les Gets. The main one is the traditional Ecole du Ski Français (Tel 50 79 75 07). Six mornings 340F (270F kids), six afternoons 300F (250F kids). 120F for one-hour private lesson in cross-country, downhill or mono. The ESF is rivalled by Ski Espace (Tel 50 79 80 08/ 50 79 74 04). Six mornings 300F (245F kids), six afternoons 280F (235F). One hour of private instruction 110F. The third and most 'alternative' school is called Ski Plus (Tel 50 79 73 55) and has a special 'a la carte' programme which includes moguls and slalom with video correction, surfing and monoskiing, a tour of the Portes du Soleil and Grand Massif, ski touring and off piste, competitions, heli-skiing (not allowed in the Portes du Soleil), paragliding (*parapente*) and hang-gliding (*delta*).

LIFT PASSES

A six-day pass for Les Gets (30 lifts) costs 492F (369F kids). This is perfectly adequate for beginners and second to third-week skiers. Better skiers will benefit from purchasing the Portes du Soleil pass for 680F (478F kids).

WHERE TO EAT, DRINK & BOOGIE

There are plenty of places to eat, on and off the slopes, mostly simple brasserie-style places. I would recommend skiers to have lunch at the top of Mont Chéry in the Belvedere restaurant. There are five restaurants at Chavannes and another one at La Turche. Down in the village, Le Schuss (Tel 50 79 71 67) is an enticing place for tea with a very calorific selection of home-made pastries, chocolates and ice creams. Nearby, Le Tourbillon (Tel 50 79 70 34), is a simple traditional restaurant, popular for its *brasserade*. This is finely sliced beef, which you cook yourself on a mini charcoal grill on the table. It comes served with a variety of spicy dips. Le Tyrol (Tel 50 79 70 55) and Le Vieux Chêne (Tel 50 79 71 93) are also good traditional restaurants. Le Magnétie Théâtre is a modern black and red cocktail bar. The owner's wife runs the popular L'Igloo nightclub which is

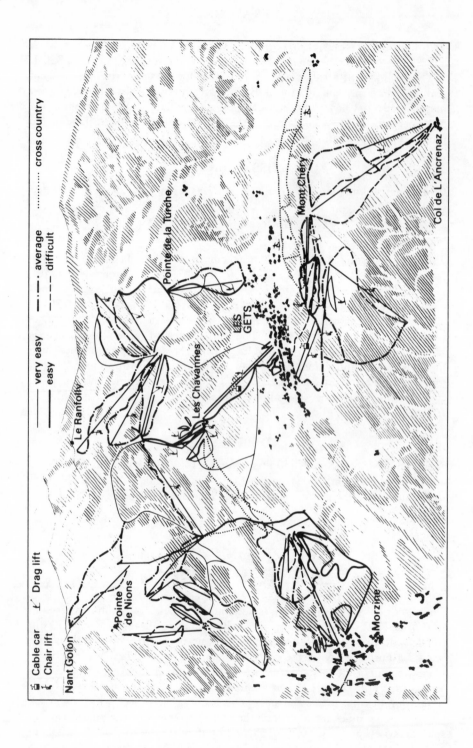

Cable car   ⼳ Drag lift

⼳ Chair lift

very easy   —·—· average   ········ cross country

—— easy   – – – difficult

Nant Golon

Le Ranfolly

Pointe de Nions

Les Chavannes

Pointe de la Turche

LES GETS

Morzine

Mont-Chéry

Col de L'Ancrenaz

open until about 4 am. This is a typical French club, where it is fun just to sit and watch. When I was there, an Annie Lennox lookalike danced everyone off their feet and a young French man in a purple glitter waistcoat demonstrated Ceroc (French rock 'n' roll dancing). There are two other night clubs in Les Gets, La Peau d'Vache and Chic 74 (in La Turche). If you just want to drink, Equateur, next to La Marmotte, has live bands and is a popular meeting place.

WHAT ELSE TO DO THERE

Hang-gliding (Tel 50 79 82 88/50 79 73 55).
Skidoo.
Swimming in Hotel Marmotte.
Two cinemas showing different films (in French) every night.
30 m of marked walks.
Massage.
Fitness room and jacuzzi in Hotel Les Alpages.
Museum of Mechanical Musical Instruments—open 2 pm-7 pm every day.

WHERE TO STAY

There is no shortage of good hotels in Les Gets. Most of these are modern and attractive chalet-style buildings. We stayed in the three-star L'Ours Blanc (Tel 50 79 14 66) which is above the main street but very close to the Mont Chéry gondola. It is a quiet but very comfortable place to stay. From 340F full board per night. If you like to be more in the swing of things, there are several good hotels in the centre. La Marmotte (Tel 50 79 75 39) is a pleasant chalet-style place, with all the balconies overlooking the pistes. The hotel has an indoor swimming pool, sauna and massage. Nearby, the Mont-Chéry (Tel 50 79 74 55) is also an attractive and comfortable hotel. A list of available apartments is available from the tourist office (see below).

IN CASE OF EMERGENCY

Doctors in resort: Four.
Chemist in resort: One.
Dentist in resort: One.
Nearest Hospital: Cluses or Thonon.
Helicopter Rescue: Yes.

HOW TO GET THERE

Nearest Airport: Geneva.
Coach connection: From Geneva airport—$1\frac{1}{2}$ hours.

FURTHER INFORMATION

Tourist Office BP 27, 74260 Les Gets (Tel 50 79 75 55).

LE GRAND BORNAND

- **HEIGHT OF RESORT**
  1,000 m.

- **HIGHEST LIFT**
  2,100 m.

- **WHY GO THERE?**
  The nearest resort to Geneva.
  Weekend skiing.
  Good skiing for beginners and intermediates.
  Not just a ski resort—an authentic French market town.

- **WHO GOES THERE?**
  Dedicated (but fun) French skiers.
  Swiss weekenders.
  Those in search of *nouvelles sensations* (snowboard and mono-ski).
  A few discerning British independents.

- **COMPANIES THAT GO THERE**
  White Roc

The first time I went to Le Grand Bornand was for a weekend. Although it is in France, Le Grand Bornand, in the Haute Savoie, is the closest resort to Geneva, so it is very popular with the Swiss. It is a small, quiet village, only 50 km and under one hour's drive from the airport. It is less sophisticated than some of the better-known French resorts such as Megève, but the prices are much cheaper. Last season a lift pass in Le Grand Bornand cost about £50 compared to £70 in Megève.

Le Grand Bornand is a typical French market town with most of the buildings surrounding a chubbily ornate church. Every Wednesday there is a market selling all sorts of local goodies, such as walnuts, home-made sausages, smoked hams, local cheeses, breads and wines. They also sell leather goods and fur hats. Le Grand Bornand originally became famous for its cheese—Reblochon. In winter, you can see it is still a farming village as the cattle are kept under the chalets. On my first day, I beckoned to what I thought was a friendly cow but turned out to be a none-too-friendly bull, which chased me all the way back to the chalet. Thankfully, the door was not locked.

You won't find anywhere more villagey than Le Grand Bornand. The locals (of the human variety!) are very friendly and the place is run by three main families. I couldn't understand why everyone kept referring to the 'bastard taxis' and the 'bastard supermarket'. It turned out that the Bastard family runs the taxis, ambulance and supermarket. The latter even sells Bastard wine—worth taking home as a souvenir, if only for the label! The rest of the village is run by the Perissins (butcher and electrician) and the Ogiers (ski enthusiasts who own a popular shop specialising in snowboarding and also run the Starski school).

300 m further up the mountain is the satellite hamlet of Chinaillon. This comprises a few modern hotels and restaurants but does not have nearly as much character as the village.

Le Grand Bornand has good facilities for children (see Ski School below). There is a baby club at Chinaillon (Tel: 50 27 00 18) for children from 18 months to 6 years old. In the village there is a mini-club for 3-6 year olds.

THE SKIING

Le Grand Bornand, in the Aravis mountains, has 65 km of varied pistes—enough to keep beginners and most intermediates happy for a week. More experienced skiers will be able to ski the whole resort in a couple of days but as it is so near Geneva I would still recommend it for weekend skiing. There is also plentiful off-piste all over the resort. A new gondola from the village takes you up to La Côte. From here you can take a chair up to the highest point, Le Lachat (2,100m), where there is a long challenging black run. Some of the steep red runs can also be quite tricky when covered in moguls. Beginners and intermediates will enjoy the long wide blue and red runs in Chinaillon and Maroly/Douche areas. The longest run is the Col des Annes, a fantastic blue piste which sweeps down the mountain, past a nunnery. Powder novices will enjoy practising just off this gentle piste.

Mono and snowboarding are very popular in Le Grand Bornand. Unlike many resorts, this is encouraged by the locals rather than frowned upon (eg the lifts *slow down* rather than accelerate to pick you up!). Queueing is not part of the peaceful Le Grand Bornand way of life. Even in peak season, we never waited more than 15 minutes. A week's lift pass includes a day at La Clusaz which offers a further 150 km of runs a bus-ride away.

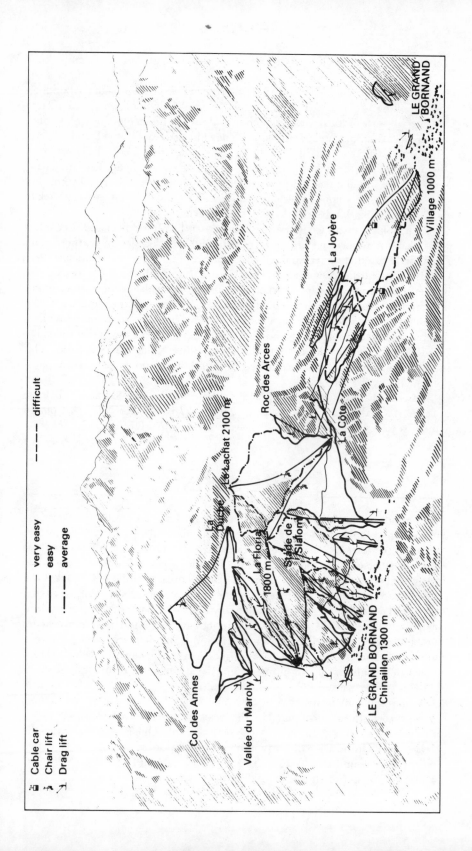

very easy
easy
average
difficult

Cable car
Chair lift
Drag lift

Col des Annes

Vallée du Maroly

La Duche

La Floria
1800 m

Stade de
Slalom

Le Lachat 2100 m

Roc des Arces

La Côte

La Joyère

LE GRAND BORNAND
Chinaillon 1300 m

LE GRAND BORNAND

Village 1000 m

CROSS-COUNTRY

There are 50 km of trails starting from the Auberge Nordique. They ski over artificial obstacles such as bridges—it all looked too much like hard work for me! You can also ski over to La Clusaz (14 km there and back). 1 km floodlit trail, one evening a week. There is a special cross-country ski school. They have an office in the village (Tel: 50 02 21 38), in Chinaillon (Tel: 50 27 00 37) and at the Auberge Nordique (Tel: 50 02 31 12). 65F (52F kids) for a morning's instruction, or 110F per hour for a private lesson.

SKI SCHOOL

L'Ecole de Ski Français in the village (Tel: 50 02 20 82) or in Chinaillon (Tel: 50 27 01 83). Six mornings (2½ hours) 300F (235F kids), six afternoons (2 hours) 230F (185F kids). Private lessons 115F per hour. The ESF run Le Club des Oursons (Little Bear Club) for 4 to 6 year olds and there is also a Jardin de Neige in the village and at Chinaillon for 4 year olds, upwards. There is also an independent school called Starski School which has a fresher approach to teaching and gives excellent lessons in snowboarding. You should spot the difference immediately—the ESF wear traditional red and blue suits, while the Starski teachers are in fluorescent pink with lime green stars. The Starski School is based at Chinaillon.

LIFT PASSES

500F for six days (450F kids)—includes one day in La Clusaz. Weekend 180F.

WHERE TO EAT, DRINK & BOOGIE

There are eight restaurants on the slopes. My favourite is Le Bournerie where you can sunbathe on the terrace and watch chickens roasting on a spit. There are also plenty of bars and restaurants in the village. The best bar is Le Panda, a dark, low-ceilinged place with posters of Diva and the Montreux Jazz Festival, a pool table, music and videos. They hold a disco every Friday night in high season, and occasionally have live bands. The Laser 6 disco is just outside the village. I found it quiet and expensive—not really worth the effort. I would recommend the Pizzeria Casanova, especially if it is still run by Maria who is most friendly and helpful. La Flambée (Tel: 50 02 32 67) serves wholesome and reasonably priced French dishes. If you're looking for something really rustic, try Chez Roger (Tel: 50 02 35 79), a mountain refuge, set deep in the snow. When I asked where the loo was, I was given a torch and pointed to the balcony. It's that sort of place! The menu is very limited, comprising a rich fondue and sometimes a speciality of the day. For pudding, there is *crème caramel* or *myrtilles* (blueberry) tart. You need to book in advance.

WHAT ELSE TO DO THERE

Not much.

Guided walks in snow shoes. Every Thursday evening they do a special snow shoe walk and fondue evening.

Hang-gliding.

WHERE TO STAY

There are 15 hotels in Le Grand Bornand, mainly small and family-run. The two-star hotel, Les Ecureuils (Tel 50 02 20 11) is near the lifts. 178-240F half board. Les Glaïeuls (Tel 50 02 20 23) is also well-located (Tel: 50 02 20 23). The English company White Roc have a pretty Alpine chalet called Qu'melles which has solid dark oak furniture and embroidered tablecloths. The chalet is only 100m from the cable car. White Roc can also arrange self-catering accommodation in apartments, 500 m from the lift station.

IN CASE OF EMERGENCY

Doctor in resort: There is a good medical centre in the resort.

Chemist in resort: One.

Dentist in resort: One.

Nearest Hospital: Bonneville.

Helicopter Rescue: Yes.

HOW TO GET THERE

Nearest Airport: Geneva.

Transfer time: 1 hour.

Train connection: Annency (32 km from Le Grand Bornand). The high speed TGV train from Paris takes 3 hours to Annency.

FURTHER INFORMATION

Tourist Office 74450 Le Grand Bornand (Tel: 50 02 20 33).

LE PRAZ-DE-LYS

- **HEIGHT OF RESORT**
  1,500 m.

- **HIGHEST LIFT**
  1,740 m.

- **WHY GO THERE?**
  Well-balanced combination of cross-country and downhill skiing.
  Breathtaking panorama.
  The ultimate rustic retreat.
  Excellent value for money, particularly in January.

- **WHO GOES THERE?**
  French cross-country skiers—unsophisticated.
  The French equivalent of the Ramblers Association.
  Anyone who wants to escape from it all.

- **COMPANIES THAT GO THERE**
  Ace.
  Red Guide.

We had quite a hairy drive up to Praz-de-Lys from the nearby town of Taninges. Although it was January, most of France was green and springlike, but this 12 km road was perilously icy with lots of stomach-churning bends. As we cautiously emerged out of the thick fir forest, sunny Praz-de-Lys stretched out in front of us. It was one of the most spectacular sights I've ever seen—a vast white canvas of sunny snow fields. It reminded me of a Lowry painting—lots of tiny figures dotted across the landscape, skiing, walking and playing in the snow, interspersed by tiny wooden chalets. Praz-de-Lys is certainly a perfect place for anyone who does not like to feel hemmed in. It is a massive plateau of snowy fields with the spectacular backdrop of Mont Blanc. The Marcely peak (2,008 m) dominates the horizon.

There is no mistaking that Praz-de-Lys is a popular cross-country resort. Every which way you look there are cross-country skiers gliding through the snow, in the woods and wonderfully open fields. There were men, women, children and the elderlyon skis—some were even 'walking' their dogs. One field was obviously designated for novices—the red-uniformed ski instructors offered a gentle helping hand to the bambi-legged beginners stumbling in the snow. Praz-de-Lys also has good alpine skiing facilities with 33 perfectly-groomed pistes and 21 lifts. In most ski resorts you have to drive or catch a lift or two to reach the skiing area. Praz-de-Lys is unusual in that the resort and skiing are mingled into one. Many of the runs start as soon as you step out of your hotel.

Although the resort has not yet been hit by commercialism, they have started to invest some money into it, and there are some modern apartment blocks on the outskirts of the village. These are ugly characterless buildings, similar to what you would find in Flaine or Avoriaz. The main village reminded me of an old Hollywood Western set—a wide street with the shops, restaurants and a cowboy saloon-bar style hotel underneath the arches. It is certainly not a chic or sophisticated place but it does have a certain simple charm of its own.

THE SKIING

Praz-de-Lys has a very good snow record. I could not understand why they had snow whilst other higher resorts nearby were green. My guide went into a complicated explanation about Praz-de-Lys' 'micro-climate' and how it is the nearest resort to Lac Leman. My French was not good enough to follow all the ins and outs, but in brief, this resort is a good bet snow-wise.

There are 50 km of pistes with 18 drag-lifts and three chair-lifts. The pistes are well groomed and patrolled by James Bond-style men on skidoos (snow bikes). The ski area is spread out across the village so you are bound to find a lift near you that connects with the main system. The skiing in Praz-de-Lys is very varied and gives you a great sense of space, as it extends over two and a half mountains. The skiing is best suited to beginners and intermediates. There is also a lot of off-piste which should keep the experts happy for a good few days. Ski touring is possible, for example over to the peak of Marcelly (2,002 m).

What I liked best about skiing in Praz-de-Lys was the fabulous views encompassing all the nearby resorts such as Flaine, La Clusaz, Argentière and Megève. It would be hard to find a more panoramic place to ski.

Directly above the village there are a couple of green runs, five blues, two reds and a black. This black run, Planey, is visible from the Hotel Chamois. Before you ski down it, walk over to the edge from where there is an amazing view of the valley and distant peaks. The run itself is only difficult for the first 50 m. The Praz-de-Lys ski area is linked to Sommand. The easiest way across is on the Bresy ski lift; this is the only lift to suffer from bottlenecks, with a maximum of 10 minutes' wait. The hardest run is the black Écheru at the far end on Sommand. This is never pisted at the top, and is very steep with large moguls. There are also some long blue and red runs on Sommand. From Sommand you can zig-zag over to Col de La Ramaz and ski over to the Praz L'Evêque chair-lift. Here there is a long steep black run which is narrow and rather moguly. Less experienced skiers can take a more gentle red route although this also has a mogul section.

CROSS-COUNTRY

The open spaces of Praz-de-Lys are enough to inspire the most ardent alpine skiers to try cross-country skiing. There are 82 km of lovingly cared-for trails with everything from nursery slopes to a well-known black run. The latter is called Chalet Blanc and is 4,500 m long and takes you in between two big cols.

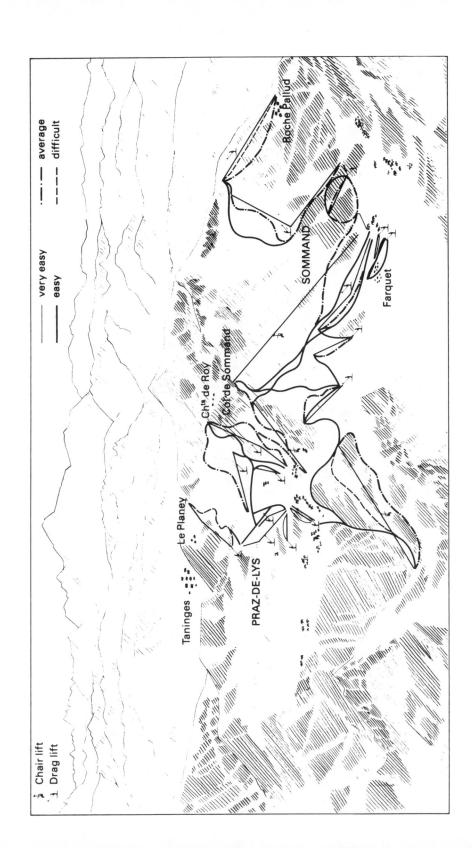

Chair lift

Drag lift

very easy

easy

average

difficult

Taninges

Le Planey

Ch.ᵗᵉ de Roy

Col de Sommand

SOMMAND

Farquet

PRAZ-DE-LYS

Roche Pallud

Every year they hold the 'Traversée de La Ramaz', a 35 km race from Praz-de-Lys to Sommand.

SKI SCHOOL

(Tel 50 34 33 68).
60F for two-hour class (50F children). Six mornings or afternoons 280F. Also lessons in cross-country, mono-ski, ski-jumping, touring and freestyle.

LIFT PASSES

315F for seven days (252F kids). Covers Praz-de-Lys and Sommand. Special January reduction 240F (240F kids).

WHERE TO EAT, DRINK & BOOGIE

Praz-de-Lys is not the place to come for gourmet wining and dining and a hectic nightlife. It is a simple, sleepy town that has a few basic restaurants, bars and a small nightclub. As the resort is part of the ski area, you can easily eat at the same places for lunch and dinner. I would recommend eating at Le Chamois, a chalet-type 'shack' perched hazardously on the edge of a hill. Outside is a sun terrace where cross-country and alpine skiers chat over a few vin chauds. Inside, the restaurant is packed with hungry skiers who have a wonderful view of Mont Blanc through the wooden shuttered windows. The patron is also the chef. He cooked us a wonderful four-course hearty lunch. We started with home-made paté and local cured ham. This was served with a large tuna salad and would have been a meal on its own. Afterwards came roast pork in garlic and shallots. Then a big platter of cheese and a choice of desserts. I chose a gloriously runny chocolate mousse whilst my friends tucked into homemade apple pie and fresh fruit salad. The local red wine was a very mellow accompaniment.

WHAT ELSE TO DO THERE

Not much unless you want to brave the 12 km drive back down to Taninges. There are plenty of places for sunbathing and 15 km of prepared walking paths.

WHERE TO STAY

There are only four hotels in Le Praz-de-Lys, the rest of the accommodation being dotted around in chalets, auberges, a youth hostel and apartments. There is nowhere deluxe. In keeping with the hearty outdoor spirit of this resort, the accommodation is mainly rustic with small one- and two-star hotels. Hotel Romeo Bagatelle II (Tel 50 34 24 26) is supposedly their premier hotel (two stars). It is a saloon-bar style building in the main high street, conveniently located for skiing, right opposite the ski school and tourist office. Hotel or apartment accommodation from 240F to 290F per night half board. The Hotel Le Chamois (50 34 22 72) (see Where to Eat, above) has much more ambience. It is not in the centre of the village, but is well-located for skiing as it is half-way down a blue run so you can ski to and from the hotel. It is worth staying there just for the views. The accommodation is clean but basic—not all the rooms have private facilities. The hotel is sometimes used for school and group bookings (usually at Easter—check before booking). From 100F per night bed and breakfast. From 150F per night half board. The British tour operator, Ace Skiing Holidays, offer excellent value package holidays to Le Chamois, from £245 half board including a six-day lift pass.

There are also several apartment blocks in Praz-de-Lys. The ones in the centre of the village look more attractive than the ugly constructions passed as you drive into the resort. Self-catering accommodation is very cheap. Four people can share a studio apartment from 1,000F for a week. Le Praz-de-Lys makes a particular effort to promote January. A week in a studio for four costs 520F per person including lift pass, or 365F per person for cross-country skiing only.

IN CASE OF EMERGENCY

Nearest doctor: Taninges. Will come up to the resort.
Nearest chemist: Taninges.
Nearest dentist: Taninges.
Nearest hospital: Cluses.
Helicopter Rescue: Yes.

HOW TO GET THERE

Nearest Airport: Geneva.
Transfer time: 1hr. Bus to Taninges then another bus to Praz-de-Lys.
Train connection: To Cluses (10 km from Taninges), then bus.

FURTHER INFORMATION

Tourist Office 74440 Taninges/Le Praz-de-Lys (Tel 50 34 25 05).

SAMOËNS

- **HEIGHT OF RESORT**
  720 m.

- **HIGHEST LIFT**
  2,113 m.

- **WHY GO THERE?**
  Beautiful old historic town near large ski area (linked to Flaine).
  Easy access, particularly by car.
  Lots going on.

- **WHO GOES THERE?**
  Sporty people.
  Unpretentious French skiers.
  A few Dutch, Belgians and Germans.

- **COMPANIES THAT GO THERE**
  Ski Scene (Intasun).

When I first arrived in Samoëns, I thought I had got the wrong place. Unlike most resorts, which are reached by winding and often perilous mountain roads, the approach to Samoëns is on a long flat tree-lined road in the base of the valley. Samoëns itself is a fascinating old French farming town, which dates back to the fifth century and certainly does not look like an ordinary ski resort. On closer inspection, a scattering of ski shops and some ski-clad tourists reassured me that I had not been led astray.

Samoëns offers some superb skiing as it is linked with Flaine and the 260 km of pistes of the Grand Massif. It is not a place for convenience skiers. The skiing is way above the low-set village and takes a 15-minute drive or ski-bus ride. I personally liked the village so much that this did not pose a problem, but if you are the sort of person who wants to spend every waking hour on the slopes, you can stay half way up the mountain in one of their new purpose-built hotels. For those who like a more laid-back holiday, the old village of Samoëns is a charming place. It prides itself in being the only ski resort in France to be listed as an artistic and historical site, the '88th town'. There is so much to see that there are two-hour guided tours of the village, twice a week. The architecture is very attractive—small, narrow streets of old stone houses and even a small château. In the centre is a cool, shady square with a majestic church and a linden tree which was planted in 1438. Every Wednesday morning the square is packed with market stalls that spill down as far as the tourist office. There is also an alpine botanical garden.

Samoëns looks a prosperous part of the Haute Savoie—the village is surrounded by plush privately owned chalets. The village hotels are mainly traditional, smart, chalet-style buildings. It is totally different from the grey, ugly, purpose-built architecture of Flaine. Although I enjoyed skiing over to Flaine, by the end of the day I was glad to escape from the hordes of Brits and the purpose-built resort's oppressive atmosphere. It was a pleasure to return for 'tea' in one of Samoëns' elegant Viennese-style tea rooms and wander at leisure round the quiet backstreets as the sun was setting.

THE SKIING

A quick glance at the piste map will show you just how extensive the skiing is. Samoëns is linked to Flaine and the Grand Massif—a total of 83 lifts and 260 km of pistes. You need to drive or catch the bus (15 minutes) to Vercland where a gondola takes you up to Samoëns (1,600 m). Here there are several hotels, some cramped apartments, restaurants, bars, ski hire and the ski school. There are a couple of nursery slopes and short blue runs for beginners. The skiing in Samoëns is mainly below the treeline. My young guide took great pleasure in pointing out the tracks of the chamois dotted through the woods. He said there was a lot of good off-piste in Samoëns. Intermediates can easily ski over to Flaine. There are runs to suit all abilities, most of them above the treeline. The runs are wide and some of the difficult ones have easier descents down the sides. There are a couple of excellent short, steep, moguly black runs and some good off-piste from Pré des Saix (2,113 m) down to Samoëns 1,600. Less-experienced skiers will enjoy the long blue and green runs leading down to the quiet village of Morillon (700 m). As the popular 'L'Igloo' restaurant is at the bottom of La Vieille chair-lift in Morillon, the green run is also used as coasting ground by good skiers. There is a fantastically long blue run from Lac de Vernant down to Les Carroz (1,140 m). At the end of the day you can ski down all the way from Pré des Saix to Vercland on a black or red run–the ski instructors often take the coolest way down the mountain, via parapente.

SKI TOURING

Ski tourers can eat fondue and stay overnight in the Refuge Bostan-Tornay at 1,763 m (Tel 50 67 01 96 or 50 90 10 94).

CROSS-COUNTRY

(Tel: 50 34 46 02).
Weekly card 85F. Daily 20F. 70 km between Morrillon, Samoëns and Sixt.

SKI SCHOOL

(Tel 50 34 43 12).
Six (2½ hour) lessons 362F (296F kids). Private lessons 111F per hour. Lessons also available in monoski, snowboard, slalom and jumping. Special powder courses. Ski touring. Kindergarten for 4-6 year olds. Baby-sitting available.

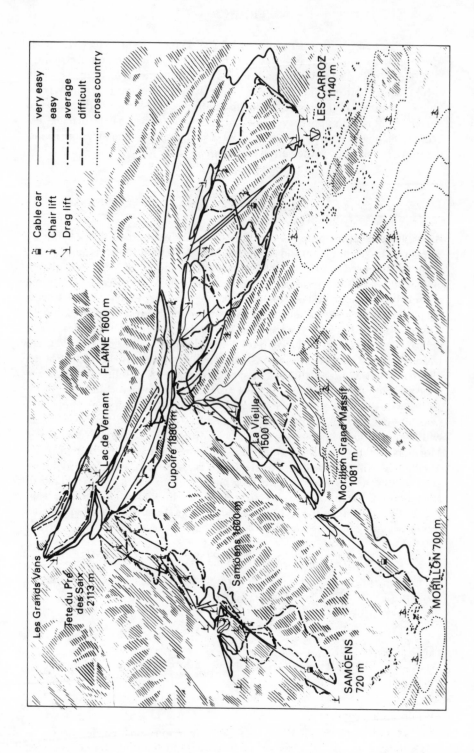

LIFT PASSES

Massif pass (covers Samoëns, Morrillon, Les Carroz, Sixt) 462F (379F kids).
Grand Massif (covers Massif and Flaine) 620F (500F kids).

WHERE TO EAT, DRINK & BOOGIE

There are three mountain restaurants in Samoëns as well as others in Flaine, Les Carroz and Morrillon.

Samoëns is a charming little place to walk around after skiing. There are a couple of excellent Viennese pâtisseries, such as A La Jaÿsinia where they serve wonderful cakes, coffees, hot chocolates, and even cocktails. There are plenty of good, simple restaurants in the village serving local Savoyarde specialities. One dish which is uniquely Samoëns is *La Soupe Chatre*. The head of the tourist office, poor man, had to use a lot of painful sign language to explain that this translates literally as 'castrated soup'! It is made from tomatoes, bread and onion, cooked for four hours, gratinéed and cut. The only place you can eat this is La Fandioleuse (Tel 50 34 98 28). Unfortunately, when I went it was closed, so I have never tried castrated soup, but I did have an excellent fondue which was specially prepared for us at Le Mini-Golf (Tel 50 34 42 83). This is a small, unpretentious bar/restaurant place that does local specialities. As we were the only people there, we had a very intimate 'fondue-à-deux' in front of their big log fire. A little less romantic is the large pinball room (popular with the local kids), next to the bar. For a more sophisticated evening, Samoëns has two new cocktail bars (Le Cafe and Le Bouly). Le Paradis Perdus (The Lost Paradise) is a nightclub that is open until 4 am. The restaurant/pizzeria La Louisiane also has dancing.

WHAT ELSE TO DO THERE

Lots!
A two-hour guided history tour every Tuesday and Friday morning.
Botanical gardens.
Cinema, showing two films each day.
Husky dog driving and pulka.
Torchlight descents.
Floodlit cross-country.
Tobogganing.
Walks and snow-shoe excursions.
Saunas and fitness rooms in hotels. Massage and beauty rooms.
Paragliding (Tel 50 34 95 80). 250F for a flight. Hang-gliding (Tel 50 34 95 80).
Taught by Michel Jardin, an ex-member of the French team. 350F for a flight.

WHERE TO STAY

There is a very good standard of hotels in Samoëns. We stayed at Neige et Roc (50 34 40 72) an attractive and comfortable hotel with its own luxurious fitness room (jacuzzi, sauna, steam etc) and lounge with welcoming log-fire. 230F-290F per night half board. Les Glaciers (Tel 50 34 40 06) is in the centre of the village and is another good quality hotel. For convenience skiing, without the character of the old village, you can also stay in one of the modern hotels at Samoëns 1,600, such as Au Rendez-Vous Des Skieurs (Tel: 50 34 40 84), 230F per night half board.

IN CASE OF EMERGENCY

Doctors in resort: Five (there's even a foot specialist).
Chemists in resort: Two.
Dentists in resort: Two.
Nearest Hospital: Cluses (20 km).
Helicopter Rescue: Yes.

HOW TO GET THERE

Nearest Airport: Geneva.
Transfer time: $1\frac{1}{2}$ hours.
Train connection: Cluses (20 km).

FURTHER INFORMATION

Tourist Office 74340 Samoëns (Tel 50 34 40 28).

LES 7 LAUX

It was a strange drive up to Les 7 Laux (literally, the seven lakes) which is between Grenoble and Chambery in the Alpes Dauphinés. The roads were good and we passed through several traditional French towns. Then we went round a bend, and came face to face with this imposing-looking structure perched half-way up the mountain. Les 7 Laux is a purpose-built resort of dark wood and glass that looks as though it has been carved out of the mountain. At first sight it reminded me of Avoriaz. There is an old traditional village directly underneath and in striking contrast to this modern resort.

All the accommodation in the ski area is in apartments although they are planning to build hotels in 1990/91. The main part of the resort is Prapoutel, a concrete and wooden high-rise. It is a good example of how a well-designed French purpose-built resort should function. You park your car, go in to the tourist office, buy your lift pass and literally step out the other side onto the pistes. Many of the restaurants and bars back on to the slopes, and the shops and tourist office are all in the main 'mall'-style development. The subsidiary stations, Pipay and Le Pleynet, are very much smaller and cater more for day-skiing and *ski-tranquille*. There is literally no development at all at Pipay apart from one bar, a shop and a couple of ski lifts. There are several villages dotted around the ski area which offer simple, rustic, hotel accommodation.

Although Les 7 Laux is a rather ugly development, it is excellent for convenience skiing and families. There is a crèche (18 months to 8 years) and a jardin de neige next to the main apartment block in Prapoutel. The children's slopes are at the top of the Debrayable du Bouquet chair-lift (can be taken on foot), next to a sunny bar. There is also a small kids' development in Le Pleynet.

- **HEIGHT OF RESORT**
  1,350 m-1,450 m.

- **HIGHEST LIFT**
  2,400 m.

- **WHY GO THERE?**
  Convenience skiing.
  'Grande Montagne' atmosphere.
  Challenging skiing in beautiful surroundings.

- **WHO GOES THERE?**
  Grenoblois and Lyonnais weekenders.
  Skiers rather than posers.

- **COMPANIES THAT GO THERE**
  None.

THE SKIING

Don't be put off by the piste map which makes it look as though there is not much skiing in Les 7 Laux. In fact, although there are only 60 runs, these are mainly long and offer plenty to entertain most intermediates for a week. There are slopes on both sides of the mountains, linking the three resorts of Prapoutel,

Pipay and Le Pleynet. The slopes are arranged in such a way that it is possible to ski in the sun all day—Le Pleynet faces south-east, Prapoutel and Pipay face north-west. The steepest pistes are at Prapoutel—this is where you will see the young sportifs bombing down the mogul fields. Pipay is more laid back, with tree-lined slopes and 'tranquille' skiing, perfect for families and children. There are some lovely long green pistes in both Pipay and Prapoutel. There is one very hard black run in Pipay called Mataru. Le Pleynet is on the other side of the mountain and links Prapoutel and Pipay with wide, high runs over a steep-sided *combe*. There is very good off-piste all over the resort. There is a high risk of avalanche in some parts, but this is kept well under control. The lift system is well devised and there is little queueing. Weekends tend to get busy although the new lifts at Pipay should have eased any bottlenecks.

Les 7 Laux will appeal to anyone who likes the hassle to be taken out of skiing. The slopes are very accessible and everywhere in the resort can be reached quickly and with little fuss.

CROSS-COUNTRY

Good. Mostly on high 1,800 m plateau. Loops up to 25 km. Superb views. Access by chairlift. Lessons available from ESF Pleynet (Tel: 76 08 03 44).

SKI SCHOOL

Ecole de Ski de Prapoutel (Tel: 76 08 02 36).
Six half-days 320F (270F kids). Private lessons 120F per hour. Lessons also available in snowboarding, telemarking and cross-country skiing.

LIFT PASSES

450F for six days (210F under 10s). 93F (46F) per day.

WHERE TO EAT, DRINK & BOOGIE

There are plenty of sunny little restaurants dotted over the mountain.
The Prapoutel complex is full of bars, cafés and restaurants and also has one nightclub. There are also four restaurants at Le Pleynet and one at Pipay. Dîner-à-deux costs about 100F per head plus wine.

WHAT ELSE TO DO THERE

Paragliding and hang-gliding (Tel 76 08 96 06).
Guided walks on snow shoes.
Energie 7 (Tel 76 08 71 91) has a gymnasium, jacuzzi, sauna, beauty salon and massage.
Cinema at Prapoutel.

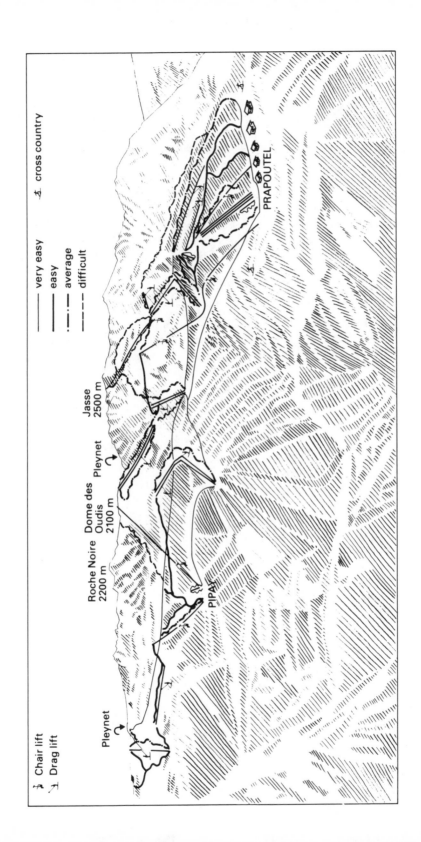

Chair lift
Drag lift

very easy
easy
average
difficult
cross country

Pleynet

Roche Noire
2200 m

Dome des
Oudis
2100 m

Pleynet

Jasse
2500 m

PIPAY

PRAPOUTEL

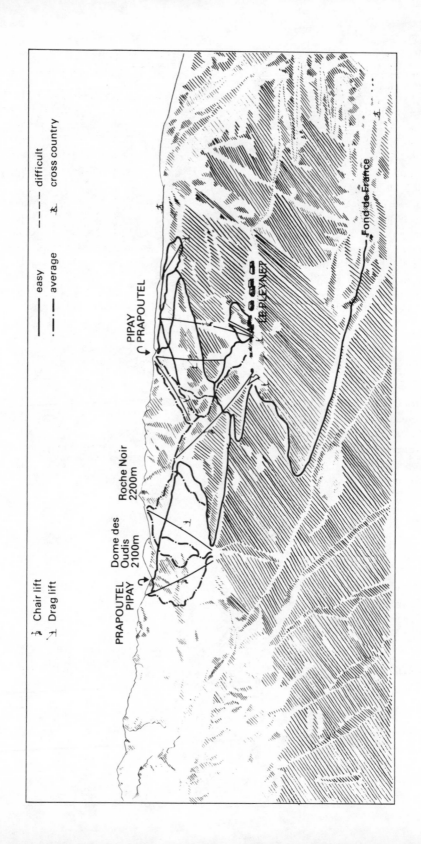

Chair lift
Drag lift

easy
average
difficult
cross country

PRAPOUTEL
PIPAY

Dome des
Oudis
2100m

Roche Noir
2200m

PIPAY
PRAPOUTEL

LE PLEYNET

Fond-de-France

WHERE TO STAY

As yet, there are no hotels in Les 7 Laux, although they have two planned for 1991. There are self-catering apartments at Prapoutel and at Le Pleynet. For example, Club Sirius has studios available from 924F per week. Further details from Club Sirius, Centre 7, Prapoutel, 38190 Brignoud (Tel: 76 08 71 68) or at Les Glaciers, Le Pleynet, 38580 La Ferrière-d'Allevard (Tel: 76 08 09 95). Prapoutel Immobilier has studios from 910F per week, Prapoutel, 38190 Brignoud (Tel: 76 08 70 51).

There are several small, rustic hotels in the nearby villages, 15-20 minutes away by car. For example, Hotel du Curtillard (Tel: 76 97 50 82) is a two-star hotel in Le Curtillard that charges 240F-286F per night full board. Hotel Le Vieux Manège (Tel: 76 71 09 91) is also a two-star hotel, in Les Adrets. 220-226F full board. Hotel des 7 Laux (Tel: 76 97 50 85) is in Fond de France, 5 km from Le Pleynet. 185F per night full board.

The tourist office staff (see below) speak English, and can arrange self-catering or hotel accommodation.

IN CASE OF EMERGENCY

Doctor in resort: One in Prapoutel. Ambulance (Tel: 76 71 41 71).
Chemist in resort: One in Prapoutel.
Nearest dentist: Theys (9 km).
Nearest Hospitals: Three in Grenoble (50-60 minutes by road, 15 by helicopter).
Helicopter Rescue: Yes.

HOW TO GET THERE

Nearest Airports: Grenoble (via charter), Lyon (via Air France).
Transfer time: 1 hour (Grenoble), 2 hours (Lyon).
Train connection: Paris to Les 7 Laux, via TGV, 4 hours.

FURTHER INFORMATION

Tourist Office Prapoutel—Centre 7, 38190 Brignoud (Tel: 76 08 17 86).

VILLARD-DE-LANS

- **HEIGHT OF RESORT**
  1,050 m.

- **HIGHEST LIFT**
  2,170 m.

- **WHY GO THERE?**
  Unspoilt French town with extensive alpine and cross-country skiing.
  Guaranteed good snow conditions—artificial snow and excellent piste
  maintenance.
  Plenty of activities for non-skiers.

- **WHO GOES THERE?**
  International hotch-potch of French, Spanish, Dutch, Germans and a
  few British.
  Lots of cross-country skiers.
  Families.

- **COMPANIES THAT GO THERE**
  Air France.

If I had not arrived at 5 pm and seen all the skiers clomping round the streets in their ski boots, I would not have thought Villard was a ski resort. You cannot actually see the ski area from this traditional French mountain village, although the two are well-connected by navette (shuttle bus) and pistes. Villard, the village, in Alpes Dauphiné, has lots of character with a large traditional church, market shops, bistros and an animated square where locals and skiers mingle. In the square there are plenty of laid-back bars and cafés, where people sit outside drinking under canopies. The village is very French, with a fountain and a statue of a bear, which is the symbol of Vercors, the local region. There used to be hundreds of bears in the surrounding woods, but now the only ones in Villard are sculpted out of stone or hanging up inside bars and restaurants. Villard's skiing is at Côte 2,000, also known as the Balcon de Villard. This comprises large purpose-built apartment blocks, shops, restaurants and hotels—not exactly beautiful but at least they blend in quite well.

THE SKIING

I skied in Villard last January when the rest of the Alps were green. Villard have spent a lot of money on their skiing facilities and it shows. They have 72 canons for making snow and take a lot of trouble in maintaining the pistes. There cannot be many European resorts where a little man darts up and down the slopes, picking up stray stones. It is very impressive. There are 130 km of pistes in all, with little queueing. I never waited longer than five minutes for a lift, even on a Wednesday afternoon, when the resort was busy with the local school kids. The Villard skiing starts at Côte 2,000 which is linked to the nearby village of Corrençon. There is a navette (free with a lift pass) from Villard to the pistes or you can take your car, although parking can be a problem in high season. There are pistes for every standard of skier, mostly wide, long and through the trees. The Canyon is an interesting run as it gets very steep and narrow in parts and you can hear your voice echoing across the mountain. Good skiers can treat themselves at the end of the day to the challenging black run, Daim, down to Côte 2,000. Villard has more black runs than anything else, but it is also possible to ski most of the area on very easy greens. There are a couple of beginners' slopes down in the village at Les Cochettes as well as a little bunny (baby) lift for the children. The child care facilities are impressive—a jardin de neige in the village, at Côte 2,000 and at the top of the telecabine Pré des Préys.

There is some good off-piste, particularly in the Corrençon area. Snowboarding is very popular, no doubt boosted by the fact that the world champion, Regis Roland, comes from Villard. It is particularly good to surf in the powdery snow of Tête des Chaudières, above Corrençon. I also saw a lot of graceful telemarkers—last year they held the French championships here.

Villard runs some very original ski courses. There is a Scandinavian Weekend which includes accommodation in comfortable alpine lodgings with its own sauna, dog-sledging, six hours a day skiing and an introduction to nordic cross-country skiing using seal-skins. The minimum skiing requirement is that you are able to snow-plough, and you also need to be a good walker. 500F for three nights, all inclusive. If you want to be really adventurous there is a seven-day Scandinavian excursion which involves staying in different hotels each night and also includes an introduction to telemarking and a visit to the local Glacière caves. 2,300F all inclusive (accommodation, equipment, lifts, instructors). For further details ring 76 95 12 58. Bernard Charriere (Tel: 76 95 93 36) is an instructor who teaches skiing on and off the piste, snowboarding and monoski. He also arranges heli-skiing over to Val Grisenche in the Italian Aosta Valley.

CROSS-COUNTRY

Villard-de-Lans is fantastic for *ski de fond*. They have 120 km of prepared paths ranging from 1 to 30 km, a 'Scandinavian centre', and a special Scandinavian long distance run of 70 km from Villard to the Vallée du Rhone. Most of the tracks are in the woods, Bois Barbu and Corrençon.

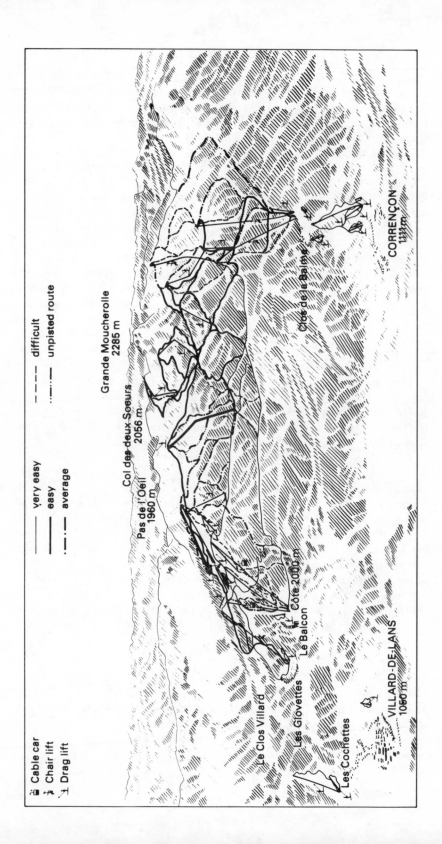

Cable car
Chair lift
Drag lift

very easy
easy
average

difficult
unpisted route

Grande Moucherolle
2285 m

Col des deux Soeurs
2056 m

Pas de l'Oeil
1960 m

Côte 2000 m

Le Balcon

Le Clos Villard

Les Glovettes

Les Cochettes

Clos de la Balme

CORRENÇON
1111 m

VILLARD-DE-LANS
1050 m

SKI SCHOOL

Villard has 100 ski instructors for both cross-country and alpine. The English-speaking instructors I met were very friendly. Six (two-hour) lessons 300F (250F kids). Private lessons 130F per hour. There are also lessons in snowboarding, mono and telemarking.

LIFT PASSES

510F for six days includes free travel on navettes (408F kids). This covers the whole area—Villard and Corrençon.

WHERE TO EAT, DRINK & BOOGIE

There are several places for skiers to eat. Le Pré du Préy, at the top of the telecabine, is a modern Alpine restaurant which serves good ski lunches (spag-bol, sausages and chips), salads and vin chaud. Altitude 2,000 is at the top of the other telecabine and Le Choucas is at the top of the Combeauvieux chair-lift in the Corrençon area. There are also two restaurants in the cross-country area of Bois Barbu. For après-ski Le Freeway in Villard is a young friendly bar with good music and a golfing theme. There are plenty of bars in Côte 2,000 but these lack the village atmosphere. In high season Villard is lively at night—there are three night clubs.

The locals certainly eat well—there are about 50 restaurants with traditional Vercors menus including gratin dauphinois (potatoes baked in cream, cheese and nutmeg), ravioli and chicken with crayfish. One restaurant tried to persuade me to have the local speciality of wild boar (sanglier) but I was not keen after having just seen one poor beast strung up in by the leg in a charcuterie! Dîner-à-deux costs 55F-180F. For about 80F plus wine you can have a good meal at La Grange (Tel: 76 95 03 67) which does fondues and local specialities. La Petite Auberge (Tel: 76 95 11 53) has traditional French food in a village atmosphere, and the pizzeria La Brèche (Tel: 76 95 03 61) is also good. Gourmets should head to Le Tetras in Hotel Christiania where the cheapest menu is 136F. This is a posh restaurant, with high ceilings, clean white linen, nice china—perfect for that romantic candle-lit dinner. Their gastronomic menu (280F) includes foie gras, smoked salmon, langoustine tails and fillet of beef.

WHAT ELSE TO DO THERE

Lots!
In summer 1989, Villard spent 100 million francs on a deluxe new sports centre which has an exotic swimming pool complete with waves, chute and waterfall. It

also has a fitness centre with weight equipment, solaria, sauna, jacuzzi and massage parlour. In the same centre there is bowling, billiards, indoor golf and even a night club.

For a taste of village life, you should watch one of the regular Saturday night ice hockey matches. These are very different from the English quick-pint-of-ale jobs—the French watch ice-hockey style and civilly drink café cognacs whilst the players beat the hell out of each other and hurtle across the ice.

For a more romantic evening you can go sledging with horses or dogs. In the daytime you can also go galloping across powder snow or learn the basics of horse riding in a paddock.

Also available: indoor tennis; mountain bike rides in the snow on specially prepared runs; and 'archery skiing' which involves shooting arrows, Robin Hood style, in the forest, but on skis.

If you speak French you can spend a more sedentary evening in the cinema— there is one in the village and in another Côte 2,000.

The nearby caves of Choranche were discovered in 1875 and have an amazing selection of stalactites. They are open all year (Tel: 75 48 64 92).

WHERE TO STAY

The three-star La Christiania (Tel: 76 95 12 51) is a friendly chalet-style hotel with comfortable rooms and a traditional atmosphere. They have an attractive dining room and an excellent gourmet menu (see Where to Eat, above), 300F-410F per night half board. La Roseraie (Tel 76 95 11 99) is a quiet two-star hotel, with a nice bar and a sauna. 195F-270F per night half board. Le Gerbier (Tel 76 95 10 50) is very centrally located with a lively bar and quiet bedrooms round the back. They have a friendly but fairly basic restaurant. 195F-270F per night half board.

IN CASE OF EMERGENCY

Doctors in resort: Four.
Chemists in resort: Three.
Dentists in resort: Three.
Nearest Hospital: There are three hospitals in Grenoble (30 km away).
Helicopter Rescue: Yes.

HOW TO GET THERE

Nearest Airport: Grenoble or Lyon.
Transfer Time: 30-40 minutes from Grenoble, $1\frac{1}{2}$ hours from Lyon.

Train connection: Grenoble, then bus. Paris-Grenoble, 3 hours.

FURTHER INFORMATION

Tourist Office 38250 Villard de Lans, BP 54 (Tel: 76 95 10 38).

Italy

There is something very special about skiing in Italy. It is best appreciated as a winter holiday rather than just a skiing week. The scenery, for one, is absolutely breathtaking. The Dolomites is the most beautiful stretch of the Alps—5,000 square km of widely varying rock formations. They look very different from the rest of the Alps—jagged teeth-like mountains which seem to glow a magical pinky grey colour in the evenings. The Dolomites are named after the Frenchman, Déodat de Dolomieu, who discovered the limestone-type rock which gives these mountains their slightly pinky-orange tinge. Gentle in parts, jagged in others, this southern range has a tremendous feel of drama and unpredictability. The mountains rise to 3,899 m, while the craggy stacks of rock, sharp cliff faces and narrow valleys are breathtaking and intimidating by turns. The highest skiable peak is the Marmolada (3,344 m), while there are another 35 peaks measuring over 3,000 m. Valleys and narrow steep passes have protected them from invasion over the centuries.

For years Italy has had a reputation for rather chaotic skiing and archaic lift systems. But the situation is now greatly improved, the Italians having put a lot of money into their resorts. In the Trentino region, for example, most of the lifts are under ten years old and the pistes are very well maintained. As this is the southernmost Alpine region, lack of snow can be a problem, particularly in the last few disastrous seasons, but many of the resorts now have artifical snow-making facilities. Although there are some internationally renowned Italian resorts such as Cortina and Courmayeur, expert skiers would be hard pushed to find anything as challenging or as extensive as the Austrian Arlberg or the French Trois Vallées. The Super Dolomiti ski pass gives access to over 1,000 km of pistes and nearly 500 lifts, but much of this is not properly connected, so unless you have a car, it could easily be a waste of money. Travelling by car is certainly one of the most pleasurable ways of skiing Italy. It will not only enable you to get more out of their pistes, but it also means that you can stop over in different villages. There is so much to explore. Cross-country skiing is also a very good way to appreciate this exceptionately beautiful part of the world, especially in Val di Fassa and Val di Fiemme.

The Italians are piste-bashing poseurs who don't like tough skiing. They prefer wide gentle open pistes where they can bomb down for an hour or so before stopping off for a mega-lunch. It is worth skiing in Italy just for the food. Unfortunately it is not as cheap as it used to be—a pizza now costs £2-£3—but it is excellent quality. It is not uncommon for the Italians to eat a leisurely five-course lunch. In some of the less commercial resorts, they even shut the lifts between noon and 1 pm. Sunday lunch is a big Italian tradition—the whole family, from great granny to the tiniest bambino, eats together. Italian resorts and hotels are very welcoming to children but they often do not have good child-care facilities. This is because the Italians are loathe to let their bambinos out of sight and prefer to leave them under the tender loving care of mama or grandmama.

Italian skiers are decidedly stylish both on and off the slopes. After skiing, they will go on parade, or *passegiata*, round the resort. Usually they will go back to their hotel to change into their sheepskins and leathers and then strut around the streets, to see and be seen.

Italian skiing is split into regions. The atmosphere varies considerably, depending whether the resort is near France, Switzerland or Austria. There are so many little 'undiscovered' Italian resorts that they could have filled a whole book. I have decided to concentrate on two regions not well-known to the British—the South Tirol on the Austrian border and the Trento valley in the north east. The South Tirol is more Austrian than Italian so I have given it a separate section. Trentino is a beautiful unspoilt area which stretches from Lake Garda (65 m) to the Dolomites (3,000 m). The capital is Trento, a delightful old town with winding streets, narrow alleys and old palaces, houses and churches. It is worth spending a day there shopping, having lunch and exploring the old city centre with its medieval buildings. Trentino has over 40 ski resorts and 520 km of pistes. There is summer skiing on the Marmolada and Tonale-Presena glaciers. The people are warm and hospitable and proudly maintain their traditional customs, dress, folklore and music. The most jet-setty Trentino resort is Madonna di Campiglio, while others, such as Moena and Andalo, are more family-orientated.

Exchange rate (June 1989): £1 = 2,180L

FURTHER INFORMATION

Italian State Tourist Office 3rd Floor, 1 Princes Street, London W1R BAY (Tel: 01 408 1254).

ANDALO

- **HEIGHT OF RESORT**
  1,025 m.

- **HIGHEST LIFT**
  2,125 m.

- **WHY GO THERE?**
  Cheap.
  Good, intermediate skiing.
  Easy access—only 1½ hours from Verona.
  Excellent Italian food.

- **WHO GOES THERE?**
  Local weekenders.
  Unglamorous Italians in Fiats and Lancias.
  School groups.

- **COMPANIES THAT GO THERE**
  Hourmont
  Snow Ranger.

The Paganella empire comprises three winter resorts—Andalo, Molveno and Fai della Paganella. Andalo is the largest of these and has the best access to the skiing. Although it does not have the charm of a Tirolean village, it is still full of character. The Paganella-Brenta plateau is framed by the great forest that spreads as far as the Paganella and by the austere and awe-inspiring scenery of the rugged Brenta Dolomites. The Paganella Massif is an enormous natural balcony with a sheer drop to the east down to the Adige Valley. The ski slopes of Andalo and Fai are on the north-west side. Andalo is fairly compact with some 1950s and 1960s hotels on the outskirts. The rest of the architecture is modern but in tasteful wooden traditional style. It is by no means as ritzy as Campiglio—in Andalo you will find Fiats rather than Ferraris. Andalo used to be very popular with the British school market although there is only one company, Hourmont, still using the resort. There are still many young Italians who coach in from Lombardy, Verona, and Emilia-Romagna. The Italians tend to look after their own bambinos, but for the tourists there is a special 'Baby Parking' service. The hotels are very welcoming to children.

THE SKIING

Andalo has the best access to the Paganella ski area. Many of the hotels are up to 15 minutes' walk from the skiing but both lift stations have ski 'garages' and car parks at the bottom. Andalo has recently invested 13,000 million lire in renewing all the lift facilities and rearranging the pistes so there are now hardly any queues except at weekends. There are 50 km of pistes. The skiing is best for beginners and intermediates—experts may find it too limited for a week. The slopes are north facing. There are some red runs below the treeline, and wide blue runs above. The more demanding skiing is mainly in gullies—wide and easier when full of snow, becoming much more tricky when the snow is scarce. There is one nursery slope in the village and another couple of narrow ones at Prati di Gaggia (1,333 m) and also at Malga Fai (1,665 m). There is artificial snow on the Teresat nursery slope in the Prati di Gaggia area. These high-level nursery areas can be chilly in early season although they do hold the sun well in the afternoon. It is possible to work out a sunny route for the day. A new six-seater gondola takes you up to Doss Pelà. From here there is a chair-lift up to the summit, Paganella (2,125 m). As there is not much sun early in the morning, it is best to stay up high until 10 am. Conca D'argento and La Selletta offer some nice easy slopes to warm up on.

Good skiers can take the rather tricky red run Caciatori 2 to Pian Dosson (1,460 m). From here, you can see the condition of the black run Olympica 2. If this looks too icy in the morning you can go over to the Dosso Larici (red) area in the Fai system. This area does not get too busy, although there is no sun until late in the day. The Paganella 2 is a long red run from Crosere (1,750 m). As the sun moves down the mountain the longer runs towards the village are a good choice but beware of the bottlenecks above Laghet. These lower slopes can be icy. In the afternoon, the sun is in the Fai area. There is a good long red run down to Santel. The old Tre-Tre course is a long off-piste route through the trees from Malga di Zambana to Santel. At about 3.30 pm it is worth heading for the Paganella summit to watch a spectacular sunset. The pistes are likely to be empty half an hour after the lifts close. The long black run is a challenging end to the day or you can cruise down the $5\frac{1}{2}$ km red run back to the village. Molveno has a very small ski area of its own. The Paganella ski area is also good for ski mountaineering in the Brenta Dolomites.

CROSS-COUNTRY

Andalo Sports Centre (Tel: 0461 58 59 07).
The cross-country facilities in Andalo are limited. There are some cross-country trails around the Lago di Andalo, ten minutes' walk from the village. There is also some cross-country up at Prati Gaggia, although this is far from ideal as you have to catch a chair-lift, involving relatively high costs and the risk of frozen tootsies. There are some more tracks in Fai della Paganella (1,030 m). Illuminated tracks at Fai and in Andalo. Instructors and waxing facilities are available.

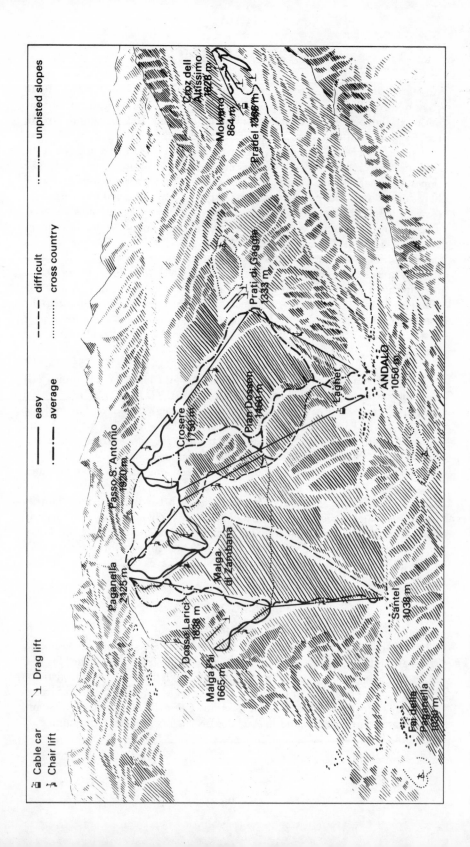

Cable car   easy   difficult   unpisted slopes

Chair lift   average   cross country

Drag lift

Croz dell' Altissimo 2828 m

Molvero 864 m

Pradel 1366 m

Prati di Gaggia 1333 m

Passo S. Antonio 1820 m

Crosere 1765 m

Prati Dosson 1460 m

Cagner

ANDALO 1050 m

Paganella 2125 m

Dosso Larici 1838 m

Malga di Zambana

Santel 1038 m

Malga Fai 1665 m

Fai della Paganella 958 m

ABOVE Another peaceful day on pretty tree-lined slopes in the Kleinwalsertal region of Austria. Eighty kilometres of pistes – mainly blue and perfect for intermediates.

BELOW One of the gentler descents in purpose-built Chamrousse in Dauphiné, France. At the other end of the scale are two downhill courses used for the 1968 Olympics.

Neck-deep in powder and no white-outs yet. Don't know what's going on underneath, but it sure feels like floating in heaven. In deep powder, remember to weight both skis evenly – and don't look down.

ABOVE Who needs pistes? Intrepid skiers head off for another day of thrills and spills in the predominantly off-piste resort of La Grave, in France.

BELOW Bastard taxis, Bastard supermarket, Bastard wine. You'll find all this and more in the pretty French town of Le Grand Bornand, where the Bastard family preside.

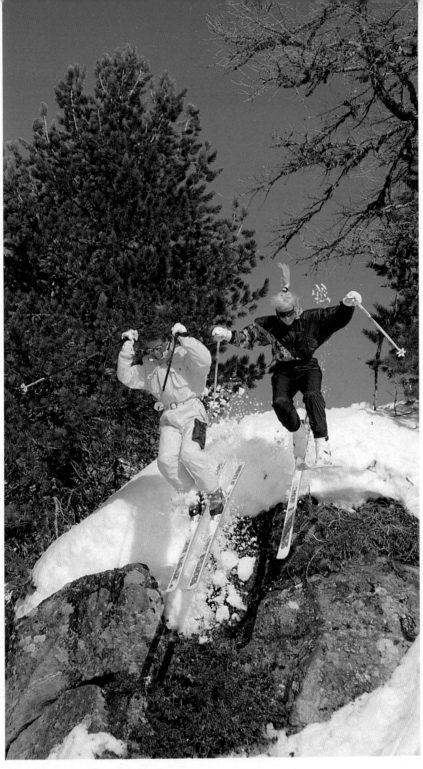

We have lift off! Another waspish leap for mankind. What do you mean you've never heard of the Flying Pigtails?

ABOVE Praz-de-Lys in France is the ultimate rustic retreat with spectacular scenery and good facilities both for cross-country and alpine skiing.

BELOW Les 7 Laux may not be the most aesthetically pleasing of resorts but thumbs up for convenience skiing and facilities for kids.

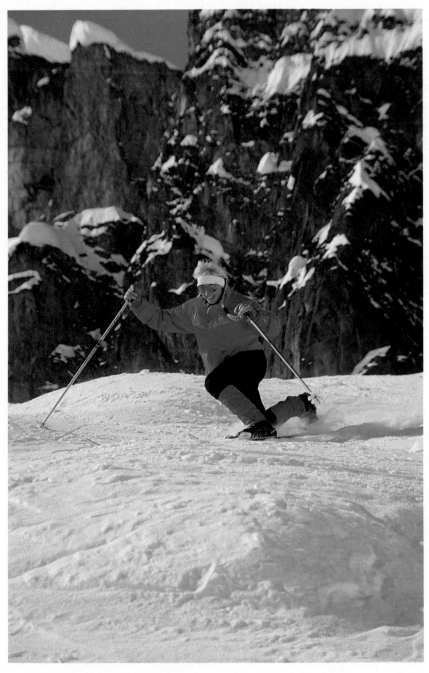

Ooops! No she isn't falling over, but is practising the highly specialised and controlled telemark method of turning, very trendy in the States.

ABOVE Ski the Portes du Soleil without having to shack up with hoorays. Down under the trees, Les Gets is a fashionable French resort, not well known to the Brits.

BELOW Once skied, never forgotten. This spectacular backdrop is the seven jagged peaks behind Wildhaus in Eastern Switzerland.

SKI SCHOOL

Scuolo Italiana Sci Brenta Alta (Tel: 58 57 02 or 58 56 80)
As in the past there have been many British school groups, English is widely (but not necessarily well) spoken. Classes are often large but they include video analysis and an end of course race. There are over 50 teachers. Six days (2-hour lessons) 60,000L at the lower station, 65,000L at the upper station. Private lessons 27,000L per hour.

The cutely-named 'Baby Parking' system takes toddlers from 2 years old, 9 am-1 pm. Kindergarten for 4-6 year olds. Ski school for children over 6 years old. Torchlight processions down the mountain every week. Cross-country lessons are also available.

LIFT PASSES

95,000L-132,000L. Ten per cent off for under 12s and over 60s. Covers Fai, Molveno and Andalo. Includes free entry to swimming pool in Andalo.

WHERE TO EAT, DRINK & BOOGIE

There are several restaurants on the slopes with lunch costing from 15,000 to 20,000L. The Rifugio at Prati di Gaggia, 300 m above Laghet near the nursery slopes, is a jolly rustic restaurant with waitress service. The summit bar at Paganella has a sun terrace with deck chairs and a spectacular panoramic view of the whole of Trentino encompassing Lake Garda, Brenta, Adamello Massif and Pale di S. Martino.

Most people are on half board so they eat in their hotels. The Agro-turistico, on the road to Fai, 1 km from the centre, has a good reputation for game. There is a lot of pasta; local specialities include game, *polenta* (maize) preferably cooked on an open fire in some *rifugio*, and strawberry or *Teroldago risotto*. There are plenty of good wines including Teroldago—a robust red that has been described as 'a man's wine'. Schiava is a light wine from Val di Cembra, ideal for lunch. After the 'passegiata' and dinner, most people go bar-hopping (Italians never 'pub crawl'). Piz Galin and Bar Central are popular haunts, particularly the Piz Galin's Pasticceria. The Piz Galin has a strong British presence and is one of the liveliest places before dinner back at the hotel. They also do good pizzas. There are plenty of small cafés, many of which serve non-Italian beers. Before heading on to one of the discos, many people drink at the Bar Central, or hotel bars such as the Bottomedi. The new 'Shuttle' disco is reckoned to be the most futuristic and sophisticated in the Dolomites.

WHAT ELSE TO DO THERE

Ice-skating (watch out you don't gamble all your money at the massive amusement arcade in the building next door!)

Swimming in a newly modernised pool. Free until 10 pm with your ski pass. Tobogganing.

It is worthwhile making an excursion to Trento to visit the historical 'old town', do some shopping and have lunch. My favourite Italian alpine restaurant is the Cantinotta (upstairs is half the price of downstairs but still expensive). The old city centre of Trento shows the medieval period in its construction, with winding streets, very narrow alleys, towers, and crumbling remains of walls.

WHERE TO STAY

The accommodation in Trentino has generally improved owing to recent government development grants. There are over 50 reasonably priced hotels and 350 apartments. Most of these are two and three-star hotels with private facilities. The Italians seem to be prepared to pay a little more for quality. In town, many of the hotels are a good 15-minute walk from the lifts. Regents Hotel (Tel: 0461 58 59 22) is 500 m uphill on the road to Fai. This is a clean, comfortable and modern hotel where the owners are very friendly. 50,000L-66,000L per night full board.

IN CASE OF EMERGENCY

Doctor in resort: One.
Chemist in resort: One.
Dentist in resort: One.
Nearest Hospital: Mezzolombardo (15 km). Fractures usually go to Trento.
Helicopter Rescue: Yes.

HOW TO GET THERE

Nearest Airport: Verona.
Train connection: Mezzo Trento Corona 15 km, then bus.
Transfer time: $1\frac{1}{2}$-2 hours.

FURTHER INFORMATION

Tourist Office: Azienda Autonoma Soggiorno 38010 Andalo (Tel: 0461 58 58 36)

MADONNA DI CAMPIGLIO

- **HEIGHT OF RESORT**
  1,500 m.

- **HIGHEST LIFT**
  2,550 m.

- **WHY GO THERE?**
  Smart Italian resort with extensive ski area.
  Spectacular setting in the Brenta Dolomites.

- **WHO GOES THERE?**
  Chic Italians.
  Italian Yuppies.
  Used to be mainly northerners, but now that Maradona (of Napoli football team) trains in Campiglio in the summer, the southern Italians also like to ski here!

- **COMPANIES THAT GO THERE**
  Snow Ranger.

Madonna di Campiglio, or Santa Maria di Campiglio, as it used to be called, is a chic, sophisticated Italian purpose-built ski resort in the Western Dolomites. It is much beloved by the Italians, who make up at least 95 per cent of the tourists. Campiglio, as it is affectionately called, is set amongst thick pine forests in the shadow of the jagged Brenta Dolomites. This smart modern resort was originally just a humble welcoming shelter, built by monk Rainondo in the 12th century to give comfort and rest to the few wayfarers crossing over the Alpine Pass with their cattle. In 1862 Giambattista Righi bought the whole of the Campiglio valley and turned it into a popular summer resort. The old Campiglio burnt down at the beginning of the century but has since been tastefully rebuilt.

Campiglio has only really been developed as a ski resort in the last 15 years. Some of the old buildings remain, including a pretty little church. The rest are new but in traditional style—a good example of how attractive a purpose-built resort can look if well-designed. The traffic system has not been so well-designed, and at weekends the resort can be chock-a-block with cars. Campiglio is a bustling, fairly compact little town with lots of smart expensive shops, tempting *pasticcerie*, cafés and restaurants. Although it is not as glitzy as Cortina, it is still an elegant resort. I was the only person in the afternoon walking round the town in a ski suit—everyone else seemed to be wearing fur coats or smart casual wear.

As far as I could see, Campiglio has two locals heros—the world-hero footballer Maradona, who trains there in the summer, and Olaf, a huge black Newfoundlander who hangs out at the Spinale ski area or the town square at tea time.

In the centre of Campiglio there is a spectacular 5,000 square metre frozen lake which is used for skating, motor bikes, and even American football.

Campiglio is predominantly an Italian resort and attracts hardly any overseas tourists. I did not see any English people there although there is one small British company, Snow Ranger, using the resort. The resort is linked into the same lift system as Marilleva and Folgarida. These are not nearly as attractive as Campiglio and attract many more Brits. So does Pinzolo, which is a larger town, 13 km from Campiglio. Many of the locals live there and the accommodation is cheaper. It has much less skiing than Campiglio and seems to attract a much more down-market clientele.

THE SKIING

Visually, Campiglio is very enticing for the skier as it is surrounded by pistes in every direction. It has 100 km of its own–150 km when you use the link with Marilleva and Folgarida. Unfortunately, the lift passes have been badly planned for good skiers, as they only include one day in Marilleva and Folgarida. You can buy day passes for the whole system. Beginners and intermediates will find plenty to keep themselves occupied for a week on Campiglio's slopes. Apart from Christmas and weekends, there is no queueing. There is good skiing for all standards. There are two nursery slopes in the village and four main ski areas—Cinque Laghi, Pradalago, Groste and Spinale. Cinque Laghi is on the western side of the village and has several fairly challenging runs including the World Cup downhill '3 Tre'. This is quite a steep and tricky red run with artificial snow facilities. The most difficult skiing is on Spinale which is reached by a chair-lift or gondola from the centre of the village. From here, you can ski over to Groste where there are some good long intermediate runs. Pradalago is a large sunny area for beginners and intermediates. From Pradalago, you can ski over to Marilleva (1,400 m) or Folgarida.

There is a lot of opportunity for off-piste—particularly over the top of Groste. There is often good powder in Spinale and Cinque Laghi.

There is a ski bus (free with the special cut-price 'White Weeks') to the various areas. The ski school is very obliging—it picks up clients from their hotels and transports them by bus to the ski areas.

If you really want to explore the beautiful Brenta Dolomites, there is a special ski touring school, Guide Alpine Val di Sole (Tel: 0463 91. 15 1).

CROSS-COUNTRY

Campo Carlo Magno Pass (Tel: 0465 41 63 3) is the cross-country ski centre.

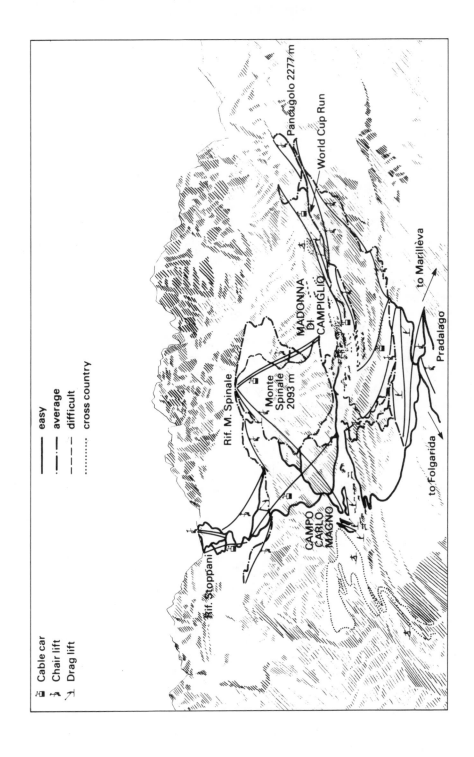

Cable car

Chair lift

Drag lift

———— easy

—·—·— average

— — — difficult

·········· cross country

Rif. Stoppani

Rif. M. Spinale

Monte
Spinale
2093 m

MADONNA
DI
CAMPIGLIO

CAMPO
CARLO
MAGNO

Pancugolo 2277 m

World Cup Run

to Marilleva

Pradalago

to Folgarida

Instructors, waxing, refreshments, changing-rooms. There are pretty trails through the woods with a total of 30 km on the Campo Carlo Magno. New competition tracks in Malga Mondifrà and Malga Dorè.

SKI SCHOOL

The official ski school, Scuola Italiana Sci Campiglio (Tel: 0465 41 14 0) has amalgamated from a handful of smaller schools. There are still a couple of independent schools, such as Scuola di Sci Cinque Laghi (Tel: 0465 41 65 0). Many of the teachers speak English. I was impressed by the way they pick up the clients from the hotels. Children are equipped with fluorescent overalls with their class and hotel name on them. Perhaps because so many of the Italians eat five-course lunches at proper tablecloth-and-waiter restaurants, ski school is only available in the morning. They operate two shifts: 9 am-11 am or 11 am-1 pm. If you are really keen you can have both. Private tuition is available in the afternoon. The ski school provides a bus (10 minutes) to the baby slopes at Campo Carlo Magno. There are special classes for the tiny children (4 year olds), the main school takes them at about 5 or 6 years old. Adults: 96,000L for six days (two hours). Children: 126,000L for six days (three hours). Private lessons 32,000L per hour.

The Cinque Laghi teaches snowboarding and there is also a special snowboarding school run by Heinz Sticki, an ex-world champion windsurfer (Tel: 0465 42 04 2). Heinz also runs special snowboard camps (Tel: 0465 41 14 0). There is also a ski-mountaineering school (Tel: 0465 42 63 4) which organises instruction in rock, glacier, and ski-mountaineering climbing, and ski mountaineering excursions with guides.

LIFT PASSES

Skiarama Dolomite di Brenta 141,000L-165,000L for a six-day pass including one day in Folgarida and Marilleva. Reductions for children available on certain weeks.

WHERE TO EAT, DRINK & BOOGIE

There are several rustic mountain restaurants where many of the Italians settle down for five-course lunches. Prices are fairly expensive by Italian standards—up to 12,000L for just one dish and a drink. There is a popular little bar in Cinque Laghi where people sun themselves and eat sandwiches, cakes and coffees.

Campiglio is a lively little town, particularly at tea time when the fur coat brigade head off to the tea bars and piano bars. Most people are on half or full board, so they eat in their hotels. There are also seven pizzerias and 19 restaurants. If you have made the most of this large ski area, you probably will not make it to one of the four nightclubs.

WHAT ELSE TO DO THERE

Ice-skating.
Public indoor swimming pool at the Centro Rainalter (Tel: 0465 42 76 6).
Saunas in some hotels.
Cinema.
Cabaret Salon Oberhofer.
Walking.

WHERE TO STAY

There are over 50 hotels in Campiglio and 22,000 beds in apartments. Christmas is ridiculously expensive and crowded. They offer special White Weeks (package deals—not available at Christmas or New Year)—from 315,000L for a week's full board in a one-star hotel to 1,280,000L full board in the most luxurious hotel in Campiglio, the four-star Grand Hotel des Alpes (Tel: 0465 40 00 0).Further details from the tourist office, see below.

IN CASE OF EMERGENCY

Doctors in resort: Two.
Chemist in resort: One.
Nearest dentist: 13 km away in Pinzolo.
Nearest Hospital: Tione (30 km).
Helicopter Rescue: Yes.

HOW TO GET THERE

Nearest Airport: Verona.
Train connection: Train to Trento (1 hour) then bus (2 hours).
Transfer time: $2\frac{1}{2}$-3 hours depending on traffic.

FURTHER INFORMATION

Tourist Office Azienda Autonoma Soggiorno, 1-38084 Madonna di Campiglio, Trentino (0465 42 00 0)

MOENA

- **HEIGHT OF RESORT**
  1,184 m.

- **HIGHEST LIFT**
  2,550 m.

- **WHY GO THERE?**
  Very friendly and cultural resort.
  Extensive sunny terrain for beginners and intermediates.
  Spectacular Dolomite landscape.
  Easy access (by car) to Super-Dolomite ski area (1,000 km)—all under one lift pass.

- **WHO GOES THERE?**
  Italian 2.2 families.
  Keen young skiers in low season.
  Culture vultures.
  No Brits.

- **COMPANIES THAT GO THERE**
  None.

It was a freezing cold evening and Signora Galbusera, the owner of the Hotel Laurino, wanted to take me on a nocturnal tour of Moena. I politely tried to explain that I was rather tired from travelling all day, and perhaps we could look at the ski lifts/ski school/après-ski bars tomorrow. She said that she wanted to show me the culture *not* the skiing, and we set off on what turned out to be a fascinating two-hour tour of the village.

Moena is an excellent ski resort in its own right as well as having handy access to the 1,000 km of Dolomiti pistes. It is also a charming large Italian village steeped in Trentino traditions and customs. Most of the buildings are clustered round a river and everywhere is within easy walking distance. Although many of the hotels have been recently modernised, they have all maintained the local flavour. There is a good selection of shops and a well-stocked supermarket. Signora Galbusera was an excellent guide. She comes from one of the oldest families in the village—her granny was the first person to open a hotel there. First stop was to see the beautiful frescoes in the 16th-century gothic and Roman church. The tall church spire dominates the local landscape, and is visible from every side of the village. Unlike many ski resorts, Moena really feels as though it has a history. Signora Galbusera told me legends and old stories about the place, pointed out the intricate friezes on the buildings and even knocked on people's doors to show me their houses. I was amazed at the locals' friendliness. One family was in the middle of dinner, yet opened up their house to a total stranger to show off their ornate sitting room ceiling! Other houses we visited had beautiful wood-panelled rooms and old tile stoves. The locals are obviously deeply religious—everywhere we went we saw Christian symbols and crucifixes. Moena still has some very old farm buildings and barns with the cows underneath. The architecture is functional—the people sleep above the barns which in turn are above the stables. The locals still speak 'Ladino', a language closely related to Latin, rather like Romansch which is spoken in the Swiss Alps.

It was the friendliness of this resort that really won me over. Signora Galbusera and her husband knew everybody's name in the hotel and did more than their fair share of introducing and matchmaking at dinner times! It's certainly not a stuffy resort—the holidaymakers are happy to shout snippets of conversation at each other across the tables. Most of the tourists are middle-class Italian families who tend to travel with three generations. This is an excellent idea for the parents who can go off exploring the Dolomite pistes, leaving the bambini with the grandparents. There are some excellent sunny bunny slopes in the centre of the village, so the grandparents can pick the children up at lunchtime and take them back to the hotels for lunch. Christmas in Moena is very family orientated, but during the rest of the season, especially during the low season 'White Weeks', there are groups of young people, and keener skiers.

THE SKIING

Moena is part of the Trevalli, a three-valley system, which links with San Pellegrino and Falcade and provides 100 km of pistes. Moena was only really developed as a ski resort ten years ago, so all the lifts are new and efficient and there is little queueing. In the village of Moena there are some very open and wide bunny slopes. This is where the ski school do their adult and children beginners' classes. There is also an extensive beginners' area in Lusia, the main ski area of Moena. Lusia is 5 minutes by navette (shuttle bus) from the village. S Pellegrino is 15 minutes away by the same navette. Trevalli is a beginners' paradise with miles and miles of easy slopes. According to the head of the ski school, 80 per cent of the skiers in Trevalli are beginners. The majority of the runs are blue and green although there are also five or six black runs. There is a 10 km run down from Cima Laste (2,500 m) to Bellamonte. From here you can catch a bus to Passo Valles (2,031 m) and ski the rest of the three valleys. Passo Valles is very open and has miles of easy slopes ideal for first-time skiers. From Passo Valles there is a drag-lift up to Mt Pradazzo (2,279 m). A run round the back of the mountain leads down to Falcade. You can then take a lift to S Pellegrino and either ski or catch the bus back to Lusia.

Trevalli has a lot of off-piste potential, particularly in the spring. Most of the skiing is below the treeline so good visibility is ensured. Every Easter the ski school does a torchlight descent down the incredibly steep mountain face from Col Margherita (2,550 m). This is so spectacular that last year about 8,000 people came to watch. Advanced skiers should buy the 'Superski Dolomiti' pass

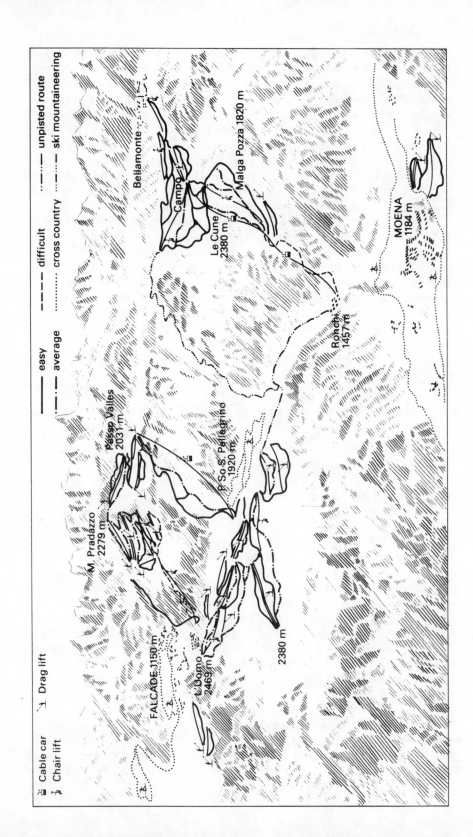

Cable car
Chair lift
Drag lift

easy
average
difficult
cross country
unpisted route
ski mountaineering

M. Pradazzo 2279 m
Passo Valles 2031 m
FALCADE 1150 m
Il Dormo 2469 m
P. So S. Pellegrino 1920 m
2380 m
Bellamonte
Campo
Malga Pozza 1820 m
Le Cune 2380 m
Ronchi 1457 m
MOENA 1184 m

which gives them access to nearly 500 lifts and over 1,000 km of pistes. There are many resorts within easy (10 km) driving distance. With a car, even the most experienced skier could spend a pleasurable couple of weeks skiing in this massive area.

CROSS-COUNTRY

Lots of people go to Moena for the cross-country skiing. 8 km trail from Moena towards Passo S Pellegrino (ski school base). Three circuits—2.5 km, 5 km, 11 km. Moena is the start of the annual 70 km Marcialonga of Fiemme and Fassa cross-country race. You can ski part of this track all year round (eg 25 km Moena-Molina).

SKI SCHOOL

The ski school seemed very friendly and efficient and has 50 teachers. 95,000L for a week, three hours a day (90,000L low season). 75,000L for a week, two hours a day (70,000L low season). Private lessons 26,000L per hour, plus 5,000L for every extra person (maximum five people).

LIFT PASSES

144,000L (120,000L low season) for six days. 101,000L (84,000 low season) kids. Includes all three valleys—Moena, S Pellegrino, Falcade. You can also buy a 'Superski Dolomiti' which entitles you to use the whole system, as far as Cortina. Six days—169,800L (141,000 low season) or 119,100L (99,100L) kids.

WHERE TO EAT, DRINK & BOOGIE

Drink is very cheap in Moena—2,630L for 2 litres of red plonk or 8,700L for a bottle of Teachers whisky in the supermarket. Wine is cheaper than beer. You can sample any wine or liqueur at the Vino Tec. The food is German-influenced with dishes such as *cannerderli* (German *knödel*), *strangolapreti* (like *gnocci*, potato pasta with spinach and cream/cheese sauce), polenta (maize), strudel and carrot cake. If you like pungent cheeses, try their local Puzone.

There are several places to eat in the mountains. Miralago is a friendly wooden chalet-style restaurant in Passo San Pellegrino, which serves cheap local food. If you don't drink any wine and eat modestly, you could have a two-course lunch at any of the alpine restaurants for just 5,500L. A more generous lunch should not cost more than 10,000L.

The nightlife in Moena is fairly low-key. There are two discos but most of the young people stay drinking and chatting in the wine bars or cafés. There are the obvious pizza places, and also some more expensive traditional restaurants such as the Malga Panna, 1 km from town. Most people have full or half board in hotels. There are several tea places to have cakes on return from skiing—these are also popular after dinner!

WHAT ELSE TO DO THERE

Ice-skating.
Snow-bikes.
Tobogganing.
Swimming in hotel pools. Saunas.
Cultural activities such as piano recitals, choral singing etc.
Church and other buildings of historical interest.
Museum of Culture in Vigo di Fassa. They are building an auditorium which will have a congress hall, squash, tennis, skating and underground parking. This is scheduled for completion in 1992.

WHERE TO STAY

There are about 55 hotels in Moena, mainly family-run in traditional chalet-style buildings. I stayed in the three-star Hotel Laurino (Tel: 0462 53 23 8). This may not have had all the latest mod cons (my bathroom was ridiculously small) but it was very friendly and the restaurant served ample portions of good Italian home cooking. It is also well-located, near the baby slopes and the bus to the main ski area. 62,000L-86,000L half board. There are at least 20 other three-star hotels and a selection of very attractive looking two-star and one-star hotels in Moena from 27,000L half board. In S Pellegrino, there is one four-star hotel, Monzoni (Tel: 0462 53 35 2) 54,000L-90,000L half board, and four three-star hotels including Arnika (Tel: 0462 53 37) which has an indoor swimming pool and sauna. 52,000L-65,000L.

IN CASE OF EMERGENCY

Doctor in resort: Tourist doctor.
Chemist in resort: One.
Dentist in resort: One.
Nearest Hospital: Cavalese (22 km).
Helicopter Rescue: From Trento.

HOW TO GET THERE

Nearest Airport: Verona.
Transfer time: $2\frac{1}{2}$ hours.
Train connection: Trento then two-hour bus ride.

FURTHER INFORMATION

Azienda Autonoma di Soggiorno 1 38035 Moena (Tel: 0462 53 12 2).

THE SOUTH TIROL

People often confuse the South Tirol with the Austrian Tirol. The South Tirol is actually part of Italy, although it is still very Austrian in atmosphere. This beautiful part of the Dolomites used to be part of the Austro-Hungarian Empire. At the end of the First World War the South Tirol became Italy's most northern province. German is still the most commonly spoken language but it changes from valley to valley. Many people speak Italian and also the local dialect Ladinish. All towns, villages, rivers and valleys have at least two names, while those in the valleys where Ladinish is spoken have a third one. This can be very confusing, so I have used just the German name throughout. The South Tiroleans are not used to British tourism, so a smattering of German or Italian would be useful.

If you are looking for total escapism, then the South Tirol is the place to come. It is full of tiny authentic villages with a charming laid-back pace of life. The climate is mild, the days are long and sunny, and there is no fog or wind to spoil the skiing. It is a very different sort of holiday from the standard one-week bombing down the pistes in a purpose-built resort. To start with, you fly to Innsbruck or Munich, which is much less frantic than arriving at Geneva. The best way to travel is probably by car as this enables you to see more of the area and stay in different places. There are also plenty of local buses. Most of the skiing is geared towards beginners and intermediates—it's certainly not the Trois Vallées but a holiday in the South Tirol is about much more than just skiing. Good skiers can invest in the 'Superski Dolomiti' pass (see page 92) which gives access to over 1,000 km of pistes. If you come here to ski, it is worth taking the time to explore the rocky heart of these mountains either by car or on cross-country skis, as downhill skiing is prohibited by the harsh terrain. The South Tirol is the perfect place to *langlauf* (cross-country ski) as there are miles and miles of virtually flat valley floors and undulating plateaux.

The South Tirol is very cheap, particularly if you stay in a pension. Extras such as wines, coffee, fruit juices and ice cream are not marked up like they are in the Alps. If you go there for a week, you are bound to put on weight as the cuisine is a delicious but calorific combination of Tirolean and Italian food, and it comes in huge portions. *Knödel* is a staple part of the local diet. This is a green, lumpy, and initially unappetising-looking pasta which is served carbonara-style with bits of bacon. It actually tastes delicious. The Pustertal ravioli are also delicious—fresh and delicate pasta parcels gently cooked and served with a buttery garlic sauce, parsley and parmesan. And if you are having a proper South Tirolean meal, there are still three courses to go, plus a lethal collection of *grappas* afterwards! They usually serve a meat course—pork, beef or local venison—in modest but succulent portions. Dumplings are a popular dish—not like the porridgy lumps of dough we get in Britain but light spicy parcels containing chopped meats and vegetables—a perfect complement to a full-flavoured goulash. There are plenty of large healthy-looking salads for vegetarians, and Tirolean vegetables, such as *sauerkraut* (pickled cabbage) and cucumber salad. Desserts include the famous *apfelstrudel,* and lemon sorbet laced with some sort of potent alcohol. Considering that there are 40 vines to every South Tirolean it's not surprising that the wine here is so cheap. They mainly make red wine (85 per cent) which is rich and smooth, but connoisseurs also praise the whites which tend to be dry, fruity and slightly *petillante*.

The South Tirol has been the link between the northern and southern civilisations for thousands of years, and is full of interesting cultural landmarks. There are over 350 castles and halls, with quaint and ancient churches, venerable monasteries, abbeys and cathedrals. You can find the most amazing Romanesque wall paintings and frescoes in tiny little villages. My reviews have centred round the Pustertal or 'Green Valley'. This has been inhabited since prehistoric times and was occupied by the Romans at the time of Christ. St Lorenzen (not far from the skiing at Kronplatz) used to be an ancient Roman military station called Sebatum. Bruneck is a beautiful old city with a maze of streets of well-preserved patrician houses. In the tiny village of Innichen you can see the twelth-century Romanesque church 'Stifskirche'. Many of the locals still use the old craftmanship techniques and the houses have wonderful carved wooden ceilings, brightly coloured window-boxes and painted rustic furniture. Each valley has its own traditional costume. The cords on the men's hats show who is married off and who is not. Red is for 'go'; green is 'already gone'.

FURTHER INFORMATION

Provincial Tourist Office for South Tirol I-39100 Bozen, Italy, Waltherplatz 22 (Tel: 0471 269 91).
Erna Low Consultants 9 Reece Mews, London SW7 3HE (Tel: 584 2841/7820). Specialises in holidays in the South Tirol.

THE HOCHPUSTERTAL

Hochpustertal is an outstandingly beautiful area at the end of the Pustertal valley, which is also home of the Kronplatz area only twenty minutes away by car (see page 116). Like Kronplatz, it is a grouping of villages (five), which all have their own identity and something different to offer the holidaymaker.

I must have seen this 'Green Valley' (as it is known), at its best when it was in brilliant sunshine. But it is easy to see why Gustav Mahler came here for inspiration. It is such a beautiful area—dinky medieval villages with onion-top church steeples, ancient chalets whose paintwork is begining to flake and yellow after scores of Tirolean winters, a bubbling stream which runs through each village, and dozens of creaking cattle sheds dotted across the hillside. Above this picturesque valley, the tree-covered slopes lead up to white-peaked mountains and the jagged crests of the Dolomites. The area is dominated by the Haunold—2,904 m of imposing limestone.

The five villages are Innichen (S. Candido) 1,135m, Toblach (Dobbiaco) 1,224 m, Sexten (Seston) 1,310 m, Niederdorf (Villabassa) 1,157 m and Prags (Braies) 1,200 m. Niederdorf and Prags do not have any skiing and are very tiny. The whole valley is very compact and 'bijou'—everything is smaller and closer together than in Kronplatz. Innichen is like a little toy town, officially founded in 769 AD.

It is a shame that the skiing in Hochpustertal does not match its superb location but they are not too concerned about the paucity of its downhill skiing, for two reasons. Firstly, the valley attracts 60 per cent of its visitors in summer when you can swim in the lake, play tennis or go mountain climbing. Secondly, it already has an international reputation as a ski resort—Toblach is the Kitzbühel of the cross-country world, famous for the Toblach/Cortina race and host to the World Master in 1991. All the locals and the majority of the visitors think that cross-country is what *real* skiing is all about. Every age group takes part, using it as a means of exercise, transport or just for enjoying the scenery. If you hate the plod-plod of city jogging amidst the carbon monoxide, this uplifting pastime will seem like heaven. And there can't be many more beautiful places to do it.

- **HEIGHT OF RESORT**
  1,173 m-1,317 m.

- **HIGHEST LIFT**
  2,200 m.

- **WHY GO THERE?**
  Outstanding scenery.
  Exceptional cross-country facilities but limited downhill.
  Pleasant environment to learn to ski in.
  The restaurants.

- **WHO GOES THERE?**
  Mainly Italians and Germans.
  Cross-country skiers.
  People who hate purpose-built resorts.

- **COMPANIES THAT GO THERE**
  Erna Low.

THE SKIING

Unlike Kronplatz, the Hochpustertal villages do not share a main ski area and

Sexten, Innichen and Toblach all have their own pistes. There are about 30 lifts and 20 km in all. Artificial snow ensures that these stay open even in conditions such as the freaky warm spell of last winter. There is not usually much queueing. It is possible to ski back to all the villages although the run down to Sexten is tricky. Sexten has the best skiing. I particularly enjoyed the long red run through the trees over towards Vierschach on the other side of the valley from the village. It is a great run to take at full speed as there are plenty of wide sweeping turns, rolling humps and a long schuss. At the bottom of this run (there is also a shorter version of it) there are two chair-lifts back to the top of the mountain. If the snow is good, it is possible to ski down to Sexten under the cable car. Three more short drag-lifts at the top make up the skiing area. There is also a long run from the top of Hahnspiel (2,200 m), through Mitterberg and down over to Moos.

The skiing in Innichen is similar, except on a smaller scale, and I got bored within a morning. If the slopes were always as uncrowded as when I was there, they would provide a good and picturesque environment for beginners but are unlikely to hold the interest of anyone more advanced. Toblach also has a small area, comprising one safe and predictable run into the village. All the villages have their own nursery slopes. According to a local, there is some good off-piste in M Elmo (2,537 m). There is a free ski bus connecting the resorts.

Although Hochpustertal does not offer extensive or challenging skiing, Kronplatz is only 20 minutes' drive away and if you buy the Superski Dolomiti ski pass and are prepared to travel there are over 1,000 km at your disposal.

CROSS-COUNTRY

This is a very well-known and much loved area for cross-country skiing, famous for the Toblach/Cortina race. The next best thing must be to *langlauf* (cross-country ski) through the stunning scenery to be found in the narrow valleys of these mountains with their sheer cliffs and buttresses. Just outside Toblach, there is an old disused railway and a lake, iced over in winter, which are just a fraction of the 200 km of double track cross-country trails of all degrees of difficulty.

SKI SCHOOL

There are several ski schools in the area. The Ski School in Sexten (Tel: 0474 70 37 5), for example, charges 60,000L-80,000L per week. Private lessons 26,000L-29,000L per hour. They also do lessons in snowboarding. There is a kindergarten for children from 4 years upwards Mon-Sat in Sexten. 35,000L-40,000L per week.

LIFT PASSES

Hochpustertal 94,300L-127,300L (74,400L-89,400L kids). 'Superski Dolomiti' Pass 141,100L-169,800L (99,100L-119,100L kids).

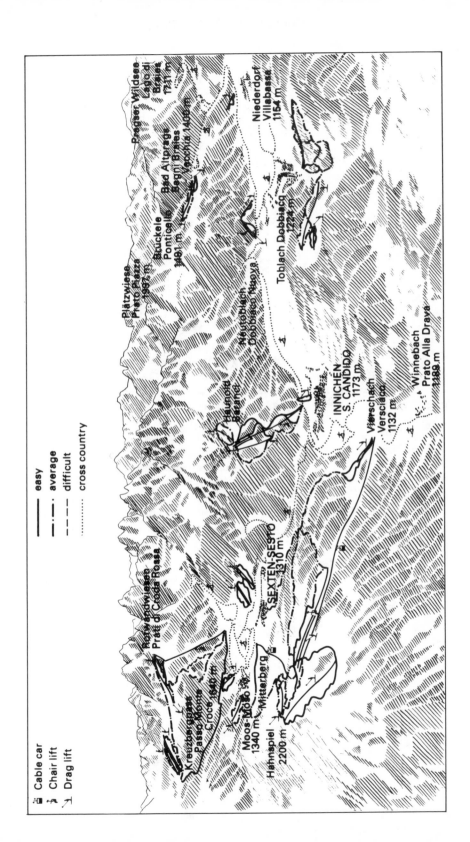

Cable car
Chair lift
Drag lift

easy
average
difficult
cross country

Rotwandwiesen
Prati di Croda Rossa

Kreuzbergpass
Passo Monte
Croce 1640 m

Moos-Moto
1340 m

Mitterberg

Hahnspiel
2200 m

SEXTEN-SESTO
1310 m

Haunold
Baranci

INNICHEN
S. CANDIDO
1173 m

Vierschach
Versciaco
1132 m

Winnebach
Prato Alla Drava
1189 m

Plätzwiese
Prato Piazza
1997 m

Pragser Wildsee
Lago di
Braies
1171 m

Bad Altprags
Bagni Braies
Vecchia 1409 m

Stuckele
Ponticello
1491 m

Neutoblach
Dobbiaco Nuova

Toblach Dobbiaco
1234 m

Niederdorf
Villabassa
1154 m

WHERE TO EAT,
DRINK & BOOGIE

I would recommend going to Hochpustertal just for lunch—there are so many wonderful little mountain restaurants and refuge huts. The quality of these seems totally out of proportion to the skiing. The Helm on M Elmo, Sexten, is a roomy self-service restaurant with a large sun terrace from where there is a most spectacular view across the middle of the Pustertal valley towards Kronplatz, as well as of tiny Sexten and Innichen below and the major-league Dolomite peaks in the distance. You probably will not remember the names—the Zwolferkopfel (3,094 m) or the Gsellnoten (2,865 m) but the sight of them is unforgettable. Innichen also has some impressive restaurants. If you grow weary of the only run worth doing, you can always relax at the Haunold/Baranci bar at the foot of the wicked 2,945 m pile of rock after which it is named. The cost of eating at these places is what I would call 'civilised' and what the Swiss would call 'charitable'. For example a ministrone cost 2,900L, a spaghetti 4,600L, goulash with knöodel 9,400L, an apple strudel 1,900L and a hot chocolate with a healthy dollop of whipped cream 1,500L.

We spent an excellent evening at Trenker House in Toblach, where Mahler stayed at the beginning of this century. This is a beautifully preserved building which has since been converted into a guest house and homely restaurant. Outside there are deer in the fields, as well as some Icelandic ponies (much prized for their sturdiness) which you can ride all year round. They serve traditional Tirolean fare—I especially remember the apple doughnut with custard. The Bad Moos in Sexten is another fine eating house. This is more modern than most of the restaurants in the area, but as well as the usual local foods they serve familiar Italian dishes such as pizza and spag-bol.

Like the Kronplatz, most of the après-ski is centred round bars and cafés where there is often dancing and spontaneous sing-a-longs. It may be a bit kitsch, but even the kitsch here seems to have a genuine feel about it. People really do wear *homburgs*, those narrow-brimmed felt hats (like trilbies), with feathers stuck in the side, and some of the mountain retreats can only be reached by horse-drawn sleighs.

WHAT ELSE TO DO THERE

Ice skating on the artificial rink in Toblach or on nearby lake in winter.
Paragliding. About £25 per flight (with an instructor).
Toboggan runs.
Swimming.
Horse-drawn sleigh-rides.
Bowling in Toblach.
Skating rink and a curling rink in Sexten. Also indoor tennis.
Walking.

WHERE TO STAY

There is everything from simple bed and breakfast places to four-star hotels. Nothing is very expensive. For example, bed and breakfast in Sexten starts at 14,000L per night. At the top end of the market are four-star hotels such as Hotel Rainer (Tel: 0474 70 36 6) in Sexten, which charges from 52,000L-99,000L per night, or the Sporthotel im Fischleintal in Sexten (Tel: 0474 70 36 5), from 46,000L-99,000L per night half board.

IN CASE OF EMERGENCY

Doctor in resort: Sexten.
Chemist in resort: Innichen.
Nearest dentist : Bruneck.
Nearest Hospital: Bruneck.
Helicopter Rescue: No.

HOW TO GET THERE

Nearest Airport: Innsbruck or Munich.
The South Tirol used to be rather inaccessible for tourists. Now Dan Air run a scheduled service to Innsbruck from £130 apex return and have introduced a new shuttle service from the airport to all the major South Tirolean resorts, including a stop off at Bruneck. £24.
Transfer time: About 3 hours.
Train connection: Munich or Verona to Bruneck.

FURTHER INFORMATION

Tourist Offices
General information from Bolzano: (Tel: 0471 99 38 08).
I-39030 Sexten-Sesto (Tel: 0474 70 31 0).
I-39038 Innichen-S Candido (Tel: 0474 73 14 9).
I-39034 Toblach-Dobbiaco (Tel: 0474 72 13 2).

KRONPLATZ

● **HEIGHT OF RESORT**
835 m-1,201 m

● **HIGHEST LIFT**
2,275 m.

● **WHY GO THERE?**
Good value for money.
Peace and quiet.
Authentic villages.
Good beginner and intermediate skiing.

● **WHO GOES THERE?**
A complete mixture of young and old.
Mainly Italians and Germans, a few Yugoslavians.
Young Italians in fluorescent gear and face paint.

● **COMPANIES THAT GO THERE**
Erna Low.

Kronplatz is the name of the main ski area which serves the town of Bruneck (Brunico in Italian) and the many other villages all around. There are about 10 villages located around the Kronplatz. These vary in size, access to the skiing and quality of accommodation although all the ones I visited were charming and unspoilt. The main resorts are St Vigil (S Vigilio) 1,201 m, Olang (Valdaora) 1,080 m, and Reischach (Riscone) 960 m.

Bruneck is a wonderful old town, which was founded in 1,250 AD and still has a medieval town centre. It is not as austere as many alpine towns and has old Tirolean architecture. There is a wide tree-lined main street, and a pedestrian shopping precinct through the oldest part of the town. There are over 40 hotels and restaurants—it is certainly worth spending an evening shopping and eating dinner there. Reischach is a sort of Upper Bruneck and is situated at the foot of the cable car which rises in two sections to Kronplatz (Plan de Corones) 2,275 m. St Vigil is an old village where they still speak Ladinish. This resort has the best access to the skiing with slopes on both sides of the village.

The South Tirol is very strict about planning permission. The buildings are small and quaint, never higher than three storeys. It will not appeal to people who like convenience skiing. The villages do not crowd around the foot of the ski-lifts. The nearest shops from our hotel in Reischach were 3 km away. Personally, I found this added to the charm of the place, as it was much less frenetic than purpose-built all-action resorts.

THE SKIING

Kronplatz is a fairly newly-developed ski area with 60 km of runs and 35 lifts. When I was there in low season, there were no queues. They have a good artificial snow system. Kronplatz is a very sunny area, approached by lifts in every direction. Sun-worshippers can follow the sun all day, skiing in the south and east in the morning and the north-west in the afternoon. From the top of the mountain (2,275 m) there is a breathtaking 360° view encompassing the Zillertaler Alpen and their glaciers in the north and the Dolomites in the south. There are slopes for all standards although Kronplatz' skiing is best suited to intermediates. The black 'Sylvester' run drops 1,000 m down to the gondola at Reischach. There are some wide blue and red runs through the trees on the Olang side of the mountain. I particularly enjoyed the pistes on the St Vigil side—these are longer and less predictable, with some steeper drop-offs and plenty of sweeping turns. The run from the top of the Pre da Peres chair-lift which takes you all the way down into St Vigil is one of the best on the mountain. If you can handle the steeper runs, you could ski down to Olang, Reischach, or St Vigil. These also all have large flat areas for beginners which are covered with artificial snow throughout the season. Advanced skiers may not find enough challenging pistes, but combined with the nearby skiing at Ahrntal, Kronplatz is beginning to offer the quantity of piste found in the big Alpine resorts. Snowboarding is very popular.

CROSS-COUNTRY

There are 250 km of carefully prepared and graded pistes in the area. The scenery is astounding and lots of the trails nice and flat for beginners. More demanding trails can be found in the valley of Anthoiz where many championships have been held.

SKI SCHOOL

75,000L for a week. 70,000L kids. Private lesson 27,000L.

LIFT PASSES

Kronplatz. Six days 113,000L-150,900L or 'Superski Dolomiti' 141,000L-169,800L.

WHERE TO EAT, DRINK & BOOGIE

There are several mountain huts to eat and drink in. Many of these are self-service, although they are certainly not canteenish in either atmosphere or food. Meals are cheap. A hamburger costs about 4,000L, a bratwurst 3,000L, chicken 5,000L. There are plenty of bars and restaurants in the village, but few of the

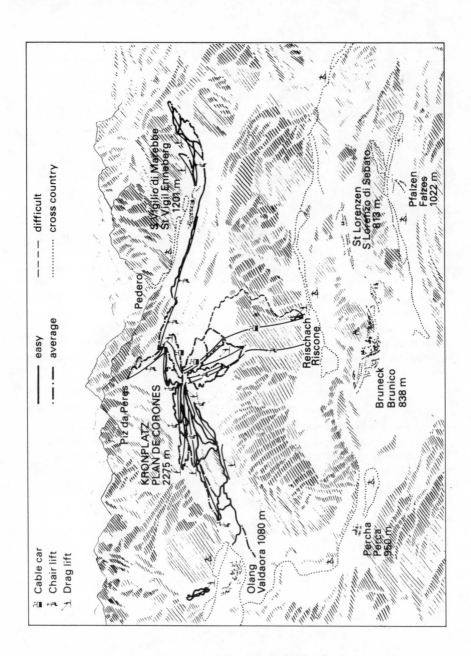

Cable car
Chair lift
Drag lift

easy
average

difficult
cross country

Piz da Peres

KRONPLATZ
PLAN DE CORONES
2275 m

Pederoi

S.Vigilio di Marebbe
St Vigil Enneberg
1201 m

Reischach
Riscone

St Lorenzen
S.Lorenzo di Sebato
813 m

Pfalzen
Falzes
1022 m

Bruneck
Brunico
838 m

Olang
Valdaora 1080 m

Percha
Perca
950 m

disco/pick-up joints you find in other resorts. Much of the entertainment goes on in the restaurants themselves. It is not unusual to bring out a guitar and start having a sing-song. The best restaurant we visited for food, atmosphere, and even price, was the Fana Ladina in St Vigil (Tel: 0474 51 17 5). This is a cosy place with low ceilings and pine walls. It is run by two sisters who have turned it into a lively and popular eating-place for the locals. They specialise in Ladinish food and make fantastic home-made grappa. You can eat the definitive five-course Tirolean meal for about £14. The Richone, in Reiscach, is a first-class restaurant. The food is, if anything, even better than at Fana Ladina but it is also more expensive and less informal.

The Tiroleans are traditional in their choice of entertainment. One restaurant I visited had a pine-panelled 'disco' with stacks of sophisticated synthesizer equipment. The music maestro of all this gear turned out to be a portly gentleman in full Tirolean costume, who proceeded to 'entertain' us with a medley of popular local oom-pah-pah tunes. Bring a good book and a pack of cards.

WHAT ELSE TO DO THERE

If you've got a car, you'll find plenty going on. If not, St Vigil probably has the best facilities out of the ski resorts.

Visit the medieval town centre in Bruneck or Michael Pacher's 'Vine Madonna' in the parish church of St Lorenzen.

St Vigil has a large sports complex, including an Olympic-sized pool, kiddies' pool, tennis, hot whirlpool and gym. St Vigil also has a natural ice-rink and a toboggan run (with its own lift).

Olang is famous for its artificial toboggan run—the scene of many international competitions.

Reischach has a modern indoor swimming pool—there is also curling on their natural ice rink.

Horse-drawn sleigh rides in St Vigil and Bruneck.

Bowling in St Vigil and Bruneck.

Indoor riding school in Bruneck.

Indoor tennis in Bruneck.

WHERE TO STAY

We stayed in Reischach at the very comfortable, modern four-star hotel—Royal Hinterhuber (Tel: 0474 21 22 1). From the outside, this looks a little like a Toblerone bar; inside the rooms are spacious and there is an excellent restaurant. The staff are very obliging—they even cooked a haggis we had brought with us to celebrate Burns Night. The hotel has a small indoor pool, sauna and resident masseur, and a private bus to take you to the slopes. 55,000L-95,000L half board per night.

Bed and breakfast at a one-star hotel starts from 6,000L. Erna Low Consultants specialise in the South Tirol. They offer reasonable accommodation such as the three-star hotel, the Reischacherhof (Tel: 0474 85 00 9) in Reischach. £20 for half board (four course meal each day) aperitif and dancing evening, free use of public swimming pool, bar, lounge, whirlpool, sauna and fitness room. £4.50 supplement per day for full board.

IN CASE OF EMERGENCY

Doctors in resort: Ten.
Chemists in resort: Three.
Dentists in resort: Seven.
Nearest Hospital: Bruneck.
Helicopter Rescue: No.

HOW TO GET THERE

Nearest Airport: Innsbruck or Munich.
Transfer time: 2-3 hours.
Train connection: Munich or Verona to Bruneck.

FURTHER INFORMATION

Tourist Offices
I-39031 Bruneck (Tel: 0474 85 72 2).
I-39030 St Vigil (Tel: 0474 51 03 7).
I-39030 St Lorenzen (Tel: 0474 44 09 2).
I-39030 Olang (Tel: 0474 46 27 7).

Liechtenstein

Driving into the tiny principality of Liechtenstein is like entering fairyland. Everything looks so clean and immaculate, with lots of pretty wooden chalets with daintily-painted shutters. You would never guess that this is, in fact, one of the most highly industrialised countries in the world.

The tiny Principality of Liechtenstein (60.66 square miles) was founded in 1719 and has a population of 28,000. Since 1806, it has been a sovereign territory under the Princes of Liechtenstein, with its own parliament or *Landtag*, and its own government. The currency is the Swiss franc and there are no frontier or customs checkpoints between these two countries. There are no trains in Liechtenstein—you have to get a bus or taxi from Sargans in Switzerland (17 km), Buchs in Switzerland (7 km) or Feldkirch in Austria (15 km). Once you are inside Liechtenstein or from Buchs, the post bus is free of charge. The capital is Vaduz where Prince Franz Josef and Princess Georgina now live. The people of Liechtenstein are of Germanic origins and speak a German dialect.

There are two ski areas, Malbun and Steg. Malbun is the main resort. Steg has a popular cross-country skiing loop called 'Valüna-Lopp' but only one ski lift. You certainly will not find any challenging or extensive skiing in Liechtenstein, and I would not recommend anyone staying there a week unless they were total beginners. But it is a very charming little place with lots of history and culture, certainly worth stopping off for a night or two if you are anywhere nearby.

Exchange rate (June 1989): £1 = 2.6 F

FURTHER INFORMATION

Liechtenstein National Tourist Office, Städtle 38, PO Box 139, FL-9490

Vaduz (Tel: 075 66288/21443), or from The Swiss National Tourist Office, Swiss Centre, New Coventry Street, London W1V 8EE (Tel: 01 734 1921).

MALBUN

- **HEIGHT OF RESORT**
  1,600 m.

- **HIGHEST LIFT**
  2,100 m.

- **WHY GO THERE?**
  Nice environment to learn to ski.
  Good for families.
  Small, quaint and friendly.

- **WHO GOES THERE?**
  Prince Charles and Princess Di.
  Prince Franz Josef and Princess Georgina of Liechtenstein.
  Papparazzi.
  Gossipy regulars.
  Lovers of all things small.
  Anyone with a big bank balance.

- **COMPANIES THAT GO THERE**
  Inghams.

No-one used to dare to go to Malbun in winter. The local farmers believed that the Malbun valley was haunted by ghosts and wicked spirits from Christmas Eve until spring. They used to flee with their livestock and 'worldly goods' to Triesenberg before Christmas Eve. It was not until the 1930s that this superstition was broken and the first Hotel Malbun opened for the winter season. In those days there was only one way to get to the resort in winter an arduous three to four-hour march, with or without skis attached to one's feet, over the Kulm to Steg and into Malbun. Thankfully, you can now get there in half an hour by bus from Vaduz, which is provided free of charge by the Principality.

Malbun has got everything that other ski resorts have, but on a miniature scale—even the nursery slope is called 'Lilliput'. The village comprises nine hotels, a scattering of bars and restaurants, a couple of shops, and a tiny chapel. Not a place to come if you suffer from claustrophobia. It is also condusive to a feeling of *déja-vu*. As it is so small, you cannot help bumping into the same people time and time again. The girl who was drinking coffee in one hotel at breakfast, served me tea in another in the afternoon, and then popped up at my hotel a few hours later! 'Life in Malbun is just one big merry-go-round', explained one genial American family who have spent so many Christmasses there that they are now counted as natives. They said it was a perfect resort for their young children as 'There's nowhere for them to get lost'. They also loved the fact that they knew everybody in the resort and everything about them. Not a place to come for an affair.

THE SKIING

Malbun has a very limited ski area. There are only six lifts and about a dozen runs but at least the lift pass is cheap in comparison to larger neighbouring resorts. A good intermediate could ski the whole of Malbun in an hour or two, but it is fine for beginners or very lazy/unambitious/doddery intermediates who just want to ski for an hour or two each day. It is also very safe for children as all the runs end up back in the village. Total novices can use the 'Liliput' practice area. Skiing is on two sides of the village. The harder runs are from the top of Sareis (2,000 m). There is one short black run down from here, which can be quite tricky. The terrain is very rocky so off-piste can be dangerous. Like the resort itself, the ski season is short and sweet—17 December-9 April.

CROSS-COUNTRY

Cross-country enthusiasts go to the nearby resort of Steg. The 'Valüna-Lopp' consists of four sections—4 km, 10.5 km, 6 km (skating), 1.7 km (floodlit), individually signposted. There are also possibilities for ski-touring. There is only one ski lift in Steg but hotel prices are cheaper (see below).

SKI SCHOOL

Considering that it is such a small resort I was surpised to find two ski schools in Malbun. The main one is Skischule Franz Beck (Tel: 075 22 63 6/22 93 4). This has ten full-time instructors—my new-found American friends raved about someone called Luki. I had an Austrian teacher called Walther, whose teaching was good but rather old-fashioned. 95F for five days, 75F children. Private 30F per hour. There's also a smaller Liechtenstein ski school, 95F for five days, 75F children. Further details from Skischule Malbun AG, Engelbert Buhler (Tel: 075 29 77 0/21 91 5).

LIFT PASSES

Cheap compared to neighbouring ski resorts—90F per week (55F children).

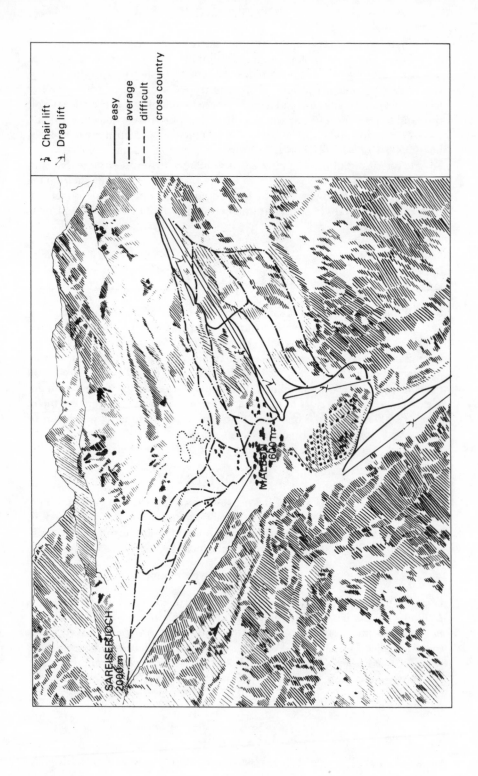

Chair lift
Drag lift

— easy
—·—·— average
— — — difficult
··········· cross country

SAREISERJOCH
2000 m

MALBUN
1600 m

WHERE TO EAT, DRINK & BOOGIE

There is only one mountain restaurant for lunch. This is on top of Sareis and serves simple food such as *Wiener Schnitzels*. If the weather is good you can lunch on the terrace and watch the cross-country skiers taking their dogs for a walk, or the hunters stalking off for the afternoon.

Life in Malbun is one big pub crawl, but as it is so small this involves more pubs than crawling. Unfortunately, alcohol is heavily taxed in Liechtenstein—about 14F a measure. The Turner Bar attracts the young sportifs whilst the Malbun Stübli bar is a small cosy place for a drink and a natter. There is live music at the Taverna bar. The Galena has tea-dancing every afternoon; do not expect anything too hip—'Rhinestone Cowboy' is about as up-to-date as they go! The Alpen Hotel is also a popular place for après-ski. Most of the eating is in the resort's hotels but some people venture down to Vaduz for a gourmet meal in one of the posh hotels.

WHAT ELSE TO DO THERE

Ice-skating.
Paragliding and hang-gliding (Tel: 075 27288).
Swimming.
Walking.
Tobogganing.
Bowling in the Hotel Malbunerhof (Tel: 075 22944).
Shopping and sightseeing in Vaduz. You can visit the exhibition of masterpieces from the famous art gallery belonging to the Prince (Tel: 075 22341), which is housed in the Englanderbau (English Building) in the main street. The Liechtenstein State Collection is in the same building. Vaduz also has a Postal Stamp Museum (Tel: 075 66259) and an Historical Museum (Tel: 075 22310). Liechtenstein is also famous for its wines—you can taste some of these in the Hofkellerei des Fürsten von Liechtenstein (wine cellars of the Prince of Liechtenstein), Feldstrasse 4, FL-9490 Vaduz (Tel: 075 21018).

WHERE TO STAY

Hotel prices in Malbun range from 25F for a single room without a bathroom to 140F for a double room with private bathroom or shower. These prices include breakfast, service and taxes. Apartments and chalets are also available from 30F-110F per day. I stayed in the oldest hotel in the resort, called the Alpen Hotel (Tel: 075 21181/21624). This opened 80 years ago and is owned by the charming Voegli family. Mrs Voegli, who must have the rosiest complexion in Liechtenstein, goes out of her way to make you feel at home. All the staff speak

English. The hotel makes its own pastries—the Black Forest gateau tastes even better than it looks. The rooms in the original hotel are old and quaint rather than luxurious—creaking floorboards etc. There is also a new annexe to the hotel with larger, more comfortable rooms and an indoor swimming pool. A single room without a bath costs from 25F per night, a double room with bath costs 80-100F per night, half board. The four-star Hotel Montana (Tel: 075 27333) is in the Inghams brochure. A single room with bathroom costs 70F-75F per night, a double with bathroom costs 60F-65F, bed and breakfast. Half board costs 20F per day extra, full board 30F per day extra. The Malbunerhof (Tel: 075 22944) has the most facilities—an indoor swimming pool, sauna, solarium, hairdresser, bowling alleys and congress hall. From 55F per night bed and breakfast for a single room with bathroom, from 90F-180F for a double with bathroom. Cheaper accommodation can be found in the nearby villages of Steg (1,300 m) or Triesenberg (884 m) . Bed and breakfast prices in Steg are from 15F-30F for a single room and from 30F-60F for a double room. There are no private bathrooms or showers. Hotel prices in Triesenberg range from 15F-57F per person. There is a regular free daily bus service connecting the resorts.

IN CASE OF EMERGENCY

There are no medical faciliites actually in Malbun.
Nearest Doctor: Triesenberg.
Nearest Chemist: Vaduz.
Nearest Dentist: Vaduz.
Nearest Hospital: Vaduz or Grabs.
Helicopter Rescue: Yes.

HOW TO GET THERE

Nearest Airport: Zurich.
Train connection: Train from Zurich to Sargans ($1\frac{1}{2}$ hours) then bus (45 mins).

FURTHER INFORMATION

Tourist Office Malbun FL-9497 Malbun (Tel: 075 26577). They have a recorded report on snow and slope conditions (Tel: 075 28080).
Tourist Office Triesenberg FL-9497 Triesenberg (Tel: 075 21926).

Norway

In some countries a child might get away with 'Sorry I'm late Miss. My bike had a puncture.' But there are not many places where they could hope to be excused on the grounds that they had forgotten to wax their skis. In Norway, and other Scandinavian countries, they possibly could. Skiing is as much part of Norwegian life as cycling is in in Holland. They have over 100 ski resorts—not only for cross-country. In 1988/89, the Norway started a big project to establish itself as a downhill destination. Twenty years ago it was a popular ski destination for British skiers (mainly cross-country), but the annual figures have plummeted from 15,000 to just 1,500. In the past it was always very expensive to get to Norway. Now, however, there are charter flights to Oslo, Bergen and Trondheim. A ski holiday in Norway does not need to cost you more than in the Alps—one week half board in Hemsedal last season (1988/89), for example, cost just £220.

Skiing in Norway is very different from skiing in the Alps. It is not nearly as macho. There are no vast intimidating mountains or massive jagged peaks. Their mountains are big enough (up to 2,000 m) for downhill skiing but much of the surrounding scenery of fjords and lakes is flat as a frozen pancake. If you like wide, open spaces you will love Norway. In Geilo, for example, you can see nearly all the pistes from the resort. Another of their main resorts, Voss, set by a lake, is only 55 m above sea level (skiing up to 945 m) but as it is north of the Shetlands it has a good snow record right up until the end of April. Although none of the resorts has a massive lift network, the pistes are wonderfully uncrowded and there is often a good opportunity for touring and off-piste.

It would be wrong to suggest that Norway's skiing can compete with the challenge and variety of the big Alpine resorts. A good skier would very soon get bored with the limited selection of pistes. But it is worth going to Norway for a totally different winter holiday experience. Why not try the wonderfully graceful sport of telemarking, a day of nordic touring, or even dog-sleigh skiing? The best time to go is in March or April (avoid Easter as there can be a lot of queueing). The days are longer, some of the lifts stay open until after 5 pm, and winter is just turning into spring.

Don't expect to find pretty alpine-style villages—Norwegian resorts tend to be rather modern and sprawling and do not have the charm or character of Austrian or Swiss resorts. The most well-known Norwegian resorts are Voss and Geilo. Geilo is Norway's equivalent of St Moritz, with expensive flashy hotels, but not as much style or as many facilities as the Swiss resort. My favourite was Voss which has a nice main street, very friendly locals and fantastic shops. The biggest disappointment for me was Hemsedal. This resort hosted the 1986 World Cup and attracts the young sporty Norwegians, but it only has a few nondescript hotels and apartments and no village centre or atmosphere. Not a place I would recommend staying. Oppdal is known as Norway's 'alpine Metropolis' and being in the centre of the country is easily accessible from Oslo and Trondheim. Oppdal has 26 alpine runs and 186 km of prepared cross-country trails. Beitostølen is on the southern slopes of the Jotunheim mountain range, about 200 km from Oslo. Although the downhill skiing is limited to 14 pistes, it has plenty of other winter activities such as husky-dog driving, horse-drawn sleigh rides, torchlit skiing, parascending and even windsurfing on snow. They are willing to arrange all sorts of special family activities. Most of the resorts can be reached by railway, which like the Swiss transport is very clean and efficient.

Most Norwegians speak perfect English. They are very warm and hospitable people who have a relaxed attitude to skiing. At Easter time, they are as happy sunbathing on the pistes as bombing down them. The food is wonderfully fresh and healthy. The *smørgasbord* is a Scandinavian cold buffet, featuring fresh and smoked salmon, prawns, langoustine, herrings, smoked reindeer, salads and many other culinary delights. At Christmas, the hotels do a special smørgasbord which often has about 40 different dishes. Christmas is very much a family occasion for the Norwegians. The trees are decorated with wonderfully dinky carved wooden decorations and there are all sorts of festivities for the children. Many of the hotels are trying to become more 'international' and the cooking is often French rather than their own traditional cuisine. This seems a shame, as the whole charm of going to Norway is sampling something different from what you would find in the Alps.

You will certainly never find crowds of lager louts in Norway. This is to prepare you gently for the bad news—alcohol is carefully restricted and very expensive (about £3-£4 for a pint of beer). You can't buy bottles of booze in the ski resort shops and there is no drinking up in the mountain restaurants. They do make up for it in their cutely-named 'after-ski'. In the winter months, *glögging* (pronounced *glugging*) starts as early as 3 pm. *Glögg* is the Norwegian equivalent of glühwein, usually served with big fat sultanas at the bottom of the glass. The Norwegians are not into rowdy Austrian-style evening entertainment. They prefer to mellow over a few drinks by the fire, listen to some quiet piano music, or simply read a good book. If you're looking to unwind, a winter holiday in Norway is the perfect opportunity.

Exchange rate (June 1989): £1 = 11 Kr

FURTHER INFORMATION

Norwegian Tourist Board 20 Pall Mall, London SW1Y 5NE (Tel: 01 839 6255).

GEILO

- **HEIGHT OF RESORT** 800 m.

- **HIGHEST LIFT** 1,900 m.

- **WHY GO THERE?**
  Swish hotels.
  The most glamourous Norwegian ski resort.
  Cross-country and easy downhill skiing.

- **WHO GOES THERE?**
  The Norwegian jet set.

- **COMPANIES THAT GO THERE**
  Ski Sutherland.
  Star Tour of Scandinavia.
  NSR Travel.
  Ski Choice.
  Bladon Lines.

Geilo is Norway's most 'jet set' resort. It is a rather sprawling village, comprising a scattering of chic ultramodern hotels, ritzy nightclubs, expensive restaurants and a diminuitive 12th century white church. The 'main' street does not have much to offer apart from a couple of exclusive-looking shops. Geilo lacks a village atmosphere—most of the action takes place inside the hotels. These are exceptionally plush, with large indoor heated swimming pools and all the trimmings: the sort of places you'd expect to find rich sugar daddies bringing their secretaries. Many of the hotels have excellent conference facilities and are full of blue-eyed Norwegian 'Mr Suits'. In Geilo people 'dress' for dinner in smart cream casual wear and lots of furs. The big hotels have night clubs, which by Norwegian standards stay open very late (3 am). The coolest way to cross the town is in a torchlit horse-drawn sleigh driven by a Dr Zhivago-type character in ankle-length fur coat. In the daytime the children speed about the streets on '*spark*', standing on the back of a toboggan and almost skating along.

Geilo is in the centre of Norway, half way between Bergen and Oslo. It's situated at the head of the Hallingdal Valley and forms the gateway to the mountain moors of Hardangervidda. Although Geilo is modern and glitzy, it still has quite a lot of history attached to it, which is evident in the ancient farm buildings all around. Viking graves were discovered nearby and the region of Hol is famous for its quality knives, tablewear and tools. The locals are also fond of folk dancing and fiddling. Geilo was developed in 1909 when they built the Bergen-Oslo railway. Many Norwegians own family *hyttes* (houses) in the surrounding mountains. The resort itself has quite good facilities for children. There is a 'Troll Klub' for three year olds, upwards, and a 'Club 15' for teenagers.

THE SKIING

The skiing in Geilo (25 km) is limited and very spread out. It is best suited to beginners and families. Good skiers would get very bored. Most of the hotels have their own transport, and there is also a public courtesy bus. It would take 45 minutes to drive round to all the ski areas. At least, as it is so spread out, queueing is not a problem—no more than 5 minutes even in high season; and snow conditions are always good as they put artificial snow on the ground as a base at the beginning of the season (November-May). It is very safe skiing—there is no huge network to get lost in. Many of the slopes are visible from the road—you can sit in the Vestlia hotel and see most of the Vestlia slopes directly above you.

The skiing in the Vestlia is mainly for beginners and families. Here there are a couple of little nursery tow lifts and a chair-lift to the top of Bjødnahovda. The long green run is called 'Bjørne Løypa' which means 'bear track' in Norwegian. This is very popular with the children as it is a long easy path through the woods. In contrast, the Hallingen is a very steep moguly black run, and even Randi-Løypa, a red run, is steep and moguly half way down. The rest of Geilo's skiing is across the fjord. There is not much off-piste in Geilo, although there is some good steep powder from the top of Gullsteinhovda (1,109 m). There is also a steep, wide black run here. One of the red runs from Gullsteinhovda is called Musikkbakken (music hall) as skiers can listen to music as they bop down the slope. From here you can cross over to the Geilohovda slopes (1,062 m). There is a wide blue run and a couple of very narrow steep blacks. A choice of pistes leads down to Slåtta and the nursery slopes. The highest pistes are at Havsdalshovda (1,173 m). These are wide beginners' slopes which usually have good visibility.

Telemarking is very popular in Geilo. Skiers walk up to Hallingskarvet (1,933 m) and ski down off-piste. Snowboarding has not yet caught on.

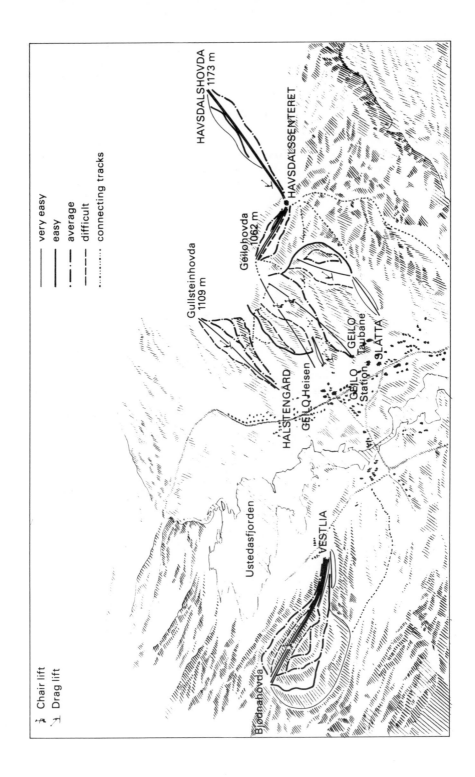

HAVSDALSHOVDA
1173 m

HAVSDALSSENTERET

Geilohovda
1062 m

Gullsteinhovda
1109 m

GEILO
Taubane

9LÅTTA

HALSTENGÅRD

GEILO Heisen

GEILO
Station

Ustedasfjorden

VESTLIA

Bjødnahovda

very easy
easy
average
difficult
connecting tracks

Chair lift
Drag lift

CROSS-COUNTRY

There is masses of cross country in Geilo—130 km of marked and prepared tracks.

SKI SCHOOL

As the skiing is so spread out there are four offices for ski school. Geilo Ski School at the Slotta Ski Centre (Tel: 067 85 875). Per Bye Ski School at Geilo Heisen (Tel: 067 85 650). Havsdalen Ski School (Tel: 067 85 901). Sport-Service Vestlia (Tel: 067 85 188).
Children from 3 years.

LIFT PASSES

540Kr for six days. Lifts close at 3.30 pm early in season, 5 pm by March.

WHERE TO EAT, DRINK & BOOGIE

Geilo has three mountain restaurants. The most popular one is Havsdal. Geilohavda is a traditional restaurant with a log fire. They often have lunchtime barbecues on the Vestlia slopes. Like everywhere in Norway, alcohol is not allowed in any of the mountain restaurants. In the short winter days, 'after-ski' starts as early as 2.30 pm-3 pm. The Vestlia has a cosy bar where a Scotsman called Alistair plays the guitar and sings in the corner. The Dr Holms Hotel also has a popular after-ski bar. There are plenty of good places to eat. I recommend Johannes Bistro (Tel: 067 85 757) where they serve first-class international cuisine. I started with snails in garlic butter (59Kr), followed by the most divine peppersteak (164Kr). The Vidda (Tel: 067 86 590) specialises in game such as snowgoose which is shot and cooked by the chef/owner. Inside it is a very pleasant restaurant—just a shame about the view of the Texaco garage! The Bardøla Hotel has a good restaurant and live music six days a week. The Highlander nightclub is a popular social point where the women get glitzed up in high heels and jewellery and many of the men wear suits.

WHAT ELSE TO DO THERE

Ice-fishing.
Sleigh-rides.
Swimming.
Dog-sleighing.
Cinema.

WHERE TO STAY

Although there are all sorts of accommodation ranging from caravans to five-star hotels, most people go to Geilo to be pampered. They certainly have a good choice of luxury hotels. The most elegant is the Dr Holms which was built in 1908 (Tel: 067 85 622). This has a wonderfully spacious lobby, a big bar with mooses on the wall and lots of carved gilt mirrors and massive oil paintings. The hotel is well situated, only 100 m from the Geilo chair-lift, and has its own swimming pool, sauna and solarium. They only do full board—740K per night, 1040Kr for a suite. The Bardøla (Tel: 067 85 400) is also an excellent hotel, which used to be a mountain lodge. It has all mod cons, such as indoor swimming pool, sauna, solarium, hairdressers, massage and jacuzzi as well as some lovely antique furniture. It is a popular place for conferences and attracts many Americans.

The Vestlia (Tel: 067 85 611) is conveniently located by the ski lifts and is half-owned by the Bardøla. They have a swimming pool, sauna, billiard room and tennis. There are some lovely pine apartments with log fires as well as hotel rooms.

IN CASE OF EMERGENCY

Doctor in resort: One.
Chemist in resort: One.
Dentist in resort: One.
Nearest Hospital: Hønefoss (180 km).
Helicopter Rescue: Yes.

HOW TO GET THERE

Nearest Airport: Oslo or Bergen.
Transfer time: $3\frac{1}{2}$ hours by train.
Train connection: On the Bergensbanen.

FURTHER INFORMATION

Tourist Office Postboks 85, 3581 Geilo (Tel: 067 86 300).

VOSS

- **HEIGHT OF RESORT**
  55 m.

- **HIGHEST LIFT**
  945 m.

- **WHY GO THERE?**
  Traditional Norwegian village in the heart of the fjord district.
  Warm, hospitable locals.
  Easy transfer from Bergen airport.

- **WHO GOES THERE?**
  Bergen weekenders.
  Norwegian families.
  Groups of young, fun-loving Norwegians, many of whom are as keen
  on suntanning as skiing.

- **COMPANIES THAT GO THERE**
  Ski Sutherland.
  Norway Line.
  NSR Travel.
  Ski Choice.

I stepped off the train at Voss on a beautifully cold, crisp night, so still I could hear someone's ski glove drop at the other end of the platform. Voss is a traditional Norwegian village, in the heart of the fjord district. It is very popular in the summer as it is near the two largest fjords in Norway—the Sognefjord to the north and the Hardangerfjord to the south. It is also Norway's best-known ski resort, having hosted several World Cup championships. Voss is only an hour and a half's train journey from Bergen. The station is right in the centre of the village, like a Swiss resort.

The village itself is distinctly Norwegian in atmosphere and style. Most of the buildings burnt down in the Second World War—all that is left is a stately 13th-century grey stone church. The village has been rebuilt very tastefully with lots of white wooden houses, like something out of the *Little House on the Prairie*. On one side of the village is a lake onto which some of the hotels and a youth hostel back. The two main streets run parallel and are attractively lined with pine trees and lots of twinkling fairy lights. It is a bustling little town, particularly before Christmas when the locals (14,000) are stocking up with Christmas goodies. Although I would not usually think of going shopping on a ski holiday, it was very relaxing to spend a late afternoon browsing round their old-fashioned shops, admiring all the hand-knitted jumpers, pewter jewellery, wooden and woven goods, and reindeer skins and horns. Best of all were the dinky hand-made wooden Christmas decorations which filled up most of my suitcase on the way home.

The locals are all very friendly and do not seem offended if you barter in the shops. Although they have a few very nice four-star hotels, the resort itself is certainly not rolling in money and they are keen to cultivate English tourists. Alcohol is not allowed in the mountain restaurants, but the young Norwegian skiers still seem quite relaxed. The resort is at its most swinging at Easter time— the young Norwegian trendies put on their shades and strip off to white T-shirts as soon as the sun comes out. There is one run that is known as the 'Sunbather's Paradise'. On a sunny day there are more people sitting on this piste eating a packed lunch than skiing!

THE SKIING

Compared to the Alps, Voss has a fairly limited ski area with only 40 km of pistes and nine lifts. But there is little queueing, plenty of off-piste and a long steep run used for the World Cup downhill. There is some good skiing in the forests and plenty of easy runs for beginners. Intermediates and advanced skiers will enjoy the off-piste route down the back of Slettafjell. This goes into the valley of Dywedalen. It starts off with some good off-piste followed by long timber trails out of the valley. You need to catch a bus or hitch-hike back to Voss. If you are feeling very energetic, you can take a day trip touring up to Lønahorgi (1,411 m) and ski back down off-piste. A cable car (next to the station) connects the village with the ski area. There is also a connecting two-seater chair-lift 4 km from the village. Most of the hotels have minibuses and there is also a local ski bus. Unfortunately, you can't ski back into the village—you either take the gondola down or ski down to the bottom of the chair-lift and catch a bus. Although it is not very high, Voss has a long ski season, from mid-December to the beginning of May. If there is snow, they will open the lifts as early as November. Before January the days are rather short and they close the lifts between 3 pm and 4 pm. From March to May the lifts stay open until 5 pm. There is a ski hire shop, Voss Ski & Surf Service (Tel: 05 510032/5118 18) at the top of the gondola. 260Kr-450Kr for six days. Telemarking, snowboards, monoski and touring equipment can also be hired. You can leave your own skis up there. Telemarking is very popular in Voss. They are also very keen on snowboarding and have even built a half pipe, which is rather surprising considering how few pistes they have.

CROSS-COUNTRY

There are eight illuminated trails (including a 4 km) and two marked trails.

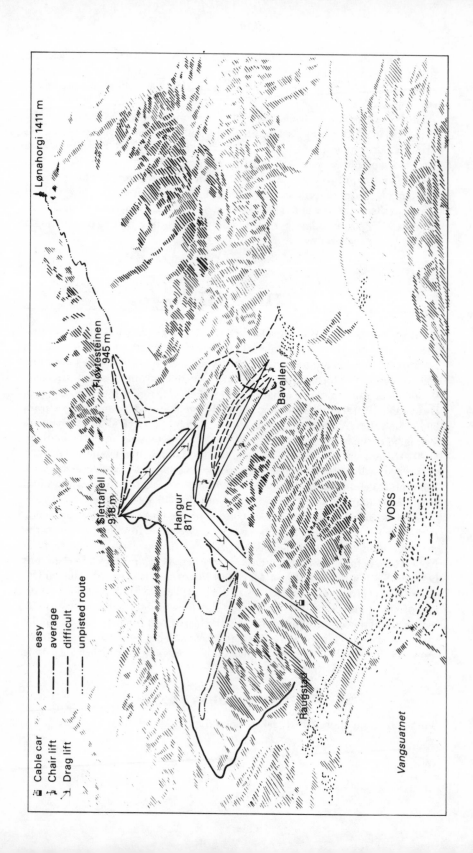

Cable car
Chair lift
Drag lift

easy
average
difficult
unpisted route

Lønahorgi 1411 m

Fløyfjesteinen 945 m

Sfettafjell 918 m

Hangur 817 m

Bavallen

VOSS

Raugstad

Vangsuatnet

SKI SCHOOL

(Tel: 05 511819/510032).
The ski school is run by the young Einar Raanilsen, who takes a modern approach to teaching and is very much into snowboarding. English-speaking instructors. Group instruction starts at 10 am at the Hangursheisen chair-lift. 300Kr for six mornings. 130Kr for 50-minute private lesson.

LIFT PASSES

600Kr for six days (100Kr-450Kr kids).

WHERE TO EAT, DRINK & BOOGIE

There are two (teetotal) mountain restaurants—one at the top of the gondola where you can get thick soup, hamburgers, hotdogs, sandwiches, cakes, etc and another popular cafe at Slettafjell where the T-bars meet.

There are four places open for glögging—Fleisher Hotel, Park Hotel, Rondo Sportell and the Stallen Pub in Hotel Vossevangen. The Fleisher Hotel is particular popular—last Easter they sold 4,000 litres of glögg!

The night life in Voss is quiet and fairly old-fashioned. The smart piano bar at the Park Hotel, with its smoochy numbers, wicker chairs and romantic view of Lake Vangsvatnet, is a popular wooing spot. Most of the people in the bar end up downstairs at the Pentagon, a flashy nightclub that won't let you in wearing jeans. The Rando disco is more casual and very popular with the skiers. Knights, in the Jarl Hotel, is a rather tacky club that is popular with English soldiers from the local military base. For a really old-fashioned evening try Fleisher's disco which usually has live bands. The discos close at 1 am in Voss (most charge 40Kr entrance). Although it is not a very late place, no one seems to get up very early and the lifts are often at their most crowded at about 11 am.

One of the things I loved best about Norway was the food and Voss has its fair share of good restaurants. All the hotels do delicious smørgasbords and lay on particularly lavish spreads at Christmas. The Fleisher Hotel has a very good traditional dining room. The manager wanted me to try a local speciality called *Smalahøve*. I wish I had not agreed. The waiter uncovered the plate to reveal a whole sheep's head, complete with eyes, nostrils and bared teeth! It had been salted, smoked and boiled. This is meant to be a delicacy, particularly the flesh above the cheek bones, but I am afraid I couldn't stomach it! The Elysee restaurant in the Park Hotel is smart and sophisticated with plush furnishings, festoon blinds and its own wine cellar. Next door, the Station is a casual restaurant, decked out in railway style, serving hamburgers (38KR) and pasta (40Kr). Red wine 65Kr for half a litre. Coffee 7Kr.

WHAT ELSE TO DO THERE

Floodlit skiing three evenings a week.
Torchlit sleigh-rides.
Hang-gliding is very popular.
Swimming pools in Fleisher Hotel and Jarl Hotel.
Cinema showing English films.
Folk museum (Tel: 05 511105).
Voss Squash Centre (Tel: 05 512350). Rackets and shoes for hire. Sauna.
Ice-fishing on Lake Vangsvatnet. You will need a State Licence (60Kr per year) available from post offices, and a local permit (from Voss tourist office, post office and sports shops).
Voss Jazz Festival—usually a weekend in March.

WHERE TO STAY

There are several very nice hotels in Voss, as well as small pensions, a youth hostel and self-catering apartments. My favourite is the Park Hotel (Tel: 05 511322), a deluxe modern hotel with an elegant dining room and piano bar and enormous plush bedrooms. 625Kr bed and breakfast per night or 2,695Kr for a week's half board. The Fleisher Hotel (Tel: 05 511155) is larger and more old-fashioned. 690Kr bed and breakfast per night, or 3,150Kr for a week's half board. The Fleisher Hotel also has some self-catering 'motel' rooms. Although these are very attractive inside, and beautifully situated on the lake, they look like ugly beach huts from the outside. Bavallslia apartments (Tel: 05 510650) are newly-built pine cabins, only 100 m from the chair-lift but a car-ride away from the village.

IN CASE OF EMERGENCY

Doctors in resort: Several.
Chemist in resort: One.
Dentists in resort: Several.
Nearest Hospital: Small hospital in Voss—very serious cases go by helicopter to Bergen.
Helicopter Rescue: Yes.

HOW TO GET THERE

Nearest Airport: Bergen.

Transfer time: 30-minute cab or bus ride from airport to Bergen railway station, then 1 hour 15 minutes.
Train connection: Direct from Bergen. 1 hour 15 minutes.

FURTHER INFORMATION

Voss Tourist Office Voss Tinghus, 5700 Voss (Tel: 05 511833 or 511716).

Spain

There are two main areas where you can ski in Spain–Sierra Nevada in the south, and the Pyrenees in the north. The most southerly Spanish mountain range is El Sistema Penibético, which has only one resort, the Solynìève (2,000 m) in Sierra Nevada. This attracts several British tour operators, but can still be recommended on the grounds that it is near the wonderful historic city of Granada and the sunny Mediterranean. The Spanish Pyrenees are on the border of France and also include the well-known duty-free principality of Andorra. Like the resorts in the French Pyrenees, the Spanish ones vary in size, age, and style; they are divided between the Catalan Pyrenees (12 resorts) and the Aragonese Pyrenees (5 resorts).

The closest Spanish Pyreneean resorts to the Mediterranean are the Catalan ones, La Molina (1,400 m) and Masella (1,600 m). These attract the locals from Barcelona but are not so reliable for snow. Cerler (1,550 m) is an attractive Aragonese rustic village above Benasque. Formigal (1,500 m) is a purpose-built Aragonese resort, in the west of the Pyrenees, quite well-known to the British. I have chosen to review the purpose-built Baqueira Beret in the Catalan, because although it is the most superior Spanish resort, with a good snow record and some very challenging skiing, it has not yet been discovered by the British market. There is also skiing in the Cantabrian Mountains (6 resorts) and El Sistema Central (4 resorts) near Madrid.

Exchange rate (June 1989): £1 = 193p

140

FURTHER INFORMATION

Spanish Tourist Office 57 James's Street, London SW1A 1LD (Tel: 01 499 0901).
ATUDEM (Tourist Association of Skiing and Mountain Resorts) in Madrid (Tel: 91 458 1557).

BAQUEIRA BERET

- **HEIGHT OF RESORT**
  1,500 m.

- **HIGHEST LIFT**
  2,150 m.

- **WHY GO THERE?**
  Skiing in the Pyrenees at its best.
  Challenging for intermediates.
  Excellent après-ski.
  Cheaper than the Alps.

- **WHO GOES THERE?**
  Spanish jet set.
  King Juan Carlos of Spain.

- **COMPANIES THAT GO THERE**
  Ski Miquel.

Baqueira (pronouced Ba-cay-da) lies in a remote setting in the Catalan region of Spain, 96 km west of Andorra. Baqueira is popular with Barcelona weekenders as the city is only 350 km away. The nearest airport is Toulouse in France. From here, you can catch a train to Montrejeau (one hour) and then it is another hour in a taxi to the resort, driving through typical Spanish villages. The mountains are wind-blown and barren-looking until you approach the resort and the scenery becomes more alpine. One of the main differences about skiing in the Pyrenees is that the slopes are on the top of the mountains rather than just two-thirds up, alpine-style. This makes everything seem very open. From the top of Baqueira you can see Aneto—the biggest glacier in the Pyrenees.

The first ski lift in Baqueira opened in 1964. In 1972 it expanded into another valley—Beret. This centre is a tiny place, comprising only a car park, lift and restaurant. Baqueira is now Spain's premier resort. This is where King Carlos has a chalet; although it is certainly no Zermatt or St Anton, it does compare favourably to mid-sized Alpine resorts and has excellent après-ski and a certain style of its own. Baqueira has its fair share of furs and Ferraris, but it is still very friendly. The village is small and compact, a purpose-built complex mainly comprising modern apartments and a few hotels under which there is a good selection of shops and restaurants.

THE SKIING

Although it cannot compare with the big Alpine ski areas such as Les Trois Vallées, Baqueira has a very respectable amount of skiing (90 k). About two-thirds of this is above the treeline. There is not much trivia (flat, linking runs) in Baqueira—the skiing has a certain 'bite' to it. It is certainly perfectly adequate for beginners and intermediates, although the true expert would probably get bored after a few days. There are, however, a couple of very challenging slopes, almost vertical couloirs. The un-prepared Escornacrabes (which literally translated means 'The place where the goats die') *is* truly terrifying. The Louis Arias and Tubo Nere runs usually have steep bumps. As it is further south than the Alps, you should get an extra hour's skiing. There are four main areas: Argulls, Cap de Baqueira, Beret and Dorsal. There has been quite a lot of money invested in the resort, and about 60 per cent of the lifts have been installed in the last three years. Three new lifts were installed in Cap de Baqueira in 1989. The equipment is modern and the pistes well-maintained. Although the Spanish have a reputation for being rather reckless skiers, they are now very safety-conscious in Baqueira. It is reassuring to know that if there is an accident they have a free mountain evacuation service.

Baqueira is like a French purpose-built resort in that the main ski-lift is only a few minutes' walk from most of the accommodation. They have recently installed a four-person chair-lift which takes you up the mountain at 5 metres a second, arriving at the first station in just $3\frac{1}{2}$ minutes. Queueing is not a problem. The first station is at 1,800 m. There are eight lifts here going up the Baqueira side of the mountain to a height of 2,500 m. On a good day you can see across the Aran Valley. The runs at the top are black. Isards is a long, comfortable, sweeping red piste. Baqueira is linked to Beret by a chair-lift to 2,100 m. A long blue run will take you down to Beret (1,850 m).

There are excellent possiblities for off-piste although skiing is restricted to the designated ski areas. Heli-skiing is also available, at a very cheap rate of about 5,000P. Skiers are dropped off at Dorsal peak, from where they ski the powder down to Montgarri. The helicopter company picks them up from this isolated village and drops them off at another peak.

CROSS-COUNTRY

This is not a cross-country resort. There are about 20 km.

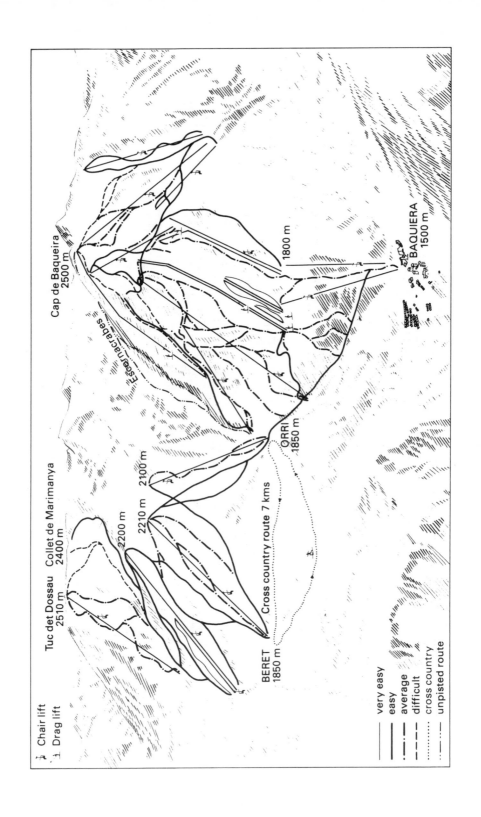

Chair lift
Drag lift

Tuc det Dossau
2510 m

Collet de Marimanya
2400 m

Cap de Baqueira
2500 m

Escornacrapes

2200 m

2210 m

2100 m

ORRI
1850 m

BERET
1850 m

Cross country route 7 kms

1800 m

BAQUIERA
1500 m

very easy
easy
average
difficult
cross country
unpisted route

SKI SCHOOL

9,400P for six days (3 hours per day). 8,300P kids. 21,100P for six days including lift pass. 17,300P kids. English-speaking.

LIFT PASSES

11,000P for five days, 15,000P for seven days. Children under eleven pay 1,400P per day.

WHERE TO EAT, DRINK & BOOGIE

Compared with the Alps, Baqueira's mountain restaurants are nothing special. There are six on the slopes. A big lunch should not cost you more than 800P. *Lomo* (pork fillet with cheese in bread) costs about 350P. The restaurant in Beret is more like a self-service canteen than an alpine mountain bar. I much preferred the one in the main ski area of Baqueira, which had neatly-laid tables, good food and a wine list. A Spanish lunchtime liqueur did wonders to my skiing in the afternoon. They serve local digestifs, such as apple liqueur, in a frosted glass. Unlike schnapps, this should be sipped rather than knocked back in one.

The après-ski is excellent, but based more on restaurants than night-clubs. After skiing, most of the Spaniards have a siesta, and then emerge at the restaurants at about 10 pm. The discos do not get going until after 1 am and stay open until 4 am. It is not surprising that the slopes are so quiet early in the morning! There are two discos, Tiffanys and Tuc Blanc, which do not charge an entry fee apart from peak nights. The Esquirro is a popular après-ski bar with draught beer and *Aranes Tapas* (hors d'oeuvres). Spanish skiers drink cocktails as they are so cheap! Expect to pay about 150P for a half-litre of beer or 200P for a good quality Spanish brandy. They do not seem to measure anything, just pour until you shout 'stop!' The Borda is a rustic restaurant which does fantastic tapas (if you go in a group, you will get about 20 dishes). The restaurant is an old barn, and the meat is charcoal-grilled. You will also get good fish in Baqueira, transported from the Bay of Biscay.

WHAT ELSE TO DO THERE

Snow carnival.
Squash.
Gymnasium.
Cinema.
Sauna.
Bowling.
Paragliding.
Heli-Skiing.

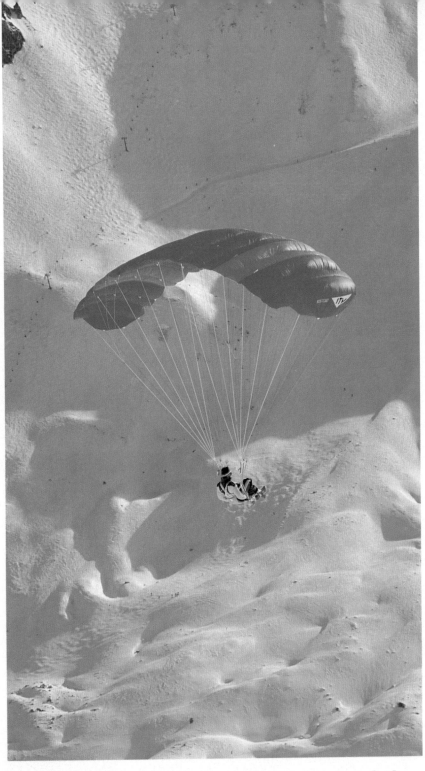

The coolest way down the mountain at the end of the day is via parapente. But James darling, where's the Martini?

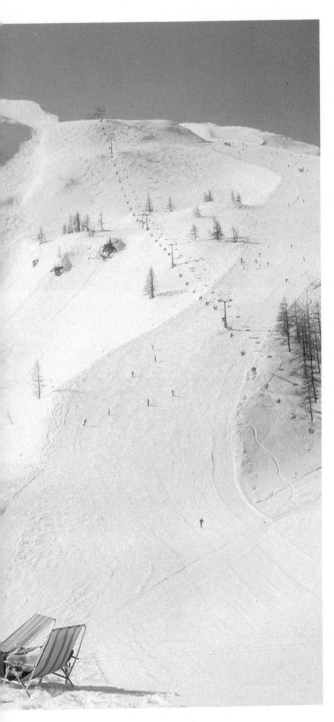

Don't know how these deckchairs found their way up to the middle of the piste in Gamskogel, Zauchensee. But why not just sit back and soak up those rays and let the others check out the moguls. Now, where's that hip flask?

ABOVE A mellow and misty day in Andalo, the largest resort in the Paganella Empire. When the cloud clears, the view of the sunset from the summit is spectacular.

BELOW A peaceful Sunday morning in the heart of Norway. Father and son escape via pulka from Geilo's glitzy hotels.

ABOVE Who cares if it gets dark early in Sweden? Lift passes include floodlit skiing. Sälen is Sweden's southermost mountain range, 450 kilometres from Stockholm.

BELOW Higgledy-piggledy wooden houses on stilts are characteristic of the Swiss Anniviers valley. St-Luc makes up in pistes (75km) what it lacks in population (100).

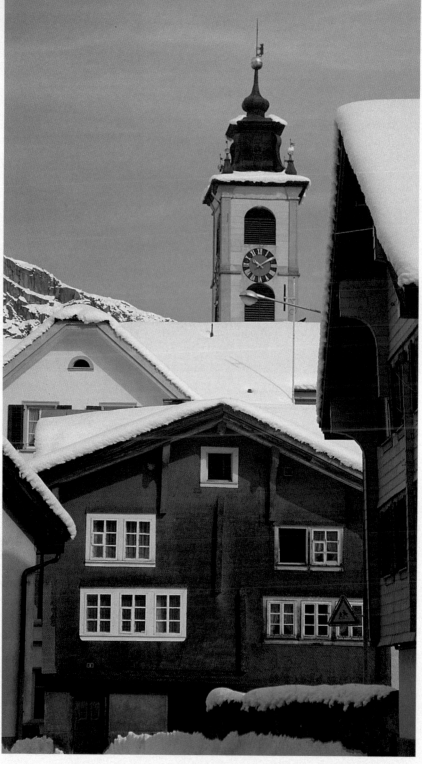

A quiet back street in the military village of Andermatt in Switzerland. The most stylish
way to arrive is aboard the Zermatt-St Moritz Glacier Express.

ABOVE Don't turkey out of the off-piste in Uludag as it's perfect for powder novices. The lifts are open 8am-8pm but close for lunch so check you don't get stuck half-way up!

BELOW Flims, one of Switzerland's most popular resorts, has still to be discovered by the Brits.

There's all the time in the world, dude, when you're coming up for air. Dig those fluorescent pants.

WHERE TO STAY

There are only three hotels in Baqueira. Montato (Tel: 73 64 50 75) is a four-star hotel in the centre. The rooms are like comfortable student rooms, practical rather than luxurious. It was apparently good enough for King Carlos who used to stay here before he bought his own chalet. The hotels all offer special packages including lift pass and ski school. 50,300P for a week at Montato, bed and breakfast, including lift pass and ski school. 42,400P for just bed and breakfast and lift pass. The Tuc Blanc is a large three-star modern hotel (Tel: 73 64 51 50). 56,100P half board, lift pass and ski school. 48,200P bed and breakfast, lift pass and ski school. 37,300P bed and breakfast and lift pass. The Ruda (Tel: 73 64 52 58) is a small three-star rustic-style hotel. 48,400P bed and breakfast with lift pass and classes. 40,500P bed and breakfast and lift pass.

Self-catering accommodation in apartments or *mulitpropiedad* (flats in hotel-type arrangements) is also available.

The only British company in Baqueira is Ski Miquel. It has hotel accommodation and also a luxury chalet (all the rooms have private facilities).

IN CASE OF EMERGENCY

Doctor in resort: One.
Chemist in resort: One.
Nearest Dentist: Viella (14 km).
Nearest Hospital: Viella.
Helicopter Rescue: Yes.

HOW TO GET THERE

Nearest Airport: Toulouse in France.
Transfer time: $2\frac{1}{2}$ hours.
Train connection: Montrejeau (1 hour from Toulouse) then taxi (1 hour).

FURTHER INFORMATION

Tourist Office Baqueira Beret Apartado 60, Viella, Lérida, Spain (Tel: 73 645025).

Sweden

Skiing is as much part of Sweden's heritage as haggis is of Scotland's. They have the longest ski season in Europe, from early November to the middle of June, and can boast an enviable snow record that puts some of the Alpine countries to shame. Sweden must be the only country in the world that celebrates its unification with a skiing marathon. The Vasa Ski Race is named after good King Gustava Wasa, who had to ski for his life in 1521 to escape an invasion of bloodthirsty Danes. Fortunately for Sweden, he made it, united the country, crowned himself and started modern Sweden. Every year tens of thousands of Swedes ski the route he followed in the world's biggest skiing event. Skiing in Sweden is usually synonymous with cross-country. This is approached whole-heartedly in an almost 'Scott of the Antartic' style, with expeditions across the wintry wilderness or through the pine forests. It is often a family affair—with mum or dad pulling little Svenn and Lena behind on *pulkas*.

The dynamic Swedish ski racer, Ingemar Stenmark, made the skiing in Sweden what it is today. Due to his amazing successes in the 1970s, skiing came to mean more than cross-country. Most Swedish skiers are proficient in both cross-country and downhill. There are 500 ski areas and over 1,000 lifts. Most of the latter are fast and modern and the pistes are well-groomed. There are four main ski areas—Sälen in the south, Åre in in central Sweden, Tärnaby-Hemavan in Lappland and Riksgränsen which is up past the arctic circle. I have reviewed them all apart from Tärnaby-Hemavan, the home of Stenmark, which features heli-skiing but has a less than optimally developed lift system. A one-day heli-tour enables you to ski 10 peaks in a day with a total of 10,000 m of vertical descent. This also includes lunch on the highest peak in the country, Kebnekaise (2,111 m).

The Swedish countryside is grand rather than spectacular—frozen lakes and magnificent pine forests without any jagged imposing alpine peaks. If you go up north in April, you might catch sight of the Lapps driving huge herds of reindeer over frozen lakes. One of the best times to go skiing in Sweden is May or early summer, when it is light nearly all day and you can combine the skiing with hiking or fishing. Riksgränsen is the only resort in the world which has lift-served skiing in the midnight sun—an unforgettable experience.

If you are looking for a hectic night life, do not go to Sweden. Booze is very expensive and many of the Swedes stay in isolated *stugas* (cottages). *The* place to go is a *dans-restaurang* where they have dinner dances, usually to live music. Don't get too excited if someone asks you to dance. The Swedes love dancing and it is often totally without ulterior motive. It is considered very rude to refuse. It is also quite normal for a woman to ask a man to dance, and you should not be offended if the person asked is obviously your partner! Signs to watch: women with a wedding ring dangling on a necklace are often showing that they are available for that evening. If someone asks you home for a cup of coffee, it usually means just that—the code for 'extras' is a glass of wine! Under no circumstances should you drink and drive in Sweden—the fines are very harsh and the police will breathalyse you at any time of the day or night. In many areas, self-caterers have to order wine or spirits from Systembolaget (State liquor store) and deliveries can be erratic.

Swedish food ranges from *korv* (hot dogs) bought from take-away kiosks in the street to a full-blown smørgasbord. Specialities include reindeer steaks, fabulous fresh open sandwiches, and waffles with cream and cloudberry sauce. The hotels tend to serve more international cuisine. Watch out for the reasonably-priced *dagens rätt* (daily special) especially in the supermarkets and cafés. The traditional Thursday evening meal is pea soup with punch (a Swedish liqueur). *Pyatt i Panna* is a cheap tasty meal of diced potatoes, onions and spam all fried together and topped with a fried egg and parsley.

The most popular type of accommodation is *stugas* or caravans, often grouped together with their own restaurants. There not many hotels, but those there are tend to be of excellent quality. Half-pension in a double room costs about 700 SEK per week. Nearly all the accommodation in Sweden has a *bastu* (sauna)—surprisingly these are often segregated in public amenities such as swimming pools. The fitness wave is no novelty in Sweden. It is by no means unusual to see a whole family going out for an early morning/evening jog or swim.

It would be unfair to compare Swedish skiing to that of the Alps as the Swedish mountains do not have the height or range. The pistes are not as steep and are generally much shorter. This is not a country for kilometre freaks or very aggressive skiers. The Swedes, in their own country, are unbelievably polite on the pistes. Although they are nearly all excellent skiers, they do not cut up less able skiers on the slopes. They exude natural style. Many of the older ones are still hooked on cross-country but the youngsters are keen to try out new skiing ideas such as snowboarding. Telemarking is very popular and they are more into alternative activities such as snowmobiling. The Swedes are also very family-conscious and offer good facilities for children. Lift passes and equipment are a similar price to that in the Alps, although you will pay a little more for tuition. Swedish instruction is of a high quality and their English is excellent. They offer a wider range than in the Alps—there are classes for veterans, women and other very specific target groups. Most schools offer a day's 'ski-non-stop' which is very hard and fast skiing, attempting to push good skiers to their limits as they aim to achieve record verticals.

The Swedish ski season starts in November (almost guaranteed as they have such good snowmaking facilities) but this is not a good time to go as there is little light and it is very cold. It really is *cold*. The temperature is often well below zero for weeks on end although it is usually quite bearable as it so dry. But don't forget your thermals! It is certainly not freezing all season. A friend of mine who worked in a Swedish ski school had to have three uniforms. One was made of down to cope with the beginning of the season (ski school is not cancelled until it gets below -25C), and he had a normal suit for the middle of the season and a spring suit for later on when it got very warm. The best time to go to Sweden is from early February onwards. Avoid Easter as it gets very crowded. The cheapest way to get there is by ferry to Gothenburg. Trains in Sweden are very cheap. Internal flights are also cheap, especially for the under-26s. If you want to drive, roads are usually well-cleared but studs are a must. Special bus and train charters by tour operators can be excellent value. Startours fly to Stockholm and include one day's sightseeing in the city.

Exchange rate (June 1989): £1 = 2.6 SEK

FURTHER INFORMATION

Swedish National Tourist Office 3 Cork Street, London W1X 1HA (Tel 01 437 5816).

ÅRE

Åre, pronounced 'Oarer', is Sweden's premier and World Cup resort. It is located in Jämtland, 650 km from Stockholm. You can either take an internal flight to Östersund or travel overnight on the Mountain Express. The train departs every Friday from Stockholm, returning on a Saturday—there are couchettes, a kid's play corner and a club car serving wine and snacks. In high season, it will be full of cool young Swedes, out for a week on the pistes. Åre is a cigar-shaped village on the main E75 Sundsvall to Trondheim road. Unless you are used to arctic conditions and have studded tyres, I would not recommend driving yourself to this resort. Crossing the ice-road over the lake at Östersund (speed limit 35 km to avoid shock waves) is best left to intrepid adventurers.

Åre is like a Swiss resort, in that the village is centred around the railway station. The social focus is the deluxe Hotel Diplomat. There is a village square, surrounded by traditional buildings. Sunwing is a new purpose-built complex above and to the west of the village. The village is surrounded by *stugbyar* (holiday villages). For example, Björnen is a self-contained complex 5 km from the village, used by the tour company Startours.

Åre is the Verbier of Sweden, the most sophisticated and expensive of Swedish ski resorts. But as with other resorts, the Swedes come here primarily to ski not to pose. Instead of parading round the streets with fur coats and poodles, the Swedes are more likely to go for an evening jog or swim. The resort does have a cosmopolitan atmosphere—there are plenty of restaurants, bars (unusual in Sweden) and discos.

● **HEIGHT OF RESORT**
550 m.

● **HIGHEST LIFT**
1,238 m.

● **WHY GO THERE?**
The only Scandinavian resort which can compete with an Alpine resort.
The charm of an Austrian village with the convenience of a purpose-built French resort.

● **WHO GOES THERE?**
Scandinavian yuppies and dinkies.
Serious skiers looking for an exclusive destination.
Mainly Swedes; also Finns, Danes and a few Norwegians.

● **COMPANIES THAT GO THERE**
Star Tour.

THE SKIING

The ski season in Åre lasts from mid-December to the end of April. The best time to go is March but make sure you avoid Easter. Åre is Sweden's largest ski area. There are 100 km of pistes with something to please every standard of skier. Even the most expert of skiers should find enough to satisfy them for a week—there are four black runs, unlimited off-piste and heli-skiing. There are also plenty of wide, open intermediate runs and 30 blue runs, several of which are very long by Scandinavian standards. It can be very cold skiing in Åre, although it is not so bad for beginners as the nursery slopes are sensibly located in the glades below the treeline. There is direct access to the slopes from the village. There is a funicular from the central square to the top of the mountain (1,238 m) and a total of 29 lifts in all. The cablecar to Åreskutan is ten minutes' walk away. Björnen is linked by lift to Åre although as these slopes are quite low they will

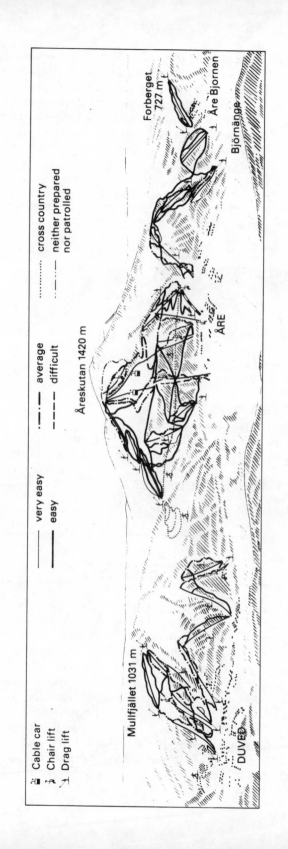

Cable car
Chair lift
Drag lift

very easy
easy
average
difficult

cross country
neither prepared
nor patrolled

Mullfjället 1031 m

Åreskutan 1420 m

Forberget
727 m

Åre Bjornen

DUVED

ÅRE

Björnänge

need good snow cover. Åre has lots of potential for ski mountaineering, touring and telemarking. There are *ratracs* to pull you up the mountain (*tolkning*). Heli-skiing costs 200 SEK for one lift, 1,000 SEK for half a day.

CROSS-COUNTRY

45 km of cut tracks. 300 km of marked trails with 10 huts.

SKI SCHOOL

109 SEK for five lessons (93 SEK children). Instructors speak excellent English.

LIFT PASSES

550 SEK (400 SEK juniors) for a week. Children free.

WHERE TO EAT, DRINK & BOOGIE

There are eight restaurants on Åre's slopes and one on Björnen's. Café Olympia at the top of the Olympia lift does meals and snacks and has a great view from the terrace. Hummel Stugan, at the top of the Hummellift, serves home-cooked pasta, a *dagens rätt* (dish of the day) and snacks.

Åre has a lively night life. The Sunwing has tea dances to live music where everyone clomps about in their moonboots. Nisses bar at Åre Fjällby is popular with the locals. There is a 'dry bar' in the older Sport Hotel which shows extremely good ski films and is popular with the more 'studenty' skiers.

When it comes to eating there is everything from a street vendor's hot dogs to the sublime smørgasborg (see Introduction to Norway, page 127). As in the rest of Scandinavia there is lots of fish, especially salmon. Reindeer with *lingonberry* (like cranberry) sauce is a local delicacy. The Marmite (Tel: 0647 502 40) is an intimate little restaurant with table d'hôte and a good wine list. Booking is recommended. If you missed their tea-time moonboot dance, Sunwing (Tel: 0647 504 30) also does moderately-priced dinner dances and special events, such as game evenings, crayfish buffets etc. For something special, I would recommend eating at Veranda (Tel: 0647 502 65) in the Hotel Diplomat. Here you can have a first-class dîner-à-deux in classic elegant surroundings with a view over Lake Åre—but it *is* expensive. At the other end of the scale, there is a cheap and cheerful pizzeria in the main square.

Åre has five discos but these charge about three times as much as you would pay in England. The Skiers Bar in Hotel Diplomat is a smooth tasteful disco open several nights a week. Bygget's and Nisses discos have live music. The in-place for the young crowd is the Country Club.

WHAT ELSE TO DO THERE

Swimming pool.
Ice-skating.
Curling.
Fitness room.
Snowmobiling.
'Pimpling'—fishing with a lilliput rod through holes in ice lying on a reindeer skin (with a hip flask).
Heli-skiing.
Hang-gliding.
Dog-sledding.

WHERE TO STAY

Aregärden (Tel: 0647 502 65) and Diplomat (Tel: 0647 502 65) are the main hotels and the hub of Åre's jet-set 'society'. These cost from 600 SEK-1,000 SEK per person. Startours organise package trips with self-catering accommodation in Björnen from £200 for ten nights.

IN CASE OF EMERGENCY

Doctor in resort: One.
Chemist in resort: One.
Nearest Dentist: Östersund.
Nearest Hospital: Östersund.
Helicopter Rescue: Yes.

HOW TO GET THERE

Nearest Airport: Östersund. One-hour flight from Stockholm.
Transfer time: One-hour bus or taxi from Östersund.
Train connection: Daily connections Stockholm to Åre (11 hours).

FURTHER INFORMATION

Tourist Office (Tel: 0647 500 10).
For accommodation contact Åre Tourist Bureau, PO Box 53, S-830 13 Åre, Sweden (Tel: 0647 512 20).

RIKSGRÄNSEN

- **HEIGHT OF RESORT**
  600 m.

- **HIGHEST LIFT**
  910 m.

- **WHY GO THERE?**
  You no longer find skiing in Argentière exclusive enough.
  Skiing in the midnight sun.

- **WHO GOES THERE?**
  The very best of Swedish skiers.
  A mixture of Stockholm yuppies and intrepid Nordic adventurers.

- **COMPANIES THAT GO THERE**
  None.

Riksgränsen, just north of the 68th parallel, is the only place in the world to offer lift-served mid-summer skiing in the midnight sun. It is located in Norrbotten Lapland, just 500 m from the Norwegian border. Until a couple of years ago, Riksgränsen was the most isolated resort I had ever been to. There were no roads there and it was only reachable by train, seaplane or on foot. You can now get there in four hours by plane and coach from Stockholm. Personally, I would still opt for the 20-hour train journey. This is invariably a raucous event—everyone brings their own drink and there is dancing in the aisles and ghetto blasters in every compartment! The train travels through four climatic zones and some of the most interesting country ever likely to be seen. In late spring or early summer, it is almost always light and the train even slows down for photos as you pass the arctic circle.

Riksgränsen is open mid-February (it is too dark before then) to the end of June. It is situated on the shores of a large lake which provides a dazzling mirror image of the midnight sun. Skiing until 1 am on powder snow which reflects a sky full of northern lights is an incredible experience. Riksgränsen is not really a resort. It is just one large self-contained mountain lodge that has been purpose-built in traditional style. It has a bed capacity of 491 in hotel rooms and apartments, a restaurant and a disco. This modern complex forms an oasis of facilities and civilisation in one of the world's great wintry wildernesses.

THE SKIING

In early season, Riksgränsen attracts the very best of Swedish hot-dog skiers. This is the place that the tough boys come to. There is a lot of kudos attached to having skied Riksgränsen—it scores ten out of ten for 'piste credibility' (page 207). However, it is not a place for beginners or skiers still needing lessons, unless they combine a couple of days' skiing with an arctic holiday in the summer. Intermediates who are not confident off-piste will find the slopes rather limiting. There are six lifts and 32 runs. Six of these are black and there is excellent potential for off-piste, although this does involve quite a lot of walking and climbing. If you are an expert skier who likes to go downhill rather than up, heli-skiing is also available. As the only people there will be staying in the hotel, there is rarely any lift queueing—five minutes at the most in a warm summer. The hotel is 400 m from a chair-lift that takes you up to the summit. From here, the slopes are either short and steep with big moguls in the summer, or long and easy. There are some excellent off-piste and bump runs down from the 'terrace' to the railway line. It reminded me of skiing late in the season in the Cairngorms in Scotland. Telemarkers and ski mountaineers will find this area a paradise.

One of the main attractions in the summer is the opportunity of skiing in the midnight sun. Every evening, the lifts re-open after dinner from 10 pm to 1 am. As booze is so expensive there is not much chance of your ski evening being spoilt by lager louts.

CROSS-COUNTRY

500 km of marked trails.

SKI SCHOOL

Free use of the ski schools are included in the *Gränspass* (see Lift Passes below). Although I would not recommend going all the way to Riksgränsen to learn to ski, it is a good place to get instruction in unfamiliar forms of skiing, such as telemarking or high-range touring. Riksgränsen claims to have the best Swedish instructors. Guides are available and often included in the Gränspass.

LIFT PASSES

The Gränspass (border pass) includes an 8-day lift pass, ski schools, special tours, high-range touring, hire of cross-country equipment, 20 per cent discount on ski equipment hire, access to sauna and jacuzzi, admittance to evening entertainments in the hotel. 1,400SEK.

WHERE TO EAT, DRINK & BOOGIE

There are no restaurants on the slopes but picnics can be organised by the tours. The only restaurant is in the hotel and serves a mixture of international and

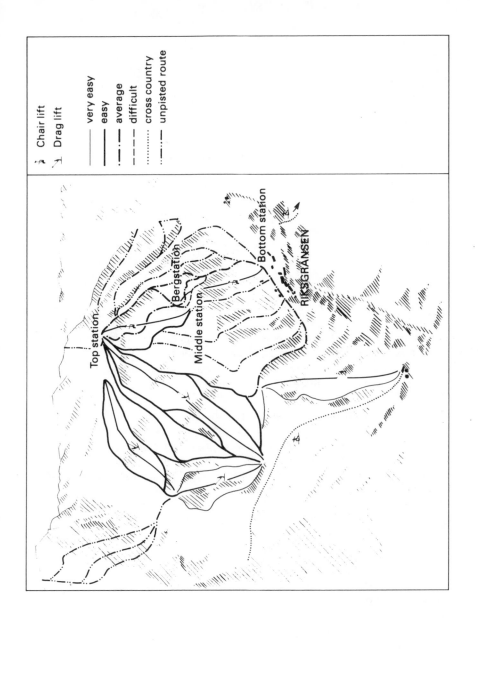

Chair lift
Drag lift

very easy
easy
average
difficult
cross country
unpisted route

Top station
Bergstation
Middle station
Bottom station
RIKSGRÄNSEN

Swedish cuisine. The après-ski is obviously also confined to the hotel. They have a happy hour in the bar—the Wolf's Paw cocktail was fun (ask for a *Vargtass*). There are live bands, a disco and the occasional fancy dress party. The 'Midsommerafton' festival is like a summer version of Halloween and culminates with a party on 22 June.

WHAT ELSE TO DO THERE

Dog-sledding.
An afternoon touring Narvik (Norway) by the Iron Ore Railway train is spectacular and worthwhile.
Square-dancing course with Anne-Marie! (only in the summer).

WHERE TO STAY

This is an easy one! The only hotel is Hotel Lapplandia (Tel: 0980 400 80) which is part of the 'Sara' chain. The hotel reminded me of an ocean liner. The atmosphere is superb and there is a wide choice of accommodation ranging from budget rooms to luxury five-star type rooms. Choose from self-catering or full board. Full board in a budget room (small, basic but comfortable huts) is for those who want a hint of roughing it or just want a bed for sleeping, but with the hotel facilities at hand. The hotel has a gymnasium, jacuzzi and sauna with panoramic view, dancing every night, evening entertainment, restaurant and bar, food store, doctor's surgery and ski workshop. From 1,330 SEK- 2,765 SEK half board in a budget room. From 2,590 SEK to 4,655 SEK half board in a standard double room.

IN CASE OF EMERGENCY

Nearest Doctor: Hotel Lapplandia.
Nearest Chemist: Prescriptions can be delivered to the hotel.
Nearest Dentist: Kiruna (130 km).
Nearest Hospital: Kiruna.
Helicopter Rescue: Yes.

HOW TO GET THERE

Nearest Airport: Stockholm then charter to Kiruna (130 km from Riksgränsen).

Transfer time: 2 hours from Kiruna to Riksgränsen by road or rail.
Train connection: 20 hours from Stockholm.

FURTHER INFORMATION

Hotel Lapplandia (Tel: 0980 400 80). As Riksgränsen *is* the hotel, they should be able to tell you everything you need to know!
Tourist Office Kiruna Tourist Board (Tel: 0980 188 80).

SÄLEN

- **HEIGHT OF RESORT**
  400-600 m.

- **HIGHEST LIFT**
  920 m.

- **WHY GO THERE?**
  Not worth going to unless you are already in Sweden.
  Nearest ski area to Stockholm.

- **WHO GOES THERE?**
  Fit young Swedish skiers, students etc.
  Back-to-nature brigade.
  Older cross-country skiers.

- **COMPANIES THAT GO THERE**
  None.

Sälen, (pronounced Saylen), lies in the province of Dalarna, known for its folksy handicrafts and 100 ski slopes. It is Sweden's southernmost mountain range, the nearest ski area to Stockholm (450 km) and the starting point of the commemorative Vasa Ski Race (see page 146). This is not a place to come without a car as it comprises a straggling group of poorly-connected villages. Sälen itself comprises only about four houses. The ski areas are dotted across the valley. It is not an area I would recommend visiting specially for a week from England, but is worth considering if you are already in Stockholm, or want a couple of days' skiing combined with some sightseeing. The architecture looks like something straight out of the Timotei shampoo advertisements—small *falu* (dark) *röd* (red) cottages with white windows. There are conglomerations of holiday villages and occasional hotels and lodges. The landscape reminded me of the Scottish borders. Below are some details of the various villages.

STÖTEN

850 m. Practically on the Norwegian border. Set under Granfjällsstöten with FIS homologated GS and slalom slope. They have 15 lifts and 14 runs (the longest is 2.4 km). There are also snow-making facilities and floodlit skiing. There is a new lodge with 45 hotel rooms, conference facilities, dance-restaurant (rather like a night club), shopping mall and supermarket. Stöten reminded me of a mini Les Arcs 1,600 in that it has everything that is needed. However, I would not choose this as a base as it is too far from the 'centre'.

HUNDFJÄLLET

This is still a bit out of the way but links with the pass to Tandådalen. It is the usual holiday village mixture of hotels and inns. There are some easy green and blue runs and some steep but very short slopes. They have 13 lifts and 20 runs (longest 2.4 km). Also snow-making facilities and floodlit skiing.

TANDÅDALEN

The skiing here is reasonably testing with four black runs and eight reds. 16 lifts and 24 runs (longest 1.2 km). Snow-making on 19 pistes and floodlit skiing. The Tandådalen Skicentre comprises a sports centre with shops and a television studio (open to the public).

HOGFJÄLLSHOTELLET

This is centred round the *Fjäll* Hotel. Most of the skiing is above the treeline so it seems higher than the other areas. But the skiing here is very tame and would only be of interest to very inexperienced skiers, families with kids or cross-country skiers who want to develop their downhill skills. There are seven lifts and a longest run of 1,200 m.

SÄLENSTUGAN

This is a tiny area, not much bigger than Hillend in Edinburgh. It has one short steep 'cliff' suitable for oscillating mogul maniacs or anyone who is trying to get the hang of speed skiing. It is used by Sälens local ski club for slalom training. I think it would be a waste of time for anyone else.

LINDVALLEN

This is the biggest and best area for reasonable skiers and is linked to Sälenstugan. Most of the runs are red. There are 22 lifts and 26 runs with a longest run of 1,800 m. All the runs have proper names like Gustav and Eva. Stina (short for Kristina) is a mile-long black run, which the Swedish call a *tuffa tjej* (or a 'black diamond' in Stateside terminology).

KLÄPPEN

This is a new area 15 km south of Sälen with only a top station bar. It is popular with the young skiers. There are seven lifts, 13 runs (three are black), all covered by snow-making facilities.

THE SKIING

Although the ski areas are not all connected by lifts, they are at least now covered under the same lift pass. The best in terms of challenge is probably Granfjällstöten with its FIS homologated giant slalom and slalom slope, but this is rather far away to stay at. The skiing in this part of Sweden is home from home for Scottish skiers. There are 100 pistes, 18 of which are black, 22 red, 35 blue and 35 green. The biggest vertical is about about 300m—it is generally about half of that. As there is not much vertical, there is limited off-piste for alpine skiers although plenty for cross-country skiers or telemarkers. The pistes are well-prepared. After a snowfall it is easy to find virgin snow off-piste. Queueing is not a problem unless you get there after the weekend buses.

The season starts in the beginning of December and ends in April. In late February and early March it becomes more temperate and the days lengthen. The best time to go here is just before or after Easter. It is very well-organised for children. There are kids' races in most areas, organised trips to see snow-making and a ski playschool every day in Kläppen.

CROSS-COUNTRY

2.5 km to 15 km cut tracks (23 km are floodlit). 140 km in total. Also 200 km marked trails. Vasaloppet is world's first and biggest cross-country race, held each year on the first Sunday in March. Participants to this 90 km race are always welome but only if entered in advance. Minimum age 19 years. Last day of entry is 31 December of preceding year. Organising Committee: Vasaloppet, Vasagatan 19, S-79200 Mora (Tel: 250 160 00). Entry fee 340 SEK. Mass start at 8.30 am in Berga, 6 km south of Sälen village.

SKI SCHOOL

There are various ski schools in the different areas. This is just a rough indication of what you may have to pay. 270 SEK for 1½ hours' private lesson (includes video) in Stöten. Kids' skischool (6-8 years 90 SEK for 1½ hours. Also mono/telemark course (two hours) 195 SEK including equipment. Ski guide (minimum three people) 100SEK for 1½ hours. Ski playschool every day in Kläppen.

LIFT PASSES

680 SEK per week for whole area (575 SEK for 8-15 year olds, 250 SEK for under-7s). Includes floodlit skiing. Enquire locally for what is on where.

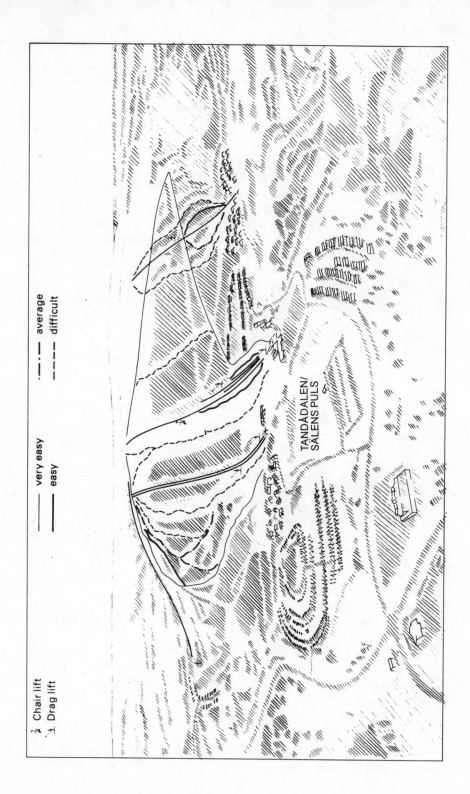

Chair lift
Drag lift

very easy
easy

average
difficult

TANDÅDALEN/
SÄLENS PULS

WHERE TO EAT,
DRINK & BOOGIE

There are no alpine-style restaurants on the slopes. Instead they tend to be at the bottom of the pistes. There are 25 restaurants in the villages and seven discos/nightclubs.

WHAT ELSE TO DO THERE

Paragliding—one-day course 450 SEK.
Para-skiing behind a snowmobile 95 SEK per lift.
Swimming pool.
Floodlit skiing.
Snowmobile safaris.
Sledge tours regularly from Lindvallen, Tandådalen, Hundfjället and GF Stöten.
Films shown regularly at Tandådalen.
Lindvallen has outdoor pool, jacuzzi, solarium and sauna.
Torchlight-skiing at New Year and Easter.

WHERE TO STAY

The quality of accommodation is very good. Families tend to self-cater in a *stugby* (holiday village) such as Tandådalen's Fritidsby. Groups can rent a *stuga* (cottage) near the lifts. Or you can take half board in a pension or hotel somewhere near the centre of the area such as Lindvallen.

IN CASE OF EMERGENCY

Nearest Doctor: Rörbacksnäs and Sälen village.
Nearest Chemist: Rörbacksnäs and Sälen village.
Nearest Dentist: Rörbacksnäs and Sälen village.
Nearest Hospital: Mora.

HOW TO GET THERE

Nearest Airport: Stockholm then charter to Mora (40 minutes).
Transfer time: One hour by bus/taxi.
Train connection: Mora then 100 km by bus or taxi.

FURTHER INFORMATION
Tourist Office Sälen (Tel: 0280 201 50).

161

Switzerland

The British have always had a soft spot for skiing in Switzerland. It was in this country that downhill skiing began. Surprisingly, it was the British who started it all, in the now well-known resort of Wengen. Switzerland still has some of the best skiing in the world. Resorts such as Zermatt are hard to match. But considering there are over 100 Swiss ski resorts, the British seem to stick to a very narrow, conservative selection comprising mainly Zermatt, Verbier, Crans Montana, Wengen, Gstaad, Klosters and St Moritz. There are plenty of other excellent resorts that have not yet been discovered.

Flims, for example, is part of the vast White Arena ski circuit and one of the most renowned resorts in Switzerland, yet hardly any British skiers go there. Andermatt is a classic Swiss resort, that has some of the hardest skiing in Europe. One of my favourite regions is Valais, in the south west of Switzerland, where there are several charming little villages with houses that are still built on stilts. The language spoken in a resort corresponds to the part of Switzerland in which it is located (ie near France, Austria or Italy). But all the resorts are distinctly Swiss in atmosphere and approach.

The Swiss must be one of the most organised nationalities in the world. They run everything with the same pristine accuracy as their watches. I travelled there for several weeks last season, and never once had to wait for a delayed bus or train. Their transport system is super-efficient. You can travel virtually anywhere on their excellent railways—spotlessly clean and never crowded, except at Christmas and Easter weekends. Most of the ski resorts have their own little mountain railways—if not, there is always a frequent PTT post bus to transport you. In many of the resorts, the post buses also act as ski buses—they are *always* on time. The airports also operate an excellent system whereby you can send your luggage direct to your resort. On the way home, you check it in at the resort station and don't pick it up again until you arrive in Britain.

The Swiss are very safety conscious. Their lift equipment is considered to be amongst the best in the world. This ranges from modern express funiculars like the Metro Alpin in Saas Fee to wonderfully archaic-looking hooded leather chair-lifts in Wildhaus. All the lifts are carefully supervised and regularly checked. If, like me, you have a phobia of getting stuck on a chair-lift, you may be relieved to know that there is a little step-ladder tucked under each chair, just in case you ever need to climb down. If you have never skied in Switzerland before, beware of making a fool of yourself on their T-bars (rarely found in France). You need to gently lean your bottom against the bar. The Swiss Ski School is rather conservative, but nevertheless has an excellent reputation. There are also some very good mountain guides and plenty of opportunity for epic touring expeditions.

Swiss resorts are notoriously pretty—you won't find any hideous purpose-built buildings; the traditional style of architecture has been carefully maintained. Most of their resorts are higher in altitude than those in Austria. The accommodation is mainly in hotels. These certainly deserve their world-wide reputation. Whether you stay in a luxury five-star hotel or a little guest house, it is bound to be clean and comfortable. Most places will turn your duvet back and even leave a little chocolate on the pillow as a night token.

The après-ski in Switzerland is not as lively as in Italy, but unlike the French, the Swiss do want more from their holiday than just skiing. Many of their hotels, three star and upwards, have their own swimming pools and there are usually lots of other facilities such as skating, curling, tobogganing and prepared walks. The nightlife is mellow and sophisticated—none of that thigh-slapping Austrian oom-pah-pah stuff! I think their food has been much under-rated. They lead the way with special alpine dishes such as fondue, raclette (melted cheese with potatoes) and *rösti* (boiled potatoes which are grated and then fried with onions, often served with bits of bacon and egg or as an accompaniment). Other typically Swiss dishes include *bündnerfleisch* (dried beef, like Parma ham) and *geschnezeltes* (veal in cream and mushroom sauce). Their pasta, especially in resorts near Italy, is excellent. Their chocolate needs no introduction, and their ice-cream is, I think, the best in the world. Wine is not so expensive if you buy local Swiss wines such as Veltliner (red) or Fendant (white) from supermarkets. In restaurants you will be able to get house wine as well as a variety of very good wines such as the Swiss Dôle. The Swiss also produce their own beer (Calanda) and have a large variety of soft drinks which are not as sweet as coke, such as *Apfelsoft* (a delicious fizzy apple juice with no added sugar). Rivella is a Swiss soft drink made from milk extract.

Many skiers have been put off going to Switzerland because of the cost of living. It is expensive, although Austria and Italy are now not far behind. Swiss resorts can actually be cheaper than some of the big French resorts such as Val d'Isère, where you almost have to take out a mortgage to buy a round of drinks in a night club. Ski passes in Switzerland are often cheaper than in other countries particularly in established resorts which have less recent investments to pay off. Quality is guaranteed. In terms of value for money, Switzerland is a good choice. They also has a very slow inflation rate (about 2 per cent) so you may not pay much more for a hotel than you would have done a few years ago. Anyone who calls himself a skier should check out what this fantastic ski nation has to offer.

Exchange rate (June 1989): £1 = 2.6 F

FURTHER INFORMATION

Swiss National Tourist Office New Coventry Street, London W1V 8EE (Tel: 01 734 1921).

ANDERMATT

- **HEIGHT OF RESORT**
  1,444 m.

- **HIGHEST LIFT**
  2,963 m.

- **WHY GO THERE?**
  Excellent skiing—on the piste, off-piste and touring.
  Long ski season (November to May) and reliable snow record.
  Old character-filled village, large enough to entertain most tame night-owls but still small enough to maintain an intimate and informal atmosphere.

- **WHO GOES THERE?**
  Serious skiers.
  The Swiss Mountain Military Service.
  The British Army (annual training).
  Anyone who dreams of a military encounter.

- **COMPANIES THAT GO THERE**
  Ski Sutherland.

On my first morning in Andermatt, I awoke to some strange grunting noises outside my hotel bedroom window. It was 8 am and the white-uniformed Swiss soldiers were limbering up in the snow. There was so much white that my camera wouldn't focus, but it would have made a wonderful picture. I soon got used to the sight of soldiers in Andermatt—in low season there were more 'Mr Uniforms' propping up the bars than skiers. Yet Andermatt is still very much a skiers' resort and has a friendly, relaxed atmosphere. It is a very attractive village, set in a high, sunny valley, to the north of the St Gotthard Pass. The narrow main street is lined by old shops, hotels and restaurants in tall traditional chalet-style buildings. There is nothing new and flashy—it has an old-fashioned charm of faded grandeur. Walking up the main street from the Gemsstock lift station, you pass several narrow side-streets, one of which leads to a beautiful old Catholic church.

A friend of mine who had once driven through Andermatt, complained that it looked dark and gloomy. The village is often in the shade but it is one of the friendliest places I've ever stayed in. One local described it as 'just one big family' and within a few days I was on *grützi* (greeting) terms with everyone from the cable-car man to the bartenders.

Before the Second World War, Andermatt used to be a fashionable resort for the British, but numbers have dramatically declined and it is now unusual to hear many English voices. Most of the skiers are Swiss, German or Italian, and because of its central location, at the 'crossroads' of Switzerland, it can get rather crowded at weekends and in holiday periods. Unless you do not mind spending most of your time queueing, it is best appreciated in low season (January or March). The most stylish way to arrive is aboard the Glacier Express— Andermatt is the half-way stop between Zermatt and St Moritz. Andermatt has been compared to the well-known resort of Zermatt, but it is much smaller, more compact and less glitzy. It is a resort for serious skiers, regardless of whether they own a fur coat or not.

THE SKIING

Don't be put off that there are not many lifts (12 plus a railway) in Andermatt. It has a deceptively large ski area with some wonderfully long challenging runs and plenty of off-piste. The two main ski areas (Nätschen and Gemsstock) are situated at opposite ends of the village, about 10 minutes' walk apart. There is a third area, further down the road in the tiny village of Hospental (1,453 m) where there are a couple of blue runs, a red and a black, and usually less queueing than in Andermatt. Even further away is Realp (1,538) which has just one drag-lift and a couple of bunny runs for real beginners. A free shuttle bus links the resorts.

The ski area that attracts the serious skiers and powder hounds is Gemsstock (2,963 m). This is reached by two cable cars. As you would expect, the views from the top are spectacular, though watch out for the perilous steps, which do not have a hand-rail. Expert skiers can take one of the wide steep black runs down the front of the mountain, and continue on a black right down to Andermatt. The less experienced can take a red which winds round the back of Gemsstock and then catch the cable car back down to the village. Gemsstock also has some excellent off-piste. You can ski down to Hospental. From here you can catch a chair-lift and then a drag and continue off-piste to Realp. The other

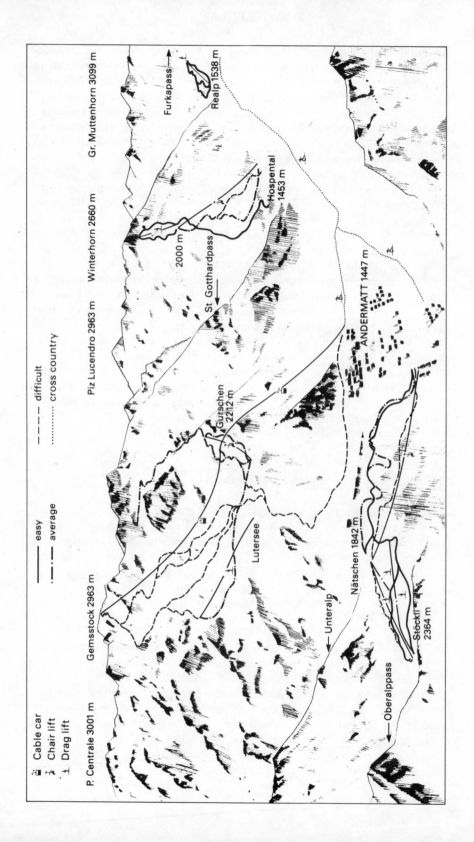

Legend:

Cable car
Chair lift
Drag lift

easy
average

difficult
cross country

P. Centrale 3001 m Gemsstock 2963 m Piz Lucendro 2963 m Winterhorn 2660 m Gr. Muttenhorn 3099 m

Furkapass
Realp 1538 m
2000 m
Hospental 1453 m
St Gotthardpass
Gurschen 2212 m
ANDERMATT 1447 m
Lutersee
Nätschen 1842 m
Unteralp
Stöckli 2364 m
Oberalppass

main ski area is Nätschen (1,842 m) which is reached by a chair from opposite the railway station. This is a very sunny area, popular with families and less ambitious skiers. As it is very near the barracks, it is also used as training ground by the soldiers. From Nätschen you can catch a drag-lift up to Stöckli (2,364 m) where there are a couple of easy blue runs as well as a black. There is also some good off-piste down from Nätschen.

Queueing can be a problem in Andermatt at weekends and in high season but most people seem to think that the runs on Gemsstock are long and challenging enough to make this worthwhile. In low season, when queueing is minimal, it is a serious skier's paradise. As it is so high, the snow is nearly always a fabulously crisp, light powder—it never gets slushy nor icy. I can't wait to go back.

TOURING

Andermatt is famous for ski touring. In spring you can trek over to Zermatt or Klosters. 'Mountain Reality' is a well-respected mountaineering school run by Alex Clapasson. They do courses in powder skiing, ski-safaris, ski mountaineering, paragliding, climbing and hiking weeks, trekking and expeditions. Further details from PB No 24, CH-6490, Andermatt (Tel: 044 20919).

CROSS-COUNTRY

20 km. This starts in Andermatt, passes Hospental and Zumdorf and ends in Realp. Classes are available through the Ski School, see below.

SKI SCHOOL

(Tel: 044 67240).
This is run by Patrick Simmen, who speaks fluent English and has several English-speaking instructors. They meet near the station Mon-Sat 9.15 am, giving two hours' instruction in the morning, and two in the afternoon. Approximately 127F per week or 37F per day. Children's classes (4½-12 year olds) available at a reduced rate. Private tuition 85F per half-day. Tuition is also available in cross-country and snowboarding. There is a special snowboarding school run by Bernhard Simmen, Bodenstr 26, 6490 Andermatt (Tel: 044 67656).

LIFT PASSES

170F (130F) for a seven-day ticket. Covers Gemsstock and Nätschen as well as Hospental, Oberalppass-Calmit, Sedrun, Rueras, Disentis. Also entitles you to 50 per cent rebate on single tickets for the Furken Oberalp railway between Realp and Disentis, Andermatt and Göschenen.

WHERE TO EAT, DRINK & BOOGIE

One of the most amusing places for après-ski is Ochsen, an old traditional wooden 'saloon bar'. On my first afternoon, I made the faux pas of asking for a hot chocolate. 'No chocolate. We're a *saloon bar*', said the Swiss-American owner Mark Russi as he curtly showed me the door. I later discovered that he'll serve you anything, and with a smile, as long as it contains lashings of alcohol. It was not long before I was addicted to his famous Irish coffees, which he serves with as much panache as if he were a cocktail bartender. Ochsen is a great place to while away a few hours by the hot stove, listening to all the local gossip. Situated in the village, rather than on the slopes, Sternen is popular for lunch, particularly in high season when the mountain restaurants are crowded. This restaurant attracts a young, sporty crowd—a big bowl of their homemade pasta should keep you going for the afternoon. Nearby is Romano and the Crew— Restaurant Spycher (Tel: 044 67753). This is a young, lively bar/restaurant run by a genial Swiss Canadian guy who makes home-made pizza and natters with the drinkers. In the evening, most people dine in the hotels. A local food fanatic/ski guide recommended the upmarket hotel Drei Könige und Post (Tel: 044 67203) as having the best food in Andermatt. The Hotel Helvetia (Tel: 044 67515) has a basement restaurant with an open chimney for grilling meat and fish. The Downhill disco is open until the early hours of the morning and although it is not the most trendy of clubs, it is still a fun and popular place to groove the night away.

WHAT ELSE TO DO THERE

Paragliding.
Skating, curling.
4 km sledge run.
Sleigh rides (on request from Hotel Sternes).
Fitness facilities in various hotels and apartment buildings.
Cinema.
Swimming in Göschenen.

WHERE TO STAY

If you're looking for flashy five-star hotels don't go to Andermatt. They haven't anything above three-star and most of these are old, family-run businesses—full of character rather than facilities. I stayed at the Badus Hotel (Tel: 044 67286) which is next to the Nätschen lift and near the station. This is a clean friendly two-star hotel run by the Danioth family. It has a pleasant, welcoming atmosphere and good simple home-cooking. It is a popular place for the soldiers to eat/drink (the barracks are nearby). In mid-season, the Badus charges from 88F half board, or from 90F in high season. Bigger hotels such as the Monopol-Metropol (Tel: 044 67575) charge up to 148F for half board, high season.

For those on a budget looking for atmosphere, there's the Ochsen (Tel: 044 67420)—19 double rooms above the popular saloon bar (see above) from 32.50F bed and breakfast. The owner of this establishment, Mark Russi, prefers to take group bookings and as it is also his home, he is reticent about taking people he does not know. Teetotallers probably won't go down very well! The Gasthaus zum Sternen (Tel: 044 67130) is an attractive old wooden chalet and popular eating house. Bed and breakfast 35F all season. The Aurora Hotel (Tel: 044 67661) is popular as it is opposite the Gemmstock cable car. They have a sauna and garage space. From 88F half board mid-season to 98F in high season.

Hospental is a smaller and quieter resort than Andermatt and would probably be good for families and cross-country. The Hotel St Gotthard (Tel: 044 67266) is run by the Bennet-Bamert family—it was recommended to me as a friendly comfortable place to stay, with good food. Further details on all the hotels in Andermatt and Hospental from Andermatt's tourist office.

_____IN CASE OF EMERGENCY_____

Doctors in resort: Two.
Chemist in resort: One.
Dentist in resort: One.
Nearest Hospital: Andermatt's Military Hospital can be used for most emergencies.
Helicopter Rescue: Available, as in all Swiss resorts.

_____HOW TO GET THERE_____

Nearest Airport: Zurich.
Train connection: Two hours from Zurich. Change onto Glacier Express at Göschenen.

FURTHER INFORMATION

Tourist Office Andermatt CH 6490 Andermatt (Tel: 044 67454).

FLIMS/LAAX/FALERA
THE WHITE ARENA

- **HEIGHT OF RESORTS**
  Flims 1,130 m, Laax 1,020 m, Falera 1,220 m.

- **HIGHEST LIFT**
  3,000 m.

- **WHY GO THERE?**
  Vast ski area—220 km of pistes.
  Smart hotels and excellent restaurants.
  Rather sprawling, so best appreciated with a car.

- **WHO GOES THERE?**
  Swiss families.
  A cosmopolitan selection of Americans, Germans, Italians, French and a few discerning Brits.

- **COMPANIES THAT GO THERE**
  Ski Sutherland.
  Swiss Travel Service.
  Powder Byrne.
  Made to Measure.

When I told some Swiss people that I was off to 'discover' Flims, they thought I must have made a mistake with the pronounciation. 'Flims/Laax', I repeated and they looked at me as though I had gone crazy. For although Flims is not well-known in Britain, it is one of Switzerland's most popular and fashionable resorts. It may not be as jetsetty as St Moritz or Gstaad, but it attracts a fair share of wealthy tourists, and is particularly popular with families.

Flims is part of The White Arena, linked to Laax and Falera. One of the first things that English-speaking people have to get used to are the rather off-putting local names, such as Crap Sogn Gion, Crap Masegn, Crap la Foppa. Before you start spluttering into your glühwein, it is worth knowing that *crap* is actually the local word for rock. Flims, which has been compared in atmosphere to Klosters, is the largest and best-known of the White Arena resorts. It is situated on a lovely sun terrace high above the valley of the Rhine in Graubunden. Flims is a sprawling village with smart expensive shops but little else to characterise it. The resort is split into Flims Dorf and Flims Waldhaus. As the lifts are in Flims

Dorf, this tends to attract the younger, keener skiers, whilst Flims Waldhaus has several old grand hotels and an older, wealthier clientele.

Laax tends to attract a younger sportier crowd (mainly German). Laax itself is an old farming village, where they still speak the local Romansh dialect. As the village is quite a trek from the lifts, most skiers stay in the new modern satellite, Murschetg, which has less character but better access to the skiing. The vast Sportshotels Rancho is down the hill from the lift station, but very popular with Germans and Americans.

If you are looking for a very simple and rustic holiday, I would recommend the tiny farming community of Falera. This is a traffic-free resort with old wooden buildings and a wonderfully romantic old church. The view across the Rhine valley to Chur, Lugnez and Gruob is quite spectacular. But be warned— you will need a car, as apart from a couple of small hotels and about four restaurants there is really nothing there. The three resorts are linked by a lift and a bus. The latter is free to lift pass holders. As everything in this area is so spread out, a car would be advisable, particularly for the evenings. Flims is also a popular summer resort with a pretty lake, swimming beach and beautiful forests for walking and horse-riding.

THE SKIING

The White Arena is a massive ski area with 220 km of pistes and an hourly lift capacity of 32,000 passengers. That's certainly enough to keep most skiers happy for a week although the standard of skiing is more suited to families and intermediates than experts. Most of the slopes are south-east facing. Skiing in the Flims area is fairly easy, although the lower slopes may suffer late in the season from a lack of snow. Beginners and day-trippers may want to economise by buying a mini-day ticket just to this area. Good skiers can take the cable car up to Cassons Grat (2,675 m). The 250 m walk up at the top of the station will certainly get your heart pumping, but the wide black steep unpisted run back down to Naraus makes it all worth while. Other hard runs in the circuit include a challenging moguly black run down from the Vorab glacier. The keenest skiers tend to stay in Laax. From here, you take a cable car up to Crap Sogn Gion. Experts can test their legs by skiing the Men's Downhill back down through the woods to Laax. There are plenty of pistes to keep the intermediate skier happy, particularly the long wide runs in La Siala area. There are also some easy runs down to Falera. The latter is directly connected to the White Arena by a chair-lift. They have their own beginners' slopes at the edge of the village. There is also a specially segregated nursery slope in Laax. Most of the off-piste skiing is in between the runs.

CROSS-COUNTRY

(Tel: 081 392035 or 081 391438).
60 km of prepared tracks. Many of the tracks go through the forest. 3 km are floodlit. The cross-country ski school is run by Danny Bazell. Group classes available.

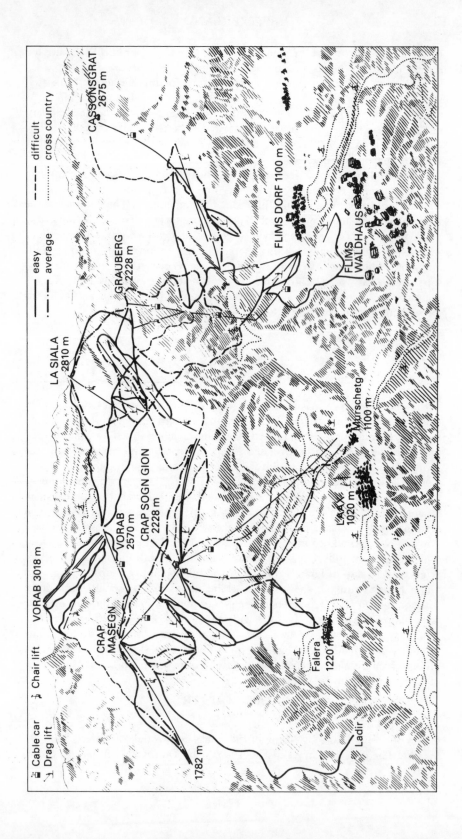

Cable car
Chair lift
Drag lift

easy
average
difficult
cross country

VORAB 3018 m

CRAP MASEGN

VORAB 2570 m

CRAP SOGN GION 2228 m

LA SIALA 2810 m

GRAUBERG 2228 m

CASSONSGRAT 2675 m

FLIMS DORF 1100 m

FLIMS WALDHAUS

Murschetg 1100 m

L'AAX 1020 m

Falera 1220 m

Ladir

1782 m

SKI SCHOOL

Flims (Tel: 081 391438).
Laax and Falera (Tel: 086 34288).
The resorts have separate ski schools with 150 instructors in all. I was shown around by Ursi Willi, who is a fabulous chirpy little teacher from the Laax Ski School. 140F for 5-day ticket (4 hours per day), 108F for children. There is no crêche but a ski kindergarten for children over 3 years old. Provision is made for their midday sleep. Also classes in snowboard, privately or in groups.

LIFT PASSES

198F for six days (99F children) covers the whole area. If you're a beginner or only there for one day you can buy a mini-day ticket just for Flims, 25F (13F children).

WHERE TO EAT, DRINK & BOOGIE

Don't come to the White Arena to lose weight as there are so many good places to eat both on and off the slopes. On the slopes I'd recommend the Tegia Larnags which is a lovely wooden cabin on the piste down to Laax. They make fabulous home-made cakes, fondues etc. It's a popular place for a 5 pm drink and it's also possible to walk back up for dinner. There are other mountain restaurants you can trek up to in the evening. The Runca is famous for its apple pies. It takes about one hour to walk up—most people toboggan down. The Foppa has a special fondue evening and sleigh-ride every Tuesday evening. The Spalegna is a tiny raclette stübli which seats about 14 people—you can toboggan home.

If you have a car the Panorama restaurant is an original place for an evening meal. Just outside Laax, in Salums, it is a small rustic restaurant where you can charcoal your food on the table. If you're feeling romantic, abandon the car and take a 30-minute walk through the woods. As it's only a small place, you do need to book. In Flims Dorf, I'd recommend the Chesa restaurant (also a hotel). They specialise in fondue. There's a wonderful open fire and you choose your own wine from the cellar. As in all of Switzerland, the wines are very expensive, about 30F for the cheapest house bottle. We also had an excellent meal at the Meiler Hotel and restaurant. Because of its location, opposite the Flims lifts, the Stenna bar in this hotel is very popular for après-ski drinks and tea-dancing. Opposite is The Pub. I'm afraid the name didn't entice me. If you get the nocturnal munchies, you can eat spaghetti until 3 am in the spaghetti house in Laax. This is next to the night club Comona which occasionally has live music.

WHAT ELSE TO DO THERE

Paragliding.

173

Curling.
Skating on the lake in Laax.
60 km of prepared walking.
Sportzentrum Prau La Selva (Tel: 081 393431) is a large spruce sports centre just outside Flims. Facilities include shooting, gym, indoor ice rink, indoor tennis, athletics stadium and football (Tel: 081 393431).
3 km toboggan run.
Sleigh rides and horse-riding (Tel: 081 392435).
Swimming in hotels or in 25 m public pool in Laax.

WHERE TO STAY

There is certainly no shortage of good hotels in this area. I stayed in the modern Crap Ner (Tel: 081 392626) in Flims Dorf which has a sophisticated bar and restaurant and an indoor swimming pool. 111F-144F half board for a single person. 192F-248F for a double room, half board. Park Hotel in Waldhaus (081 300181) is a five-star hotel with excellent facilities and a string of faithful regulars. 175F-215F half board for a single person. 310F-430F for a double room, half board. The English company Powder Byrne have an apartment in Flims catered for by chalet girls. The Chesa (Tel: 081 392338, has 20 rooms and charges 50-65F half board for a single person, 90F-130F for a double room, half board. The cheapest accommodation you'll find is about 29F bed and breakfast in a guesthouse. This sort of accommodation is apparently very sought-after, although personally Flims is not a place I'd go to on a budget. Laax has lots of apartments and some big modern hotels. Sportshotels Rancho (Tel: 086 30131) is a massive modern complex with apartments/studios/rooms and all sorts of sporting/leisure facilities. Falera only has two hotels. One of these, Le Siala (Tel: 086 332332) has four stars, a cosy bar, indoor swimming pool, sauna and keep fit room. It's popular with the Swiss and Germans and also has a big American group who return every year. 90F half board.

IN CASE OF EMERGENCY

Doctors in resorts: Four in Flims, one in Laax.
Chemists in resorts: One in Flims, one drugerie in Laax.
Dentists in resorts: One in Flims, one in Laax.
Nearest Hospital: Illanz (11 km).
Helicopter Rescue: Available, as in all Swiss resorts.

HOW TO GET THERE

Nearest Airport: Zurich.

Train connection: $2\frac{1}{2}$ hours from Zurich. Train to Chur, then bus (17 km).

FURTHER INFORMATION

Tourist Office Flims CH-7018 Flims-Waldhaus (Tel: 081 391022).
Tourist Office Laax CH-7031 Laax (Tel: 086 34343).
Tourist Office Falera CH-7153 Falera (Tel: 086 33030).

SAINT-LUC

● **HEIGHT OF RESORT**
1,650 m.

● **HIGHEST LIFT**
3,000 m.

● **WHY GO THERE?**
Tiny, peaceful Swiss resort.
Beginners' and intermediate skiing.
Total escapism.
For a sun tan.

● **WHO GOES THERE?**
Swiss families.
Young Swiss, Belgian and Dutch skiers.
Youth groups who want to go ski touring.
Astrologers!

● **COMPANIES THAT GO THERE**
None.

There used to be only one way up to Saint-Luc—by mule. In 1875 an English tourist complained that 'It is *such* a long, hard trek up!' Thankfully, we took a less bumpy route by car, although a couple of the hairpin-bends still had my heart a-flutter. The resort itself could not be more relaxing. It is perched up high in the Valaisanne mountains, and is renowned for its Mediterranean climate and long sunny days. The minute we stepped out of the car, I breathed in the tranquillity. Above us were clear blue skies and whichever way we looked we saw snowy peaks including the Weisshorn, Mont Blanc, Dent-Blanche and the Matterhorn.

The resort was originally called *Louk*, a celtic word for forest. It used to be inhabited by Celts, then the Romans, followed by the Burgondes. The people that live there now are called the Anniviards. There are only about a hundred of them. At the beginning of the century, Saint-Luc was a popular summer health retreat for the British aristocracy. Now there are no English companies, and even the Tourist Director does not speak any English.

Like nearby Zinal, the architecture is typical of the Anniviers valley. Most of the buildings are old timber houses, built up on stilts. Photos from the 1920s suggest that Saint-Luc has hardly changed in the last century. You can still see the original timber house that was described as *ancienne* in 1924! Part of the village was burnt down in 1845 and again in 1858. The locals were careful to preserve the remaining antique chalets, and tastefully rebuilt more houses out of stone. It is a self-sufficient little place, with its own church, mill and wine cellar. In the main street you can see the original village bread-oven, now only used once a year, the second week in January.

The resort was opened for skiing in 1960 and they now have 75 km of pistes. The village is still very unsophisticated with only four hotels, a few restaurants, ski stores, a supermarket and a couple of little gift/card shops. The resort makes good use of its notoriously sunny climate—most of the restaurants and hotels have large south-facing terraces. Saint-Luc is also known as 'the resort of the stars' and takes a bizarre interest in astrology. They have built a special astrological pathway up in the mountains, where you can observe ten different planets at marked stops. The walk is 2 km, starting at Tignousa (the sun), finishing at Hotel Weisshorn (Pluto).

THE SKIING

Considering it is such a small resort, Saint-Luc has a very respectable amount of skiing (75 km) and is perfectly adequate for families and inexperienced intermediates. There is only one chair-lift up from the village, so in high season queues are likely. This lift takes you up to the main ski area and a fantastic new high-tech restaurant. From here, you can go up to the top of Le Col des Ombrintzes. Good skiers can cross over to the north-facing side of the mountain and ski down off-piste. From Le Col, you can either take a blue run down towards the tiny resort of Chandolin or head back down to Tignousa via a blue or black (more like red). In the Chandolin area there is a steep challenging black run, a couple of blue runs and a long 'motorway' red run. Bella Tola (3,026 m) gets very windy at the top. The black run is often not prepared and is fantastic in new powder. There is also a very long blue run which goes right the way back to the village. The bottom half of this run is through the forest and is more like a red run. There are good possibilities for off-piste and touring in St Luc. It takes about one hour to ski off-piste from Pas de Boeuf to Obereuns.

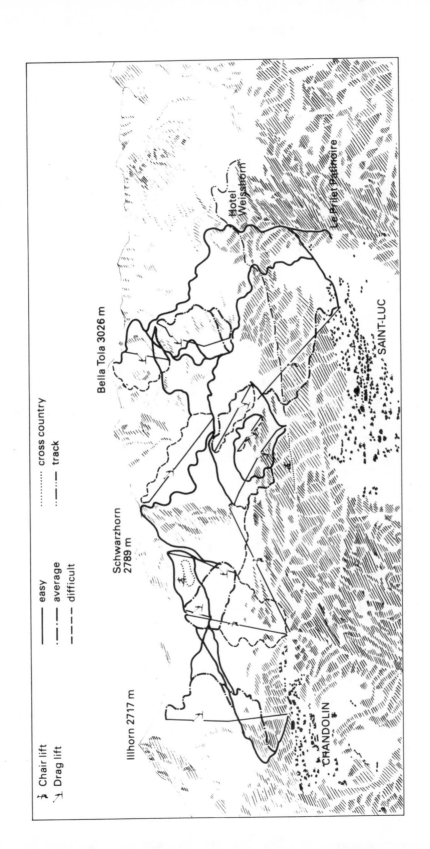

Chair lift
Drag lift

———— easy
—·—·— average
— — — difficult

·········· cross country
—··—··— track

Illhorn 2717 m

Schwarzhorn
2789 m

Bella Tola 3026 m

Hotel
Weisshorn

Le Prilet Patinoire

CHANDOLIN

SAINT-LUC

CROSS-COUNTRY

Not a good resort for cross-country. Only one 5 km trail through the forests. Useful if you are staying at Hotel Weisshorn, though.

SKI SCHOOL

(Tel 027 651412).
This small school is supposed to have at least one English-speaking instructor. Six half-days 78F (6-12 year olds 68F). During high season 4-5 year olds will be looked after.

LIFT PASSES

Six-day pass 122F (78F kids).

WHERE TO EAT, DRINK & BOOGIE

The new high-tech restaurant Tignousa at the top of the chair-lift is a wonderfully panoramic place for skiers to have lunch. The rustic Cabane Bella-Tola is also popular. The food in the Bella-Tola is excellent. In the village, the Hotel Favre and La Fougère both have splendid sun terraces. I sat outside at La Fougère and dined on homemade soup, local cheese, a glass of red wine and a coffee. The bill came to about 30F—very pricey. Le Chasseur has a big charcoal grill and is popular for après-ski and evening meals. Most people in Saint-Luc stay and drink in their hotels. There is also a disco in Hotel Beau Site and another one called Roc-Arolle.

WHAT ELSE TO DO THERE

Not much.
There's a natural ice skating rink, and a sauna (open to the public) in the Hotel Bella-Tola. Don't forget the astronomy evenings.

WHERE TO STAY

The most unusual place to stay is in Hotel Weisshorn (Tel: 027 651106). This is perched like an eagle's nest, half way up the Tornot mountain. From the village, it looks like something out of James Bond. The only way to get there is on skis or by walking 1½ hours through the woods. You have to carry your own luggage—on the chair-lift! In this case, there is a lot to be said for travelling light. After skiing or walking as far as Chalet Blanc du Tornot, the hotel will come and pick you up (for a small fee) in their ratrac. The hotel is not supposed to be very luxurious, but it is certainly in a novel location. 48F half board.

The most refined hotel in the village is Bella-Tola (Tel: 027 651444). This has been owned by the same family for four generations and is like a beautiful old Victorian villa with waxed-pine floors, ornate painted ceilings, wooden shutters and wrought iron balconies. The hotel is full of antiques and paintings including oil portraits of all the aristocratic-looking family. It is the sort of elegant place where you can imagine the Victorian ladies stepping onto the lawns with their parasols. 90F per night half board.

The Hotel-Pension Favre (Tel: 027 651128) is a more basic hotel but with a very pleasant large sun terrace. From 50-58F per night half board. If you are looking for something really basic, you can stay in one of the mountain huts (popular with youth groups). The Cabane Bella-Tola (Tel: 027 65 15 37) caters for group bookings (dormitory accommodation) and charges from 30F per night full board.

IN CASE OF EMERGENCY

Nearest doctor: Vissoie.
Nearest chemist: Vissoie. There is a small depot in Saint-Luc.
Nearest dentist: Sierre.
Nearest Hospital: Sierre.
Helicopter Rescue: Available, as in all Swiss resorts.

HOW TO GET THERE

Nearest Airport: Geneva.
Transfer time: $2\frac{1}{2}$ hours.
Train connection: Sierre, then bus.

FURTHER INFORMATION

Tourist Office CH-3961 Saint-Luc (Tel: 027 651412).

WILDHAUS

- **HEIGHT OF RESORT**
  1,100 m.

- **HIGHEST LIFT**
  2,262 m.

- **WHY GO THERE?**
  Spectacular scenery, set beneath the Seven Peaks.
  Particularly good for families.
  Very friendly farming community and real community spirit.
  50 km of novice and intermediate skiing.

- **WHO GOES THERE?**
  Swiss and German families.
  Zurich weekenders.
  Snowboard whizz-kids.

- **COMPANIES THAT GO THERE**
  Ski Sutherland.

'There are more cows (1,600) than men (1,250) in Wildhaus!' was the first thing the jovial tourist officer, Roland Lymann, told me. Not that there is much evidence of this in the winter—the cows have been tucked away in their stables further down the valley, and most of the farmers are teaching on the ski slopes. But it is rather reassuring to know that there are soft green pastures rather than craggy rock fields underneath the snowy slopes you are whizzing down.

Wildhaus is a very safe, old-fashioned resort in eastern Switzerland that seems to have been untouched by commercialism. It offers a respectable 50 km of skiing, linked by ski lifts and bus to Unterwasser and Alt St Johann. These resorts are in the Churfirsten Paradise which comprises seven impressive jagged peaks as well as the highest peak in eastern Switzerland, Säntis (2,501 m). Wildhaus is the best-known and largest resort in this region. It is not as pretty as some Alpine villages as the resort is rather straggling, with the hotels, restaurants and a few basic shops spread out along one main road. But the seven peaks form a dramatic backdrop, and whatever the village lacks in aesthetics, it makes up for in charm. The people are exceptionally warm and friendly. The tourists are mainly Swiss families, although it is also beginning to attract a younger clientele due to the keen snowboarding school. There are quite a few Germans (Lake Constance is only 30 minutes' drive away), a few Dutch, but hardly any British.

Wildhaus is certainly not a posey resort. The local hero is Karl Alpiger, who is one of the top fifteen racers in the world. If you catch him when he's not training, he may turn out to be your ski school instructor. The resort has has its fair share of local eccentrics, such as one old dear who regularly skis back home along the streets in the moonlight after a late-night session in one of the bars. I wonder what his wife says?

Children are particularly well-catered for in Wildhaus. The 'Wildy' Children's Programme comprises a special children's ski school, weekly races, a babysitting service, horse-drawn sleigh rides and the puppet theatre. The latter is the cultural highlight of Wildhaus. This dinky munchkin-sized theatre has been converted out of an old stable and only seats about 30 people. The locals have joined forces to entertain the tourists with puppet shows. These are delightfully presented, with weekly performances for both children and adults. Unfortunately it's all in German, so unless you speak the lingo you will have to be content to watch the cute little figures bobbing up and down.

THE SKIING

Although there is not a great deal of skiing directly above Wildhaus, the lift system enables you to ski Unterwasser and Alt St Johann under the same pass. This network comprises 50 km of easy slopes, perfect for intermediates and families. If you like to ski amongst beautiful scenery, this is just the area for you as the seven peaks are quite spectacular, especially when they are tinged a pretty pink by the setting sun. Some of the views are absolutely breathtaking. From Chäserrugg, you can can look across to Germany and Austria; whilst from Gamserrugg, you see Liechtenstein and Austria. If you are staying in Wildhaus there are two chair-lifts up to Oberdorf. One of these deserves to be a museum piece. The chair is sideways on to the mountain, complete with a faded leather hood. From Oberdorf you can ski back down on one of three reds or a blue. Or you can take another chair up to the top of Gamsalp and ski a couple of blacks or a red. If it is not too windy, you can carry on up to Gamserrug (2,076 m). Here there's a steep narrow black down to Oberdorf, or you can chicken out and take a less challenging red run. It is not difficult to ski over to Unterwasser (includes some gentle off-piste). A funicular from Unterwasser will take you back up to Iltios. Above Unterwasser is the Chäserrugg, which at 2,262 m is the highest pisted peak. Here, there's a choice of a black or a long red run. The black starts steep and moguly and then evens out into an enjoyable long cruising run. There is often good powder skiing either side of this piste. Intermediates will enjoy the quite challenging but wide 'motorway' red run down from Stöfeli to Iltios. Floodlit skiing is also available. In the springtime, the ski schools often take the students to Säntis where there is a wonderful 8 km south-facing off-piste run down to Upper Toggenburg. This is fantastic in the *firn* or powder snow. If the snow is good it is also possible to ski all the way down to Grabs.

Snowboarding is taken very seriously in Wildhaus. They hosted the 1988 Swiss National Snowboarding Championships and have their own ardent snowboard school run by Erich Koch, Dorf, 9658 Wildhaus (Tel: 074 51543). Special packages are available.

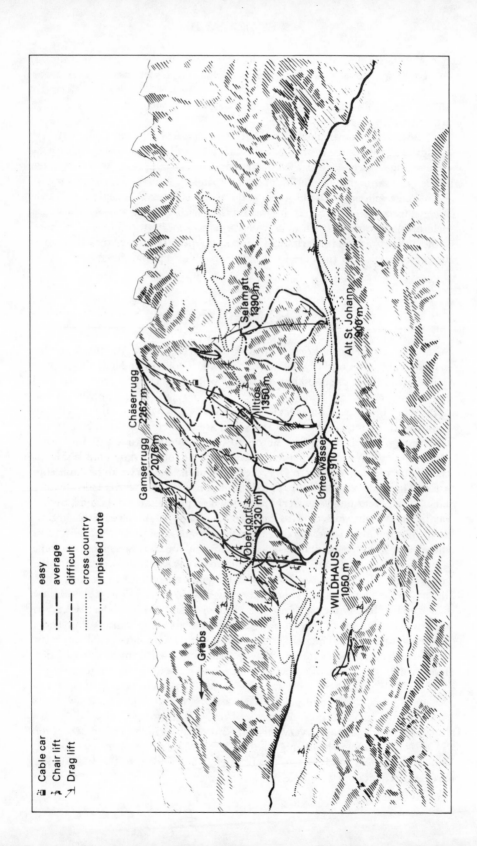

⊞ Cable car	─── easy
⊶ Chair lift	─·─·─ average
⅄ Drag lift	─ ─ ─ difficult
	········ cross country
	─··─··─ unpisted route

Gräbs →

Gamserrugg
2076 m

Chäserrugg
2262 m

Oberdorf
1230 m

Selamatt
1390 m

Illtios
1350 m

Unterwasser
910 m

WILDHAUS
1050 m

Alt St Johann
900 m

CROSS-COUNTRY

40 km. At 1,200 m, the panoramic Oelberg-Oberdorf-Selamatt trail is 25 km long and can be skied until well into spring.

SKI SCHOOL

Wildhaus ski school (Tel: 074 51722) takes pride in specialising in a 'personal service'. There are about 30 permanent instructors and up to 60 in high season. Five or six of these speak good English. They sell special packages of ski school and lift pass combined. This is very good value. 235F for six days' lessons plus six-day pass. Includes four hours of lessons each day, a day trip, race and special prize-giving evening. 140F for children. Private lessons 160F (four hours). The ski school takes children from 3 years upwards. 2-3 year olds can go to kindergarten.

LIFT PASSES

143F covers all three ski areas. 99F for children. A day's pass just for Wildhaus costs 29F.

WHERE TO EAT, DRINK & BOOGIE

There are plenty of good mountain restaurants, two of which are on Gamsalp. The cosier of these is the Michel Stübli where people (literally) get hammered— the tradition is that the last person to hit a nail into the tree stump buys the drinks. There is a fantastic view from the Chäserrug restaurant over to Walensee (Lake Walen) and Flumserberg. My favourite alpine restaurant is Gade (on the way down to Unterwasser). This has been converted out of an old stable and is famous for its coffee schnapps. It is also good for lunch and dinner. We had a delicious home speciality of ham baked in bread followed by a wonderfully rich white chocolate mousse. I would also recommend eating in the Friedegg Hotel. The latter does not have a bar, but most of the other hotels, such as Toggenburg, Alpenblick, Alpenrose and Sonne, have public bars. The Schönenboden is a small hotel with a simple rustic restaurant, just outside Wildhaus near the lake.

The nightlife in Wildhaus is certainly not sophisticated but there are a couple of discos. The Sternen is populated mainly by the teenage Rick Astley brigade whilst the James Club in the Hotel Hirschen attracts a slightly older (20-35 years old) clientele.

WHAT ELSE TO DO THERE

Wildhaus is very popular for curling—some people spend the whole week in the curling rink. There are weekly introductory courses.

Ice-skating.
Tobogganing.
Firing range.
30 km of cleared walking trails.
Sleigh-rides.
Indoor tennis (10 km away in Grabs).
Swimming for the public in three hotel indoor pools.
Eight public saunas.
Fitness room.
Puppet theatre.

WHERE TO STAY

I would recommend staying in the three-star Hotel Toggenburg (Tel: 074 52323) which is close to the chair-lift, and very comfortable and clean with its own fitness facilities (sauna, solarium etc). 75F-95F per night half board. The nearby Hotel Friedegg (Tel: 074 51313) run by the Wyss family is a smaller hotel, with no bar, but excellent food and a friendly atmosphere. 76F per night half board. The four-star Hotel Alpenrose (Tel: 074 52121) is a good place to pop in for lunch if you are skiing over from Wildhaus to Unterwasser. It also looks a comfortable, tastefully decorated place to stay. 86F per night half board.

IN CASE OF EMERGENCY

Doctors in resort: Two.
Chemist in resort: There's a drugerie which will order prescriptions.
Dentist in resort: Nearest is 10 km away.
Nearest Hospital: Grabs, 10 km away.
Helicopter Rescue: Available, as in all Swiss resorts.

HOW TO GET THERE

Nearest Airport: Zurich.
Train connection: About 1½ hours from Zurich. Change at Wil for Nesslau. Then post bus to Wildhaus. Or Zurich to Buchs and then bus to Wildhaus.

FURTHER INFORMATION

Tourist Office Wildhaus CH-9658 Wildhaus (Tel: 074 52727).

ZINAL

● **HEIGHT OF RESORT**
1,670 m.

● **HIGHEST LIFT**
2,895 m.

● **WHY GO THERE?**
Pretty, unsophisticated Swiss village.
Peace and quiet (not if you stay with Club Med!)
You want to take to the skies.
To sample a Club Méditerranée all-inclusive holiday, in a traditional
Swiss village.

● **WHO GOES THERE?**

Vividly-dressed French Club Medders.
Hang-gliders.
Parapenters.

● **COMPANIES THAT GO THERE**

Club Méditerranée.

When I arrived at 4 pm in this tiny little Swiss village, high up in the Anniviers valley in Valais, I was dazzled by all the brightly coloured birds of prey which were swooping down upon us from the skies. On closer inspection these 'birds' turned out to be sporty youngsters who had coolly opted for the quickest way down the mountain, via parapente (parachute) and skis. Every couple of minutes another one would take off from the top of the mountain and float gracefully down to hover just above the village. Peacock-like, they would then attract further attention by doing a couple of laps of honour in the air. The vivid colours of the parachutes clashed exotically with the fluorescent ski suits of the fliers. They were so agile that landing looked easier than stepping off a chair-lift. One by one they silently alighted on a snowy patch just opposite the lift station. Within a couple of minutes their parachutes were packed away in their knapsacks and they were off for some serious liquid refreshment. It was quite a shock to find this trendy new sport such a craze in the small, unsophisticated resort of Zinal.

Zinal is a tiny traditional village, 30 km from Sierre in eastern Switzerland. The Anniviers valley has five ski resorts (see also Saint-Luc). The architecture of this region is very distinctive and attractive—higgledy-piggledy houses made of wood and raised several feet off the ground on stilts. Most inhabitants use this basement space for storing logs or animal fodder. In some of the bigger houses, the animals are kept there in the winter. On the houses, there are several carvings of the local sport, *combat de reines* (cow-fighting). Although it was actually the British who opened the first hotel in Zinal in 1859, there are hardly any British tourists there now. The skiers are predominantly Swiss and French (because of Club Med).

The resort is neatly divided up into three sections. As you drive into the resort, you enter the 'commercial' sector—the 'high street'. This comprises the tourist office, ski school, a couple of ski shops, supermarket, butchers, gift shop and a hairdresser's. That is all. A few metres down the road is the hotel area where there are a handful of old establishments. There is nothing grand or flashy. Hotel Club Méditerrannée has more beds (500) than all the others put together. This tiny little village is brought to life by all the hearty French holidaymakers who prance around in their dazzling ski suits and do their best to boost the parapenting craze. At the far end of the resort is 'Le vieux village'—a pedestrian zone of old wooden houses, lovingly preserved by the Amis du Vieux Zinal. These are wonderfully doddery timber buildings, mainly owned by local farmers. Zinal really does have a village atmosphere and all the locals that I met, including the tourist office, the ski school and the hôteliers, were warm and hospitable. It is the perfect place to get away from it all and have a really simple, unstressed holiday. I look forward to going back.

THE SKIING

Zinal's ski area is very high, and goes up to nearly 3,000 m. They usually have very good snow conditions, with lots of light powder. Everyone catches a gondola up in the morning to Sorebois (2,438 m). As this is the only way up, there will probably be queues in high season (February and Easter). Unless they take to the skies with a parapente or hanglider, skiers keep their feet firmly on the ground in Zinal—there are no chair-lifts, just eight drag-lifts. This apparently gives access to 70 km of pistes although, as it is so compact, a good skier could probably ski it all in a day. The skiing in Zinal is mainly easy intermediate cruising, although there are a couple of blacks to test the more expert legs. I met several good skiers who said they were quite happy with the skiing in Zinal—there is plenty of off-piste potential and also opportunity for ski-touring. However the true expert would not find enough challenge or variety in the skiing. Apart from a red run home through the trees, the skiing in Zinal is all above the treeline. It is very safe for families as it is in a confined area. For children and beginners, there are a couple of baby runs and two easy blues down from Combe. The fun-loving Club Med influence is present even on the slopes. We were stopped a couple of times by their GO (Gentils Organisateurs) and offered a lump of sugar with a swig of brandy.

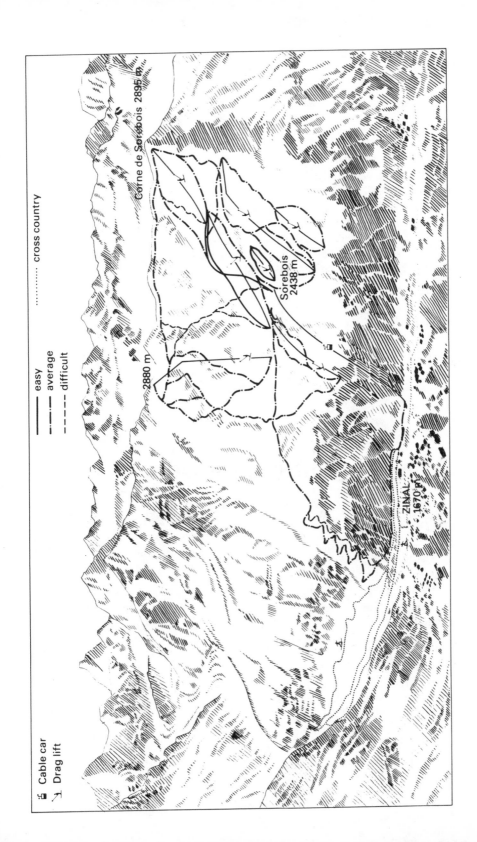

Cable car

Drag lift

—————— easy

—·—·—·— average

— — — — difficult

················ cross country

Corne de Sorebois 2895 m

2880 m

Sorebois
2438 m

ZINAL
1670 m

CROSS-COUNTRY

Although some people do go to Zinal for the cross-country skiing, there only are 12 km of prepared trails. There are some very easy routes which are ideal for beginners.

SKI SCHOOL

(Tel: 027 651035/027 651373).
The head of this small friendly ski school, Benoist Germann, is an excellent guide and teacher. He greatly improved my technique in just a morning's intensive instruction. Zinal is not a good place to bring very young children. The ski school will not accept them under 6 years old. Club Med have fantastic facilities for children—but they also will not look after children under 6 in Zinal. Six half-day ski school tickets 77F (67F kids). 100F half-day private lesson. Lessons in snowboarding and mono-ski are also available.

LIFT PASSES

126F (77F kids) for six days.

WHERE TO EAT,
DRINK & BOOGIE

At lunchtime the skiers eat up in Sorebois. There are only two restaurants—a self-service one for the public and a special restaurant for Club Med guests only. Both have sun-trap terraces with excellent views. Unless you stay at Club Med, and get involved in their boisterous home entertainment, there is not much après-ski in Zinal. There are several bars and cafés, and one disco called L'Alambic which stays open until 3 am.

But the best recommendation is the food. Valaisanne cuisine is quite delicious. Although raclette is served elsewhere in Switzerland, it actually comes from this region. Their strong-flavoured cheese is melted onto a plate and eaten with boiled potatoes. The downstairs café in Hotel Le Besso is often full of young people dining cheaply on raclette and Fendent (local wine). For a starter Le Besso serve another regional speciality called Assiette Valaisanne. This is very tasty cured beef. Opposite Le Besso is La Ferme restaurant (Tel: 027 651363), a high-ceilinged farm-lodging with a big charcoal grill. This is also a popular place for après-ski. If you go to Zinal you should not miss eating in the evening at Hotel Le Trift. The hotel is owned by Yvan and Jacqueline Genilloud who have become well-known for their gastronomic creations. The wooden-beamed restaurant is very pretty with white lace tablecloths and fresh spring flowers, whilst their gourmet food would surpass any expectation.

WHAT ELSE TO DO THERE

Unless, like me, you are the sort of person who gets vertigo stepping out of a bus, it would be a shame to miss the opportunity of trying parapenting in Zinal. The school is run by Philippe Briod, L'Arellaz, 3961 Zinal (Tel: 027 652810 or 027 651370). He charges 100F for a lesson. If you are already a proficient parapenter you can hire one for 15F per flight, 60F for the day or 250F for the week. The school also offers hang-gliding. Your first ten-minute lesson, accompanied by a pilot-costs 100F.

A natural ice-skating rink where they hold a weekly 'ice disco'.

Flatotel Les Erables (see Where To Stay, below) has a large indoor swimming pool that is open to the public and a small fitness centre. You can also have a sauna, solarium, or massage there. The swimming pool is free for anyone staying at Les Erables or Club Med.

In March 1989, Zinal organised its first Euroskiathlon which involved downhill and cross-country skiing as well as a 5-10 km run.

WHERE TO STAY

The largest hotel in Zinal is owned by Club Méditerranée (Tel: 027 651383). A Club Med holiday is a totally unique concept, ideal for anyone who wants to shed all responsibility. Everything is organised for you by their Gentils Organisateurs (GO). These talented workers will arrange your lift pass, ski hire and lessons, sing and dance for you in the evenings (and even on the slopes) and entertain your children. Anyone with children should definitely consider a Club Med holiday, as they do a grand job of taking them off your hands for as long as you want/need. Some people may find it rather like an upmarket Butlins. It is certainly not a place for romantic twosomes. Meals are a communal affair (but the food is first class both in quality and quantity). There is (amateur) entertainment every night. This is performed in French, so if you do not speak the lingo you will miss a lot. If you do not have a college-campus sense of humour you probably will not laugh anyway.

For a more sedate holiday, I would recommend staying at Hotel Le Trift or Hotel Le Besso. Le Trift (Tel: 027 651466) is a small, family-run business. Although it is spotlessly clean, the bedrooms are very tiny and boxlike. Only a few of them have private facilities. What they lack in space, they make up for in courtesy. The staff were very friendly and served us a fantastic breakfast every morning of piping hot fresh coffee, orange juice, croissants, muesli, home-made bread, cheese and jams. 44F-56F per night for a single room with bathroom, 88F-112F per night for a double room with bathroom. If you stay here you should definitely make the most of their excellent cuisine and pay an 18F daily supplement for half board.

Hotel Le Besso (Tel: 027 653165/66) is run by Jim Casada, who is quite a local character. His rooms are bigger and slightly more luxurious, all with private facilities. 54F-70F for a single. 90F-114F for a double. Flatotel Les Erables (Tel: 027 651881/82) is a large modern complex, very popular with the Germans.

This can either be used as a hotel (two and three-bedroom rooms are available) or you can rent an apartment. Special packages are available. An apartment for 4-6 people costs from 316F per person for a week. Includes half board in the centre's restaurant.

IN CASE OF EMERGENCY

Nearest doctor: Vissoie.
Nearest chemist: Vissoie.
Nearest dentist: Sierre.
Nearest Hospital: Sierre.
Helicopter Rescue: Everywhere in Switzerland.

HOW TO GET THERE

Nearest Airport: Geneva.
Train connection: Sierre. $2\frac{1}{2}$ hours from Geneva airport. Then bus (one hour).

FURTHER INFORMATION

Tourist Office 3961 Zinal (Val d'Anniviers) (Tel: 027 651370).

Turkey

In the 1970s no one thought about going on holiday in Turkey. In the last few years it has become *the* trendy holiday destination. Most people associate Turkey with beaches and summer holidays. There is in fact plenty of opportunity for skiing, and the British company Club Turkey have set up a special winter skiing programme. The ski season is from December to April.

There are five mountain ranges, with 89 mountains over 3,000 m high. At the moment there are seven ski resorts, although two more are planned. The best-known and most developed resort is Uludag on Mount Olympus, about four hours' drive from Istanbul. Most of the other resorts are very small and primitive, usually comprising just one lift and a hotel. Erzurum, in eastern Turkey near the Russian border, is a bleak, shabby resort with just a small T-bar and an excruciatingly long (3,300 m) single chair. This gives access to lots of wide open deserted powder bowls. To take advantage of this immense potential the Turks are planning to build more lifts in Erzurum. As they are so near the Russian border, resorts like Erzurum have a Siberian climate, which drops to minus forty degrees in the dead of winter. The airport often has to close because of too much snow.

It is unfair to compare skiing in Turkey with skiing in the Alps. The lift systems are unsophisticated and the Turks have not yet developed large ski areas. But the ski days are long (lifts are often open from 8 am-8 pm) and they have a good snow record. More importantly, a ski holiday in Turkey is a different cultural experience. The skiing is probably best appreciated when combined with a few days sightseeing in Istanbul, or if you go in April, a few days on the beach.

191

FURTHER INFORMATION

Turkish Tourist Office 170 Piccadilly, London W1 (Tel: 01 734 8681).
Club Turkey Sixth Floor, 113 Upper Richmond Road, London SW15 2TL (Tel: 01 785 6389).

ULUDAG

- **HEIGHT OF RESORT**
  1,800 m.

- **HIGHEST LIFT**
  2,543 m

- **WHY GO THERE?**
  Two-centre holiday combining skiing with sightseeing in Istanbul. A different type of ski holiday.

- **WHO GOES THERE?**
  Tanned Turks.
  Piste poseurs.

- **COMPANIES THAT GO THERE**
  Club Turkey.

Skiing has always been considered a luxury by the Turks, and is only pursued by the rich and privileged. Uludag is the Cortina or St Moritz of Turkey. It is their most developed resort and attracts a glitzy Turkish clientele of businessmen and film stars. About 80 per cent of the people who go to Uludag do not even ski! The Turks prefer the posing to the pistes and certainly do not have the obsessive French boy-racer mentality of skiing all day. Fashionably dressed, they like to ski for an hour or two, if at all. Many of them do not even leave the bars, where they are busy looking beautiful with their suntans and shades.

Uludag is a purpose-built seventies-style resort, near the town of Bursa, south of Istanbul and west of Ankara. Although small, it is well-equipped with modern hotels and restaurants, as well as indoor swimming pools, skating rinks, squash courts, jacuzzis and gymnasiums. The hotel lobbies have a selection of smart boutiques, jewellery shops and hairdressers—you will even find a Bennetons! It is all very laid-back, and it is not unusual to walk in and have your hair cut at 10.30 pm at night.

The resort is situated at the foot of Mount Olympus, surrounded by a pretty forested mountainscape. Although it does not look much different from an Alpine resort, Uludag has a unique Islamic feel about it. Seven kilometres beneath the resort is the mosque of Sahilan, quite spectacular when covered with snow. This can be reached by skiing down the road. The English company, Club Turkey, organises ski barbecues near this mosque—the skiers are entertained by travelling musicians.

THE SKIING

The Turks started skiing in Uludag in the fifties. The ski area is limited, but there is no queueing apart from in 'semestre', the Turkish school holidays (last week in January and first week in February). There is not enough challenge or variety to occupy the serious skier for a week but there is plenty of mileage for beginners and unaggressive intermediates. There are 25 pistes and twelve lifts. The nursery slopes are right in the centre and it is possible to ski from your doorstep. The slopes are not very long but they are well-pisted and sufficiently varied with lots of trees. Many of them have music playing from speakers on the lifts, creating an almost 'carnival' atmosphere. It is certainly a very laid-back place to ski. From February, if there are people who want to ski late, the lift-men will turn on the floodlights and keep the lifts open until 8 pm. Turkish ski resorts are not for those who like skiing all day as they always shut the lifts at lunchtime (this has been known to happen with people half-way up!).

One of the best things about Uludag is the off-piste. As there is nothing very steep, it is particularly good for learning powder skiing. If you are fit, and really keen, you can take a two-hour hike up to the summit Zirve (2,543 m) from where you can carve your way down a monster off-piste route. The huge expanses of un-pisted snow are pure bliss. If you are not so fit, but just as keen and have £25 in your pocket, you can be taken to the top by helicopter. The Turks do not seem to have caught on to alternative skiing as yet. The solitary mono-skier in the resort was a striking sight.

CROSS-COUNTRY

There are six or seven tracks in Uludag. There is also fantastic potential for cross-country touring through the National Park. But be warned: never do this without a guide as not only can you get lost but there are bears and wolves in the woods! No joke.

SKI SCHOOL

The Turkish for ski is 'kayak' so if someone offers you kayak lessons, don't think they're trying to get you down to the beach. The ski school instructors speak English. Reports about the school are good. £30 for six days, two hours a day. £7.50 private lesson.

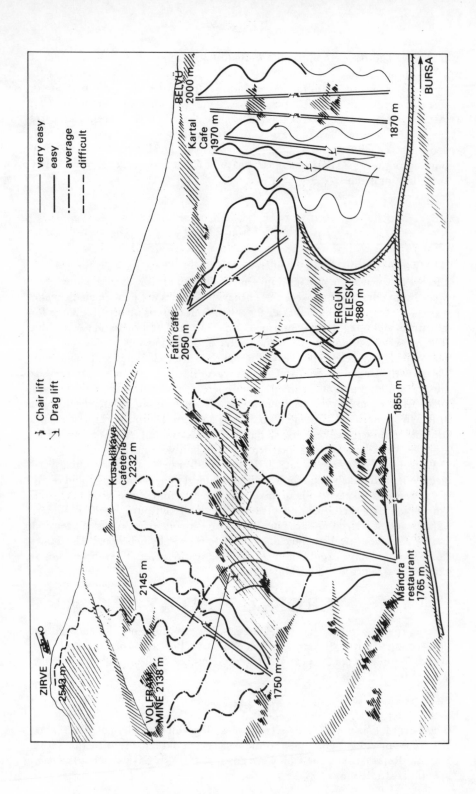

ZIRVE
2543 m

very easy
easy
average
difficult

Chair lift
Drag lift

VOLFRAM
MINE 2138 m

2145 m

Kusaklikaya
cafeteria
2232 m

1750 m

Fatin cafe
2050 m

BELVÜ
2000 m

Kartal
Cafe
1970 m

1870 m

ERGÜN
TELESKI
1880 m

1855 m

Mandra
restaurant
1765 m

BURSA

LIFT PASSES

You used to have to buy different tickets for all the lifts. Thankfully, there is now one combined pass—£28 for a week.

WHERE TO EAT, DRINK & BOOGIE

Although it can be quiet in the week, Uludag comes to life at the weekend when the resort is full of furs, flashy cars and suntans. The Beceren Cafe, at the bottom of the slopes' is packed with poseurs who do not ski, but exercise themselves by changing outfits three or even four times a day! The best restaurant in the resort is probably Mandra which is open for both lunch and dinner. This is a bright lively restaurant with a log fire and large windows overlooking the pistes. The food is cheap—lunch costs anything from 75p to £5. A beer is about £1, the same as in England. Considering that it is a Muslim country, I was surprised to see that alcohol was freely available. Most of the hotels have bars and there are seven discos in the resort. The bars are very atmospheric and often have Turkish singers. *Sharap* is the Turkish version of glühwein.

It is definitely worth visiting Bursa which is 36 km away. The most novel way of getting there is by cable car. This 30-minute ride down the mountain costs the equivalent of 65p-75p and gives an amazing view of the approaching city. The cable car ends up near the Green Mosque. Alternatively, it takes an hour by taxi or *dolmus* (minibus) from the resort to Bursa. Bursa is like a mini-Istanbul and the main thermal resort in Turkey. There is an old natural hot spring bath (from the Byzantine period) where you can pamper yourself with a *kese*, a vigorous scrub-down with a rough glove and an even more vigorous massage. Bursa was the original capital city of the Ottoman Empire and is famous for its donar kebabs. This is nothing like the greasy counterparts sold in England, but is the original Turkish dish served with yoghurt (Turkey is *not* a place for vegetarians—most of the food is lamb or beef). There is also a special silk market in Bursa and a bazaar which sells everything from leatherwear to oriental carpets. If you would like to watch a bit of authentic shimmying and shaking, visit the Taylan nightclub which has belly dancing most evenings.

WHAT ELSE TO DO THERE

Two ice-skating rinks.
Two full-size swimming pools.
Squash courts.
Gymnasiums.
Saunas and jacuzzi.
Turkish baths in Bursa.

WHERE TO STAY

There are 14 hotels, ranging from wooden chalets to big modern complexes. The most luxurious is the The Kervansaray, a high-tech hotel with an impressive range of facilities such as an indoor swimming pool, night club, casino, squash, gym, in-house laundry service and shops. Club Turkey do packages to this hotel from £429 for a week, half board. The Grand is more 'faded' but still popular and has an indoor swimming pool, ice-skating rink, hairdresser, sauna, massage, gym, shops, disco, casino and even its own helicopter service. From £419 for a week, half board with Club Turkey. The Ergün is a small hotel with 20 rooms, all with their own fridge and satellite TV. From £389 for a week half board.

IN CASE OF EMERGENCY

Doctor in resort: There is a doctor and clinic in the resort where they will plaster and repair fractures.
Nearest chemist: Bursa (36km).
Nearest dentist: Bursa.
Nearest hospital: Bursa.
Helicopter rescue: Available.

HOW TO GET THERE

Nearest airport: Istanbul.
Transfer time: Four hours.

FURTHER INFORMATION

Club Turkey Sixth Floor, 113 Upper Richmond Road, London SW15 2TL (Tel: 01 785 6389).

Directory

COMPANIES

Ace Skiing Holidays 1 The Holm, Moffat, Scotland DG10 9JJ (Tel: 0683 20441).

Across-Country Skiing Holidays Inntravel, Hovingham, York, YO6 4JZ (Tel: 065 382741).

Adventure Express 2 Church Street, Chesham, Bucks, HP5 1HT (Tel: 0494 791400).

Air France Holidays Georgian House, 69 Boston Manor Rd, Brentford, Middx TW8 9JQ (Tel: 01 568 6981).

Austro Tours 5 St Peters Street, St Albans, Herts AL1 3DH (Tel: 0727 38191).

Bladon Lines 56-58 Putney High Street, London SW15 1SF (Tel: 785 3131).

Club Méditerrané 106-110 Brompton Road, London SW3 1JJ (Tel: 01 581 1161).

Club Turkey Sixth Floor, 113 Upper Richmond Road, London SW15 2TL (Tel: 01 785 6389).

Erna Low Consultants 9 Reece Mews, London SW7 3HE (Tel: 01 584 2841/7820).

Hourmont Olivier House, 18 Marine Parade, Brighton, East Sussex BN2 1TL (Tel: 0273 677777).

Inghams Gemini House, 10-18 Putney Hill, London SW15 6AX (Tel: 01 785 7777).

Made to Measure 43 East Street, Chichester, West Sussex PO19 1HX (Tel: 0243 533333).

Mogul Ski Holidays Royal Chambers, Station Parade, Harrogate, North Yorkshire, HG1 1HQ (Tel: 0423 69512).

Norway Line Tyne Commission Quay, Albert Edward Dock, North Shields, Tyne and Wear, NE29 6EA (Tel: 091 296 1313).

Norwegian State Railways Travel Bureau 21/24 Cockspur Street, London SW1Y 5DA (Tel: 01 930 6666).

Norwegian Travel Service Church Gate, Church Street, Woking, Surrey GU21 1DJ (Tel: 0483 756871).

Pegasus Ski Italy River House, Restmor Way, Hackbridge Rd, Wallington, Surrey SM6 7AH (Tel: 01 773 2323).

Powder Byrne 50 Lombard Road, London SW11 3SU (Tel: 01 223 0601).

Red Guide Permanent House, Clifton Street, Blackpool FY1 1JP (Tel: 0253 23939).

Ski Choice 27 High Street, Benson, Oxford OX9 6RP (Tel: 0491 37607)

Ski M & M 3/1 Abercorn Gardens, Edinburgh, EH8 7BL (Tel: 031 669 8100).

Ski Miquel 460 Corn Exchange, Hanging Ditch, Manchester M4 3BY (Tel: 061 832 2737).

Ski Red Fox Home Lea, Portsmouth Rd, Esher, Surrey KT10 GPII (Tel: 0372 67643 April to December or 0425 279986 during the ski season).

Ski Scene (Intasun) Intasun House, 2 Cromwell Avenue, Bromley, Kent BR2 9AQ (Tel: 01 290 0511).

Ski Sutherland Church Gate, Church Street West, Woking, Surrey GU21 1DJ (Tel: 04862 70383/70696. For their Norwegian Travel Service tel: 04862 756871).

Ski Tonic Tudor Court, Heathlands Road, Wokingham, Berks, RG11 3AS (Tel: 0344 777877).

Ski Total Total Holidays, 10 Hill Street, Richmond, Surrey TW9 1TN (Tel: 01 948 6922).

The Ski Venture Gwalia House, Tresaith, Cardigan, Dyfed SA43 2JL, Wales (Tel: 0239 810361).

Snow Ranger Suite 228/9 Linen Hall, 162 Regent Street, London W1R 5TB (Tel: 01 439 1255).

Star Tour of Scandinavia 209 Edgware Road, London W2 (Tel: 01 706 2520).

Supersports Lymington Rd, Highcliffe, Christchurch, Dorset. (Tel: 0425 273526).

Swiss Travel Service Bridge House, Ware, Herts SG12 9DE (Tel: 0920 463971).

Waymark Holidays 295 Lillie Road, London SW6 7LL (Tel: 01 385 5015).

White Roc Ski 69 Westbourne Grove, London W2 4UJ (Tel: 01 792 1188).

FURTHER INFORMATION

The Ski Club of Great Britain 118 Eaton Square, SW1W 9AF (Tel: 01 245 1033). £24-£34 annual membership. Membership entitles you to use their London clubhouse and excellent resort and snow information service, reductions on holiday bookings and shops, free subscription to *Ski Survey* magazine, equipment centre and special holidays including cross-country and ski touring.

Ski Solutions 206 Heythorp Street, Southfields, London SW18 5PA (Tel: 01 944 1221). Free information on available ski holidays.

Planes, Trains & Automobiles

PLANES

Travelling by air is still the quickest and simplest way to get to most ski resorts. Independent travellers can often buy just flight seats from tour operators and scheduled flights are cheaper if booked in advance. Try to avoid travelling at weekends in peak season. Saturdays at Geneva airport are complete bedlam and should be avoided at all costs. Package holidays usually include return transfers to the resort from the airport. If you are travelling independently, you can often buy a ticket on one of these transfer coaches. There are also usually public transport facilities to the resorts either by bus or train. Below is a list of selected airlines offering scheduled flights from the UK to airports near European ski resorts.

AIRLINES

Air Europe The Galleria, Station Rd, Crawley, West Sussex RH10 1HY (Tel: UK linkline 0345 444737).
Scheduled flights to: Geneva, Munich.

Air France 158 New Bond Street, London, W1Y OAY (Tel: 01 499 9511).
Scheduled flights to: Nice, Toulouse, Lyon.

Austrian Airlines 50 Conduit Street, London W1R ONP (Tel: 01 439 0741).
Scheduled flights to: Salzburg, Linz, Vienna, Graz and Klagenfurt.

British Airways Written enquires should be addressed to British Airways

Travel Shops, 65/76 Regent Street, London W1R 7HG (Tel: 01 897 4000 for reservations).
Scheduled flights to: Most European airports.

Dan Air New City Court, 20 St Thomas Street, London SE1 9RJ (Tel: 01 378 6464).
Scheduled flights to: Berne, Bergen, Innsbruck, Montpelier, Nice, Toulouse, Oslo, Perpignan, Zurich.

Pilgrim Air 44 Goodge St, London W1P 2AD (Tel: 01 580 2831).
Scheduled flights to: All Italian airports.

Swiss Air The Swiss Centre, 10 Wardour Street, London W1V 4BJ (Tel: 01 439 4144).
Scheduled flights to: Geneva, Zurich, Berne.

THE SHORT BREAK

Weekend skiing is the perfect answer for anyone who is short of time rather than money. The travelling time obviously needs to be kept to a minimum, so a flight and a short transfer (under $1\frac{1}{2}$ hours) is essential. For example, Le Grand Bornand in France is less an hour's drive from Geneva. Swiss Air flies from Heathrow to Geneva on a Friday night, enabling you to ski all day Saturday and Sunday, and fly back first thing Monday morning, to be at work in London by 9.30 am. Or if you can take one day off work, this will give you three days' skiing. Weekend skiing is not cheap, costing about the same as a package week. But it is ideal as an 'extra' holiday and very therapeutic for the stressed worker. I was surprised how relaxing such a short break could be—it felt as though I had been away twice as long.

There are many companies which offer weekend skiing. Also check the Sunday papers for the latest deals.

Powder Byrne 50 Lombard Road, London SW11 3SU (Tel: 01 223 0601).

Ski Choice 27 High Street, Benson, Oxford OX9 6RP (Tel: 0491 37606). Tailor-made packages (short and long breaks) to wide range of European resorts.

Ski La Vie 28 Linver Road, London SW6 3RB (Tel: 01 736 5611). Weekend skiing in Switzerland.

Ski Les Alpes 207 Down House, Broomhill Road, London SW18 4GQ (Tel: 01 871 5117).

Ski Whizz Crescent House, Angel Hill, Bury St Edmunds, Suffolk IP33 1UZ (Tel: 0284 750505).
Tailor-made packages, mainly to France.

White Roc Ski 69 Westbourne Grove, London W2 4UJ (Tel: 01 792 1188). Weekend breaks to resorts with short transfers, such as Le Grand Bornand.

TRAINS

The authentic way to travel to a ski resort is by train. In countries such as Sweden and Norway, this can be very atmospheric, with spectacular scenery, and is an excellent way to meet people. Travelling by train is more functional in some countries than others. I would certainly recommend travelling by train in Switzerland which has one of the most efficient railway networks in the world. Most skiers fly to Zurich or Geneva from where there are rail connections to nearly all the Swiss resorts. The trains are always punctual. If you want to travel all the way by train, the high speed TGV train goes from Paris to Geneva, Lausanne or Berne.

Many Swiss ski resorts have their own train stations. If not, they can always be reached by an equally reliable post bus service from the nearest station. Luggage and skis can be checked in at Zurich or Geneva airport, direct to the resort. Although this is a very efficient service, the luggage sometimes does not arrive at the resort until the following morning. Make sure you take everything needed for that night with you. On the way back the luggage can be checked in at the station straight through to the UK flight destination, provided you are flying from Basel, Geneva or Zurich.

Travelling by train in a well-organised country such as Switzerland gives you the freedom to visit different resorts. The Swiss Holiday Card entitles you to unlimited travel on the Swiss Railways and most alpine post buses and lake steamers. This costs £92 for 15 days (further details from the Swiss National Tourist Office, see page 164). If you get the opportunity, I would certainly recommend travelling by Glacier Express which goes from Zermatt to St Moritz, stopping at Brig, Andermatt, Chur and Davos. The whole journey takes 7 hours, but is thoroughly enjoyable as it passes through such spectacular Alpine scenery. This is certainly the best way to see Switzerland.

If you are travelling to France you can put the car on the train. SNCF (French Railways, 179 Piccadilly, London W1V OBA; Tel: 01 491 0346) have trains from Paris to St Gervais (between Chamonix and Megève, useful for Le Grand Bornand, Samoëns, Les Gets or Praz-de-Lys) and to Grenoble (useful for La Grave, Chamrousse, Les 7 Laux and Villard-de-Lans). They are also now offering a direct 12-hour journey from Calais to Moutiers in Tarentaise. It is ideal for anyone travelling to resorts such as Tignes, Val d'Isère, Les Arcs, La Plagne, Trois Vallées. The train leaves Calais at about 8 pm, arriving 12 hours later in Moutiers. This avoids the major bottlenecks, so you can unload the car at leisure and be on the slopes by lunchtime. On the way back, there is an overnight sleeper leaving Moutiers on Saturday evening. Such a trip avoids the traffic and aggravation of driving to this part of France and also give you an extra day and a half on the slopes.

Further details about travelling by train is available from the various tourist offices.

AUTOMOBILES

Ski-drive holidays are best approached as a special kind of holiday. They enable you to explore different resorts, see more of the country, and take everything but the kitchen sink with you. It is of particular advantage to have a car in an area such as the Dolomites in Italy as it enables you to take advantage of their vast, but not that well-linked, ski area. It also gives you the nomad opportunity of hopping from one village to another—there are so many delightful undiscovered places in this part of Italy, that many people say it can only be fully appreciated when travelling by car. But if you have less than a week to spare, it is probably not worth driving all that way.

Most people choose self-drive for freedom rather than economy. Unless there are four or more of you travelling, a self-drive holiday is not cheap. Most package tour operators only give about £35-£75 off for each person travelling by car. Once you have added up the cost of the Channel crossing, motorway tolls, petrol and overnight accommodation, it will probably work out much more expensive than you anticipated.

Self-drive is a good choice for families, as the kids are safely under your supervision and there should hopefully be room for all their odds and ends such as toys, potties and plastic trays.

When choosing a resort to drive to, check that it is not car-free. Some resorts, such as Zermatt in Switzerland, do not allow cars in the centre. Leaving your car in a freezing unguarded outdoor car park, miles away from the hotel, rather defeats the convenience of driving (especially when you then have to carry all the luggage, potties, plastic trays etc!). *Never* park facing uphill, as if there is a heavy snowfall it will be very difficult to get out. Some resorts have underground parking—a definite plus.

Driving holidays need a little careful preparation. You should always carry your driving licence, international driving permit (available from the AA or RAC), insurance certificate, registration document, passport and Green Card with you. The AA (Tel: 0256 20123) and RAC (Tel: 01 686 2525) offer continental driving packages which include roadside assistance, vehicle recovery, delivery of spare parts and letters of credit for any repairs and alternative travel home. The AA Overseas Routes (Tel: 0256 493748) offer computerised routes to all European destinations, £8.95 (£3 surcharge if you are not a member), and they have a free *Motoring Abroad* brochure. The RAC has a marked-map service for Europe, free to members (£6 non-members).

If you are travelling in France, Spain or Italy, you will have to pay to use their motorways. In Switzerland you are required to pay yearly tax, about 30F, payable at the Swiss National Tourist Office in London, at the AA, or at the Swiss frontier. In Austria you do not usually pay, apart from the Brenner autobahn and the tunnels. There are no tolls in Germany or Belgium. Make sure you have enough foreign currency on you. Credit cards are not widely acceptable in foreign petrol stations. If you are going to Italy you can buy special petrol coupon packs which include petrol and motorway tolls—these are available from the AA.

The preparation for driving in the mountains is important. Snow-chains or special tyres are a *must*—in some countries like Austria it is illegal to drive without them in your possession. It is best to hire the chains in this country from somewhere like the AA, as they are quite expensive to buy. Four-wheel drives handle alpine roads much better than two-wheel drives. The car should be serviced before you go, and the headlights adjusted for driving abroad. Remember to take a first-aid kit (in Austria this is compulsory), a warning triangle (compulsory in most countries), a rear view mirror on the left-hand side of the car (compulsory in Italy), fire-extinguisher, spare tyre, jump-leads, anti-freeze and a torch. A spare plastic windscreen is a good idea and do not forget a good map and a dictionary! The best way to transport skis is in one of those modern fibreglass-top boxes, as this protects them from the elements.

Below are a few of the companies operating ferry and hovercraft crossings to the Continent.

Brittany Ferries The Brittany Centre, Wharf Road, Portsmouth PO2 8RU (Tel: 0705 827701).

Hoverspeed Maybrook House, Queens Gardens, Dover, Kent CT17 9UQ (Tel: 0304 240241).

P&O European Ferries Channel House, Channel View Road, Dover, Kent CT17 9TJ (Tel: 0304 203388).

Sally Line Argyle Centre, York Street, Ramsgate, Kent CT11 9DS (Tel: 0843 595522). Also sells ski packages to Austria.

Sealink Charter House, Park Street, Ashford, Kent TN24 8EX (Tel: 0233 47047).

CAR HIRE

The ultimate luxury must be to fly and then hire a car at the airport. This avoids the hassle of waiting around for transfers and enables you to have a car at your disposal for the duration of your stay. If there are only two of you, or you are travelling on your own, this can work out very expensive, but the big companies such as Avis offer special packages and with four travelling it can work out quite economical. As long as you choose a reputable company, the budget cars should be perfectly adequate, even though they do not have much zip. When you order the car, tell them that you will need snow chains and a roof rack.

A word of warning: if you hire the car in Switzerland (eg Geneva) it will take unleaded petrol. This is fine, until you decide to head into France. Their alpine garages are not equipped with unleaded petrol, so do make sure you have a full tank when crossing the border, or you may have to dash back into Switzerland for a top-up!

Avis Rent-a-Car Ltd Trident House, Station Rd, Hayes, Middx, UB3 4DJ (Tel: 01 848 8765). Below are some of the airports where Avis car hire is available: FRANCE Geneva (French side), Grenoble, Lyon, Nice, Perpignan, Toulouse. SWITZERLAND Geneva, Zurich. AUSTRIA Innsbruck, Klagenfurt, Linz, Salzburg, Vienna. ITALY Bologna, Florence, Pisa, Venice, Verona.

SWEDEN Kiruna, Ostersünd, Stockholm. NORWAY Bergen, Oslo, Stavanger, Trondheim. TURKEY Istanbul.

INSURANCE

Finally, wherever you decide to go, and however you decide to travel, do not forget to get properly insured. Douglas Cox Tyrie specialises in winter sports insurance and has various packages available. Further details from: **Douglas Cox Tyrie Ltd,** 100 Whitechapel Road, London E1 1JB (Tel: 01 247 8888 or 24-hour ansafone 01 377 1336).

Exotic Ski

Many skiers have a very limited view of the world—there are the Alps and the Rockies, but that is about all. It is in fact to possible to ski in all sorts of faraway places. This chapter is for all you globetrotters who are looking for something a little more unusual. Some of these may be very primitive with perhaps only one lift. I am not suggesting that anyone should book a fortnight's skiing in somewhere like Morocco. But if you are going there on holiday anyway, it is nice to know that you can leave the beach for a day and pop up to the mountains for a few hours' skiing. And while all your friends are discussing the merits of Verbier, there is nothing like a casual mention of 'When I was skiing in Sahoro, Japan', to boost your piste cred.

The USA and Canada have some wonderful undiscovered slopes. Unfortunately, it would take a whole book to do them justice so I have not included them below. I have not included the Eastern Block countries either, as several of these, such as Yugoslavia, are being snapped up by the British package tour operators for cheapo-cheapo holidays. I have included Finland as it offers some very unusual and magical winter holidays.

Below, then, is a personal pick of worldwide destinations—I have given them marks out of ten for piste credibility. As I have not totted up quite enough points myself yet, I am afraid none of the places below can be personally recommended. The tourist boards should be able to give you further information about skiing in their countries.

ARGENTINA

Piste cred: 10.
Ski season: July to early October.

The Andes in Argentina is the second highest mountain range in the world. The skiing is in the south of Argentina, mainly in Bariloche. The most famous slopes are Cerro Catedrel, 19 km from Bariloche. Here there are 26 km of pistes and several lifts. Queueing can be a problem in July and August. They hold a Fiesta de La Nieve (snow carnival) every August. There are also slopes 5 km out of Bariloche, on Cerro Otto and at López, Dormilón and La Ventana.

Las Lenas is a small modern resort which was built in 1982, 1,180 km west of Buenos Aires. There is a special Ski Lenas plane from Buenos Aires to Marlargue (two-hour flight). A 50-mile bus ride takes you to the resort. Las Lenas looks a little like a French purpose-built resort and is said to have the 'best skiing south of the equator'. The runs are good for intermediates and have wonderful names such as Jupiter, Apolo and Neputo. There is also some very good off-piste. The Swiss and Italian teams train here.

FURTHER INFORMATION

Argentinian Embassy 111 Cadogan Gardens, London SW3 (Tel: 01 730 4388).
Omni Plus Ltd 20A Chalcot Square, NW1 8YA (Tel: 01 722 0308). Organise holidays to Argentina.

AUSTRALIA

Piste cred: 9.
Ski season: June to September.

Skiing in Australia has been compared to skiing in Scotland. The mountains are not very high and are not renowned for powder or spring snow. Many of the resorts are very small, and some are just 'day areas' which can only be used by club members. The main attraction for the British skier seems to be that the Australian ski season is our summer. The skiing takes place in the Snowy Mountains in the south-east of Australia, in two states: New South Wales and Victoria. In New South Wales most of the resorts are in the Mount Kosciusko National Park. Mount Kosciusko (2,230 m) is the highest mountain in New South Wales. The main resorts are Thredbo and Perisher Valley/Smiggins Hole. The Victoria resorts are near Melbourne. Mount Buller is the biggest resort in Australia, and twinned with Mount Stirling offers both downhill and cross-country. It is only three hours' drive from Melbourne. They have recently started a A$90m development project. Mount Buffalo was the first Australian ski resort to have a lift system. Mount Hotham is said to have some of the most challenging skiing in the country. Mount Stirling has the most extensive range of cross-country trails (60 km) in the southern hemisphere. Falls Creek is Victoria's classic alpine village, with artificial snow-making facilities. Ski touring, snow camping and trekking across the 'roof' of Victoria are also available.

FURTHER INFORMATION

Victorian Tourism Commission Victoria House, Melbourne Place, Strand, London WC2B 4LG (Tel: 01 240 3974).
Tourism Commission of New South Wales 66 The Strand, London WC2N 5LZ (Tel: 01 839 6651).

CHILE

Piste cred: 10.
Ski season: May to December.

Chile is the snow paradise of the southern hemisphere, situated between the Pacific Ocean and the high, snow-covered Cordillera de Los Andes. The season varies according to the latitude and altitude of the resorts. In the zone from Portillo to Chillán, ski resorts open June-October, during which Chile hosts many national and international competitions. There is usually deep powder in July and spring snow starts in mid-August. In the area south of Chillán, spring skiing starts in September.

Portillo (2,850 m) is probably the best-known ski resort in South America. It is 150 km northeast of Santiago, Chile's capital, in Cordillera de los Andes. There are seven main runs and seven lifts—the Roca Jack slope is notoriously difficult, with 305 m out of 835 m vertical. There are not as many queues here as at Bariloche in Argentina. The luxury hotel faces Lake Inca. Farellones, only 48 km from Santiago, is a popular weekend resort for Chileans. Lagunillas is 64 km from Santiago, near the picturesque village of San José. The ski resort Chillán is well known for its hot springs. Cerro Mirador, only 12 km from Punta Arenas, is the world's most southerly ski resort and one of the few places where you can ski with a sea view. The season is May to October. Skiers stay in the city, 8 km away. There is a mid-way lodge with food, drink and equipment.

FURTHER INFORMATION

The Chilean Consulate 12 Devonshire Street, London W1 (Tel: 01 580 1023).
La Federación de Ski de Chile Casilla 9902, Santiago, Chile.
Omni Plus Ltd 20A Chalcot Square, NW1 8YA (Tel: 01 722 0308). Organise holidays to Chile.

CYPRUS

Piste cred: 5.
Ski season: January to March.

Cyprus has a very short ski season from January to the end of March. There is only one resort and the facilities are very limited but it is one of the few places in the world where you can ski, and then an hour's drive later be swimming or sunbathing on the beach. The skiing takes place on Mount Olympus (1,900 m). In March, you can can clearly see sails dotted on the distant blue sea from the ski slopes. The nearest resort to the ski area is Troodos (1,850 m), but Platres (1,230 m) is also not far away. There are four slopes, rather cutely named Aphrodite, Hermes, Dias and Hera. The Cyprus Ski Club owns the four ski lifts and can provide tuition and equipment. The Club accepts tourists as temporary members. The most important activity is the annual International Skiing competition which takes place towards the end of February.

FURTHER INFORMATION

Cyprus Tourism Organisation 213 Regent Street, London W1R 8DA (Tel: 01 734 9822).
Cyprus Ski Club Federation PO Box 2185, Nicosia, Cyprus (Tel: 02 44 19 33).

FINLAND

Piste cred: 6.
Ski season: October to May.

Finland has a long ski season from October to May. Cross-country is the main type of skiing but they do have some limited and gentle alpine pistes. There are 119 ski centres that feature downhill skiing. The longest slope is 2,500 m long; most of them are about 550 m. About a third of the centres also have artificial snow. Early and late season ski-packages are offered at prices from 550 FIM. A five-day holiday package includes accommodation in a hotel room or log cabin with shower, a ski lift card, access to maintained cross-country ski tracks and four hours of tuition in cross-country or downhill skiing.

As Finland is such a long country (1,000 km from Helsinki in the south to Utsjoki in the north), the temperature and snow conditions vary considerably. The farther north you go, the more deeply forested and mountainous the country becomes. In December and January the sun never actually rises in Lapland in the far north, but in April they often have up to 16 hours of sunshine every day. Expert cross-country skiers should try skiing on the fells of Lapland where there are literally thousands of square kilometres of hard, easily-traversed snow and 300,000 reindeer. Ski treks are also available. Other winter activities include ice-fishing, snowmobiling, reindeer-rides, windsurfing on the snow or ice, dog sleigh-rides, hang-gliding, ice-driving courses and even snow sculpture competitions.

Do not forget the ubiquitous Finnish sauna. In winter, the Finns often finish off a sauna with a roll in the snow or a dip in the lake. But please, do not try this if you have high blood pressure or a heart condition. Finally, the children will love Finland at Christmas (provided they are old enough to cope with the cold) as they can visit Santa Claus Land, near the town of Rovaniemi on the Arctic Circle.

FURTHER INFORMATION

Santa Claus Land Maakuntakatu 10, 96100 Rovaniemi, Finnish Lapland (Tel: 960 17203).

Finnish Tourist Board 66 Haymarket, London SW1Y 4RF (Tel: 01 839 4048).

Waymark Holidays 295 Lillie Road, London SW6 7LL (Tel: 01 385 5015 or 01 385 3502) arrange special Lapland pulka tour/cross-country skiing.

Goodwood Travel Ltd 'Flights of Fantasy' St James's House, 78 Castle Street, Canterbury, Kent CT1 2QZ (Tel: 0227 763336). Christmas Concorde to Lapland.

Finlandia Travel Agency 130 Jermyn Street, London SW1Y 4UJ (Tel: 01 930 5961/839 4741). Christmas in Lapland.

Finnchalet Holidays Dunira, Comrie, Perthshire PH6 2JZ (Tel: 0764 70020). the total winter experience—cross-country skiing, snowmobile safaris, reindeer round-ups and ice-fishing.

Canterbury Travel 248 Streatfield Road, Kenton, Harrow, Middx HA3 9BY (Tel: 01 206 0411). Father Christmas tours to Lapland and 'Lusosto Experience' where if you feel really adventurous and hearty you can stay in a Lapp tepee.

GREECE

Piste cred: 6.
Ski season: December to April.

The highest mountain in Greece is Mount Olympus (2,917 m) although this is only used by hardy ski-tourers as there is no uphill lift transport. The oldest resort is on Mount Vermion in the central Macedonian mountains, but the largest resort is at 1,600 m-2,000 m on Mount Parnassus, above Delphi, in central Greece. There are 12 ski lifts, two self-service restaurants, a ski school and equipment hire. The ski area has an impressive view across the blue seas from the Gulf of Corinth to the Gulf of Euboea. Skiing can be combined with visiting the archaeological sanctuary of Delphi, or a dip in the sea. Accommodation is available in the surrounding areas with hotels at Delphi, Arahova and Itea, and smaller pensions and rooms at Amfiklia, Polydrosso and Agoriani.

FURTHER INFORMATION

National Tourist Organisation of Greece 4 Conduit Street, London W1R OPJ (Tel: 01 734 5997).
Parnassos Ski Centre EOS Amsikleias, Greece (Tel: 010 30 234 22640 or 22280).

INDIA

Piste cred: 10.
Ski season: December to April.

The Himalayas is the highest mountain range in the world. India's premier resort is Gulmarg, 2,730 m, in Kashmir. The nearest airport is Srinagar which is regularly serviced by Indian Airlines from Delhi—the flight time is one hour. Jammu and Kashmir Department of Tourism runs a helicopter service to Gulmarg from Srinagar. Alternatively, you can catch a bus to Tangmarg and travel by jeep the remaining eight kilometres. Gulmarg has chair and drag lifts—the pistes are most suitable for beginners and intermediates. There are English-speaking instructors. Advanced skiers can go heli-skiing. Ski mountaineers can take a number of popular but uncrowded routes with fantastic views of the Himalayas and the Vale of Kashmir. There is also cross-country skiing in a fine conifer forest. Accommodation ranges from budget ski cabins to hotels. All sorts of food are available including Indian, European, Chinese and local Kashmiri. The other main skiing area in India is Kufri in Himachel Pradesh.

FURTHER INFORMATION

The Government of India's Tourist Office 7 Cork Street, London W1X 2AB (Tel: 01 437 3677/8).

Ski Moghuls The Airline Centre, 66a Streatham Hill, London SW2 (Tel: 01 674 9652). Ski holidays to the Himalayas.

ISRAEL

Piste cred: 5.
Ski season: December to April.

The only ski resort in Israel is on the north-eastern slopes of the Hermon range (1,600-2,100 m). The highest peak offers a stunning panoramic view of the Golan Heights, Upper Galilee, the Hulah Valley, the Qalat Nimrod Crusader Fortress, the Birket Ram Lake and the Banya Spring. The ski slopes have been compared to those found in New England—not particularly lofty, but still a challenge to intermediate skiers. Weekends can get crowded. The longest run is 2 km. Skiers can check on conditions by phoning the ski site 9 am-3 pm or Moshave Neve Ativ, the holiday village which runs the ski site (open 8.30 am-3.30 pm) throughout the day. There is a cafeteria and ski hire, and accommodation close to the ski area includes the kibbutz guest houses of Hagoshrim, Kfar Gilad and Kfar Blum, hotels in Metulla and Kiryat Shmona and the youth hostel of Tel Hai. It takes about 3 or 4 hours to drive up from Tel Aviv, but the roads are sometimes closed due to heavy snow.

FURTHER INFORMATION

Israel Government Tourist Office 18 Great Marlborough Street, London W1V 1AF (01 434 3651).

Hermon Ski Site Israel (Tel: 067 40121).

Moshav Neve Ativ 12010, MP Ramat Hagolan, Israel (Tel: 067 41185 or 46479).

Israel Ski Club POB 211, Givatayim, Israel.

JAPAN

Piste cred: 10.
Ski season: December-April.

Skiing was introduced to Japan by an Austrian called Major von Lerch, as military training at the end of the Meiji Period in 1911. There are now over 5 million skiers in Japan, which makes them one of the largest skiing populations in the world. The Japanese take their skiing very seriously and dress in smart, one-piece suits with all the latest equipment. Japan has a good snow record and hundreds of ski areas but these do get very crowded at weekends, Christmas and New Year. The best snow is usually between early January and March. You should book everything in advance, including seats for trains and buses. Rental ski equipment is easy to obtain but *remember* that the Japanese have very small feet so they may not have boots in your size!

Yamagata is one of the most popular skiing areas. Zao, one of its resorts, has 12 slopes and 8 courses, with several lifts, cables and gondolas. There is a 'snow monster' course through trees, which have been fantastically distorted by snow. There is night skiing until 9 pm. The resort is 45 minutes by bus from Yamagata station. Zao Bodaira is popular with families, schools and cross-country skiers. There is also downhill through 'snow monster' trees. The season is December to April with a ski festival in April. The resort is 50 minutes by bus from Kaminoyama Station. Tengendai Ski Resort is 50 minutes by bus from Yonezawa station. This is a downhill resort with good powder and a course through natural 'snow art', the famous 'toothbrush' trees.

Spring and summer skiing (April to July) is available at Gassan which is two hours by bus from Yamagata station. Hakuba is 220 km from Tokyo on the main island of Honshu. It is well-known for its *onsen* (hot springs) as well as for powder snow and challenging skiing. The resort comprises old wooden farmhouses, ski lodges, *minshuku* (family-run guest houses) and lots of rice paddies. Naeba (1,789 m) is the largest resort on Honshu and two hours by *shinkansen* (bullet train) and bus from Tokyo.

The French tour operators, Club Méditerranée, who organise fully comprehensive holidays, have opened up a village in Japan. This is Sahoro, on the northern island of Hokkaido, 140 km from Sapporo. The resort is at 400 m with the highest skiing at 1,100 m. There are 15 pistes lined with tall white birch trees.

FURTHER INFORMATION

The Japan National Tourist Organisation, 167 Regent Street, London W1 (Tel: 01 734 9638/9).
Club Méditerranée SA, 106/110 Brompton Road, London SW3 1JJ (Tel: 01 581 1161).

KOREA

Piste cred: 7.
Ski season: December to March.

There are five Korean ski areas all between 40 minutes and three hours from Seoul. Equipment and instruction is available at all the resorts. Chonmasan Family ski resort (812 m) is only 40 minutes' drive from Seoul and has four slopes and six lifts. The Chonmasan Lodge has a choice of Korean-style Ondol rooms or bunk beds, various restaurants, a cocktail bar and a sauna. Yongin Leisure ski resort is 50 minutes' drive from Seoul. Night skiing is available. There is a restaurant serving Korean and Western meals, a cafeteria and the Yongin Mountain Hotel. Alps ski resort is just north of Mt Soraksan National Park. The resort is 4½ hours' drive from Seoul or an hour's bus ride from Sokch'o airport. There is a 1,500 m downhill course, five other slopes and three chairlifts. Night skiing is available.

Hotel rooms are available but for those who prefer a more rustic experience, there are cabins with bunk beds and a fireplace. Mt Soraksan and several beaches are close by. Bears Town resort is 40 minutes' drive from Seoul, near the historical monument Kwangnung (a royal tomb) and an arboretum. It has four slopes, and five lifts. The longest slope is 2,500 m. Yongpyeong (Dragon Valley) resort has Korea's best average annual snowfall, ten slopes and 12 lifts. Yongpyeong (750 m) is set on the slopes of Mt Palwangsan (1,458 m) near the Taegwallyong Pass. It is about 3½ hours' drive from Seoul. Night skiing is available; also bowling alley, restaurants, ski shop, disco and billiards room. The Dragon Valley Hotel has an indoor swimming pool, sauna and health clubs. Alternatively, accommodation is available in the Yongpyeong Hostel. The Yongpyeong Snow Sculpture Contest is a big event in Korea where the contestants have to use ladders to climb up and chisel two-story high snowballs into works of art. They also have a Snow Festival with fireworks, torch-lit skiing and other festivities.

FURTHER INFORMATION

Korean National Tourism Corporation 2nd Floor, Vogue House, 1 Hanover Square, London W1R 9RD (Tel: 01 409 2100).
Or the following numbers in Korea:
Alps (Tel: 02 546 6962).
Bears Town (Tel: 02 546 7210).
Chonmasan (Tel: 02 744 6020).
Yongin (Tel: 02 744 2001).
Dragon Valley/Yongpyeong (Tel: 02 548 2251).

MOROCCO

Piste cred: 6.
Ski season: December to May/June.

The highest mountain in Morocco is Toubkal, 4,165 m. The Atlas mountains stretch 700 km from Agadir and the Atlantic shore towards the north. There is a smaller range in the north of Morocco called the Rif which separates the Mediterranean coast from the Gharb plains and the Taza beach.

Most of the ski resorts are in the Atlas mountains. They have a surprisingly long season from December to May or June. The ski resort of Michlifen is situated in an area of cedar forest, less than one hour from Fes and Meknes. The crater of Michlifen is a wide natural ampitheatre. There are four pistes (up to 215 m in length), one lift and a beginners' lift. Azrou is a village on the foothills of the middle Atlas mountains. It has easy access (15 km or 20 km) to two small ski stations in the Habri and Hebri mountains.

The Oukaïmeden is in the high Atlas, at 2,600 m, near the Toubkal summit, 75 km from Marrackech. Although this is a high resort, altitude sickness should not be a problem—2,600 m in Morocco is not like 2,600 m in the French Savoie region (vegetation generally stops at 1,600 m in Europe, while it is still thriving at 2,000 m in the Atlas.) This resort has the highest ski-lift in Africa with a length of 1,600 m and an inclination of 750 m. There are seven other ski-lifts ranging from 200 m to 800 m in length. There are many other areas in the Atlas mountains that do not have facilities or ski-lifts but where you can go ski touring.

FURTHER INFORMATION

The Moroccan National Tourist Office 174 Regent Street, London W1R 6HB (Tel: 01 437 0073).

NEW ZEALAND

Piste cred: 9
Ski season: May to November.

The skiing in New Zealand is in the Southern Lakes—the main season is from July to October. Most of the skiers are locals rather than tourists and many of the ski areas can only be reached by air. Like Canada, heli-skiing is popular as there are not many lifts. No one stays at the ski areas, or 'skifields' as they call them in New Zealand. Instead skiers base themselves either at Queenstown or Wanaka.

Queenstown is halfway between two skifields—Coronet Peak and The Remarkables. In Queenstown there is opportunity for plenty of other activities such as white-water rafting, golf, horse-trekking, jet boating on the Shotover River, shopping, flightseeing and sightseeing. Coronet Peak was New Zealand's first international ski resort and has a reputation for good skiing and powder. The Remarkables is just across the valley and offers easier slopes for beginners and low intermediates. The upper slopes are more challenging and have a spectacular view across Lake Wakatipu and Queenstown itself. Heli-skiing is also available here or you can take the heli-taxi across to Coronet Peak. Both resorts come under the same lift pass so you can ski one in the morning and the other in the afternoon.

Wanaka is a smaller town, just over an hour's drive away from Queenstown. It has access to two ski fields. Treble Cone is a very scenic skifield with a fantastic view over Lake Wanaka. It is best known for expert skiing but the management have worked hard over the last couple of years to increase the amount of beginner and intermediate skiing. Heli-lifts to the summit of Treble Cone are available. Cardrona is half way between Wanaka and Queenstown, and is known as a family field, with gently rolling terrain as well as steeper slopes. Mount Cook ski region is a couple of hours' drive to the north. Guided helicopter tours of the glaciers are available with the Alpines Guides company. They have rights to 1,500 square kilometres of terrain, incorporating over 60 runs, so you can ski here for days and never do the same run twice. The highest mountain in New Zealand is Mt Hutt (2,743 m) which is an hour from Christchurch. The

215

skiing here is mainly intermediate and they have the longest ski season in the country—May to November.

FURTHER INFORMATION

New Zealand Tourist Board The Haymarket, London SW1Y 4TQ (Tel: 01 930 8422).
The Skiing Kiwis PO Box 6666, Wellesley Street, Auckland 1, New Zealand (They have a London phone number: 01 930 8422). Organise skiing holidays in the Southern Lakes.

PERU

Piste cred: 10.
Ski season: June to August.

When it comes to skiing, Peru is really for the tough guys and the trekking brigade. There are no organised ski resorts but the Cordillera Blanca mountains (7,000 m) are guaranteed to have snow and the Peruvians have held ski competitions here during the last two or three years. The first week in June is known as the Semana del Andinismo in Huaraz, the heart of the Peruvian Andes. Events include photographic exhibitions, conferences, hang-gliding, climbing demonstrations and high-mountain skiing. It is the official start of the walking and climbing season in the Cordillera Blanca and Himalayan mountains. The main attraction is the national slalom ski competition which takes place at the Glacier Pampa-Rahu which means 'snow-capped mountain of the plain'. This provides the highest natural run in the world (5,200 m). If you want to ski, you have to climb up the glacier for three hours–not for the faint-hearted. As the skiing is so high up you will need to be very fit. The Austrian team ski there in the summer for high-altitude training.

There are no hotels or tourist facilities up on the glaciers—skiers stay down in the valleys. An annual ski event/holiday called Adventure takes place in July and involves skiing down the glacier. It mainly attracts the locals but there are also a few tourists, particularly the Germans and French.

FURTHER INFORMATION

Peruvian Tourist Board 1st Floor, 10 Grosvenor Gardens, London SW1W OBD (Tel: 01 824 8693).
Omni Plus Ltd 20A Chalcot Square, NW1 8YA (Tel: 01 722 0308). Organise holidays in Peru.

Ski Alternatives

This book has been aimed at the alpine skier. But as it is all about discovery, I have included some examples of what the French call winter *nouvelles sensations*. This refers to new trends of getting down the mountain, such as floating through the powder on brightly coloured snowboards/monoskis, or taking to the skies like exotic birds of prey attached to a parachute or hang-glider. There are now no bounds to where skiers can go—they are hitching helicopter rides to the highest peaks, or even using parachute-type canopies as their personal uphill ski-tows. Speed-freaks are hurtling down chutes of ice on bits of steel, and freestylers are doing somersaults in the air and jumping over giant mogul fields. I have also included information on the more traditional types of skiing, cross-country, telemark and touring, as these are currently undergoing a big revival and are all an excellent way to find undiscovered terrain. I hope you find something that takes your fancy.

BOBSLEDDING

There are three types of bobsledding—bobbing, luge and Cresta. The bob looks like a giant metal bullet. It is made of compact steel and fibreglass and has basic suspension, brakes and steering. There are two or four-rider sleds which at full speed can screech down the chute at about 120 kilometres per hour. Crash helmets are obligatory. It may be a good idea to take

217

out life insurance before you do this one, as it has a higher fatality rate than any other Olympic sport.

If you are the sort of person who loves big dippers and giant water chutes, the luge might appeal. Whoever rides the luge would have to be fairly brave (or mad) though, as you are clad in a synthetic suit and flung feet-first down an icy chute at speeds of up to 135 kilometres per hour. A luge weighs about 50lb and has upturned runners. 'Joyriders' lie on their backs, fully reclined, with their feet projecting past the runners, unable to see where they are going. There are bars either side of the seating shell to hang on to. The luge is steered by a combination of shoulder pressure or by a stronger pressure of the legs on the runners. Steering the luge is a very precise skill, that takes years to master. There are two types of luge tracks. The *kunstbahn* is an artificial track with high-banked corners and the *naturobahn* (growing in popularity) is a natural track, usually a mountain road.

'The ultimate laxative' is how a Boston stockbroker described the Cresta. And boy, you would have to be terribly constipated to contemplate this one! It is a chauvinistic little set-up—men only. Women are only allowed to ride once a year, in an end of season unofficial race. And then only if you are 'lucky' enough to be the wife or girlfriend of one of the members. There is only one Cresta run in the world and that is in the Engandine valley, between the exclusive, chi-chi Swiss resorts of St Moritz and Celerina. It is run by Lt-Col Digby Willoughby, late of the Gurkhas, whom sports writer Ian Wooldridge described as 'the most autocratic administrator of any sports venue in the world'. If your face, wallet, or stripey shirt do not fit, you will not be given a ride. And maybe it is better if you are not. For the Cresta is even more terrifying than the luge, because this time you are going down the icy chute head-first.

The élite few who try the Cresta run are kitted out in crash helmet, metal-backed gloves and boots with teeth in the toe caps. Their elbows are protected by steel plates and there are leather bindings on the knees. This protective gear is not just for show. To reduce speed, the rider has to ram those toe-cap teeth into the ice. Poor old Errol Flynn dug his in all the way to achieve the slowest descent of the Cresta ever recorded. The elbow plates are protection against the Cresta Kiss—a rather gruesome experience when the skin gets ripped off by colliding with the ice walls.

As a beginner you will not be subjected to the whole run, but will start below the Clubhouse. You will be ordered 'into the Box'—a rectangle of ice, defined by two purple lines. Inside is your steed—a 60lb slab of steel. Beginners lie down head-first on their tummy and cling on to the bars at the side. The *arbeiter* (or worker) stands at the side of you with a foot on the runners to stop you charging off. When he lets go, you're off for what will probably be the most terrifying experience of your life. The most dreaded corner is the Shuttlecock. But at least, if all goes wrong, and you are flung off at this point, you will have the privilege of automatically becoming a member of the Shuttlecock Club and wearing their Club Tie. Sporting chaps, aren't they?

FURTHER INFORMATION

British Bobsleigh Association 50 Sullivan Road, London SW6 3DX (Tel: 01 351 5120).

Powder Byrne 50 Lombard Road, London SW11 3SU (Tel: 01 223 0601). Powder Byrne have joined forces with the International Bobsleigh School at St Moritz (not to be confused with the Cresta) to offer special bobsleigh courses. You will do up to six runs a day, and your progress will be videoed (remember to smile—you are supposed to be enjoying it). You need your own crash helmet with chin protection. There are cheaper rates for the under 26s.

Great Britain Luge Association Contact: Chris Dyasson (Tel: 0223 358438 eves/ 0223 350800 day). This is the governing body of the luge. Chris Dyasson runs beginners' courses in Austria. Experienced lugers are trained abroad and can join regular racing sessions.

St Moritz Tobogganing Club Contact the London Secretary Lady Brabazon (Tel: 01 736 3705).

CROSS-COUNTRY SKIING

Cross-country, or 'Nordic' skiing, as it is often called, is the oldest and most traditional form of skiing. It dates back over four thousand years to when it was used in Scandinavia and Russia as a form of transport during the long snowbound winters. Ever since alpine skiing took off, the majority of skiers have dismissed cross-country as just a tame sport for the elderly and the dowdy back-to-nature-brigade. This image is now changing, and cross-country skiing is being marketed as a trendy, athletic sport, and starting to attract young sporty skiers in bright lycra leggings and vibrant clothes.

Cross-country skiing is easier to learn than alpine skiing and can be practised by people of any age or fitness level. It is one of the best types of exercise as it is low impact, has a minimal risk of injury, and is excellent for increasing cardiovascular efficiency. Weight-watchers may be interested to know that it can burn up 400-700 calories per hour. The health benefits are very similar to jogging but there is less impact on the legs.

Cross-country skiing, like jogging, gives a tremendous sense of freedom. It can be done anywhere, through snowy fields, across frozen lakes, or along forest trails. The cross-country skier can go up, down, or just amble along on the flat. One of the main joys is not being reliant on lifts—it is the perfect sport for getting away from it all. In some countries, such as Sweden, it is possible to travel for miles and miles without encountering another skier. One stressed British businessman told me that it was the first time in years that he could actually 'hear' himself think.

There are two main types of cross-country skiing: touring and track. Touring is the authentic Nordic skiing, that is still practised in Scandinavia, and is similar to hiking or backpacking on skis. This is either done along marked (but unprepared) trails, or off the trails. These tours are usually made in groups, and can last several days, staying overnight in rustic huts.

Track skiing is more usual in the Alps. Here, most cross-country skiing is on trails which have been specially prepared and cut to provide track-marks for the skis. These trails are usually very picturesque, down in the valleys through the trees. Skating is a fast version of the sport done on flat, packed snow.

Cross-country skiing is cheaper than alpine skiing. There is no need to buy a lift pass and the equipment costs less. Cross-country skis are longer and thinner than alpine skis. Track skis should be lightweight with a minimum sidecut (ie they should be nearly the same width the entire length of the ski). Cross-country touring skis are slightly wider with more sidecut (ie top and bottom should be wider than the middle) in order to give more stability in the rougher terrain. Ski poles are longer than for alpine skiing and should come up the armpit when the pole is in the snow. Anyone who has suffered bruised shins or crushed toes from clumpy alpine boots will appreciate how lightweight cross-country boots are. They look like training shoes or football boots. Only the toe is attached to the binding, so that the heel can lift up for the kick-glide movement which propels the skier along. For freedom of movement and so as not to overheat, it is best to wear several layers of lightweight clothing rather than one bulky Michelin-style item.

It is easiest to learn cross-country skiing on prepared tracks. Many resorts have special nursery areas that are very flat. Cross-country tracks are colour-graded like alpine pistes, according to their difficulty. It is worth taking a few lessons to get started. The basics of cross-country skiing are similar to walking. The simplest move, called the 'diagonal stride' is a gliding motion. The skier strides the left leg and ski forwards, at the same time pushing with the right pole, and vice versa. The aim is to get the maximum glide. Arm and leg movements should be fluid. The skis stay in a parallel position in the tracks. To go uphill the cross-country skier uses the herringbone technique or side-stepping (both used in alpine skiing). To go downhill the alpine snowplough can be used, although this is more difficult on cross-country skis. Beginners will spend most of the time on the flat. Also see Telemarking on page 222.

FURTHER INFORMATION

Highland Guides Nordic Ski Centre Ski Road, Aviemore, Scotland, PH22 1QH (Tel: 0479 810729). Runs courses in cross-country skiing and telemarking. Weekend courses available. 40 km of waymarked ski trails and prepared tracks in the Aviemore hills.

Ski Club of Great Britain 118 Eaton Square, SW1W 9AF (Tel: 01 245 1033). The Ski Club has lots of information (for members) on touring and cross-country, and run special holidays and tours for all standards at low rates.

British Ski Federation Brocades House, Pyrford, West Byfleet, Surrey KT14 6RA (Tel: 0932 336488). For information on competitive cross-country skiing.

London Region Nordic Ski Club c/o Phil Jackson, 173 Nursery Road, Sunbury-on-Thames, Middlesex (Tel: 09327 89849—this is a home phone number so please ring at reasonable hours). The club has information packs and puts enthusiasts in touch with each other. They also have information on resorts and hotels in Scotland.

Waymark Holidays 295 Lillie Rd, London SW6 (Tel: 01 385 5015). Organise cross-country holidays in the Alps, Norway and Finnish Lapland, Canada and Czechoslovakia.

Across-Country Skiing Holidays Inntravel, Hovingham, York YO6 4JZ (Tel: 065 382741). Organise cross-country holidays in Switzerland and France.

HANG-GLIDING

The best way to avoid the lift queues and crowded slopes is to take to the air. Hang-gliding, or 'delta' as it is called in France, is the nearest you will get to a bird's-eye view of a ski resort. The hang-glider takes off on skis, suspended in a metal harness from a wing-like 'sail'. Normally, he or she just dangles there, although it can be done in a sitting position. The hang-glider is steered by a control frame and a shift of weight. The basic principle is that if you lean to the right the hang-glider will turn right; lean back and it will soar higher, lean forward and it should start to descend. It is more complicated than paragliding (see page 224) and if you are going to take it up properly you will need to learn about thermals to maintain the height and increase the flight distance.

On a ski holiday, hang-gliding is more of a joy-ride. It is used as a way of getting *down* the mountain. Novices are not allowed to hang-glide on their own, but must be accompanied by a qualified pilot. A first flight will only take 10-15 minutes. In a ski resort, hang-gliders usually take off on skis as this facilitates the take-off and landing. A skilled pilot will slow the hang-glider down until it is nearly stationary so landing is like 'stepping off a bar stool'. If you get hooked, there are about 20 schools in the UK. A good second-hand glider costs from £500 and a new one from £1,000 to £2,000.

FURTHER INFORMATION

British Hang-Gliding Association Cranfield Airfield, Cranfield, Bedfordshire MK43 OYR (Tel: 0234 751688). They have details of the registered schools in this country.

HELI-SKIING

Heli-skiing is the ultimate way to ski undiscovered slopes and virgin snow. It opens up a world of unlimited off-piste, completely cut off from all commercialism. It is the most exhilarating, and perhaps terrifying, experience I have ever had. The helicopter dropped us off, James-Bond style, at the top of a mountain. It was a quiet and lonely moment when our helicopter flew off into the distance, and all contact with the rest of the world was cut off. There was now no going back, no gondola to take us down if we chickened out.

We were warned before we went up that heli-skiing is only for expert, experienced skiers. It would be unfair of a 'gutsy' intermediate to 'give it a go' as this could put the rest of the group at risk. It is important to be able to ski well in *all* conditions. Although there may be virgin powder fields from top to bottom, there could equally well be 3,000 m of heavy crud. Most heli-skiing is done in the spring when there is usually powder at the top, crud half-way down, and spring snow at the bottom. Although heli-skiing companies pick the sunniest, clearest days, the weather in the mountains can change very quickly and it is impossible to predict accurately the snow conditions. A good guide is essential. This has to be a fully qualified mountain guide rather than just an instructor. Most guides are equipped with a two-way radio, a rope and a pick-axe (just in case some poor unfortunate skier happens to fall down a glacier or crevasse).

If you decide to go heli-skiing, you need to be physically fit (see page 230, Fitness, Intermediate Plateau). A couple of hours' skiing through heavy crud is enough to exhaust the strongest muscles. It may take half or even a whole day to get down the mountain and there is no cosy little bar to stop off for liquid refreshment. This is skiing for the tough guys and it should be taken seriously.

Mental attitude is also very important. You *must* feel confident. If you are likely to throw a wobbly the minute that helicopter disappears out of sight, do not go! You need to trust the ski guide and your own ability and be skilled enough to do exactly what you are told to do. Even if you are a brilliant skier, you must also have the discipline not to charge ahead. At a tricky section, we were ordered to ski ten metres apart, to do only one turn and *not to fall*. We were not even allowed to talk—the only thing we seemed to be allowed to do was breathe, and I am not even sure I was doing that!

The mountain guide had instructed us what to do in case of an avalanche. The idea is to traverse downhill out of the way of the oncoming avalanche. If this fails, skis and poles should be abandoned, and you should try and swim upwards doing the breaststroke. At first this sounded like a real doom and gloom story, but it is actually no more pessimistic than being given emergency instructions on an airplane. In theory, heli-skiing is no more dangerous than normal skiing off-piste. In practice this is not the case, as you are much more isolated. In normal off-piste skiing the pistes are not far away if a problem arises, but when you are heli-skiing you are stuck in the middle of nowhere and totally reliant on the guide's and your own ability. As with any off-piste skiing, it is a good idea to wear a bleeper that can be picked up by the rescue team in case of an avalanche.

Heli-skiing is paid for by the lift and can cost anything from £25 upwards. It can also be paid for by vertical footage. There are several specialist companies (see below).

As long as it is approached sensibly, and the risks are understood, heli-skiing is a remarkable experience. It opens up a whole new world of skiing. Human beings can conquer any mountain that they desire. The thrill of skiing down virgin slopes in brilliant sunshine is unrivalled. I have never experienced anything that gives such an amazing sense of freedom. One of the best places to go heli-skiing is in the Canadian Rockies as there is such vast potential. Heli-skiing is also available in Europe although it is banned in some countries such as France.

FURTHER INFORMATION

Ski Venture Gwalia House, Tresaith, Cardigan, Dyfed SA43 2JL, Wales (Tel: 0239 810361). This company organises heli-skiing in the States and Europe. They also offer holidays based around all sorts of *nouvelles sensations* such as paragliding, hang-gliding, snowboarding, mono-ski and even snow-mobiling.

Canadian Mountain Holidays, Powder Skiing in North America Ltd, David & Tessa Brooksbank, 61 Doneraile Street, London SW6 6EW (Tel: 01 736 8191). Accommodation in remote lodges where the heli-skiing actually takes place. Trips include 100,000 vertical feet (usually six to eight lifts a day). Available in eight areas in the Canadian Rockies.

Ski Scott Dunn 17 Aynhoe Rd, London W14 OQA (Tel: 01 602 8029).Six-day powder courses with Swiss mountain guide including heli-skiing from 3,048 m. Takes place in Champéry, Portes du Soleil. The week includes two heli-lifts.

Powder Byrne 50 Lombard Road, London SW11 3SU (Tel: 01 223 0601). Powder courses including heli-skiing. Based in Grindelwald in the Jungfrau region, Switzerland.

MONO-SKIING

Mono-skiing was one of the original *nouvelles sensations* pioneered by the French. It was seen as a fun, gimmicky alternative to skiing, brilliant for off-piste, but it never really took off in other countries. There are still some loyal French mono-skiers, but it has now been greatly outshadowed by snowboarding (see page 225). This is probably because snowboarding has captured a more fun-loving image, while good skiers complain mono-skiing mucks up their skiing technique.

A mono-ski is about three times the width of a normal ski. The mono-skier wears ordinary ski boots which are clipped into bindings close together in a parallel position to the ski. Normal ski poles will do, but it is better to use ones that are 5-10 cm longer as the arms need to be in a higher and wider position for balancing.

The first thing to learn is how to propel yourself along on the flat. It is much too strenuous to just pole along, so you should take one foot out of the binding and push yourself along like on a skateboarder. *Never* do this on a slope or the ski will slide away and you will end up in a nasty heap at the bottom. As a beginner it is much easier to use a chair-lift rather than a poma or T-bar. Pay particular attention when getting on to a poma or you could end up being hoisted several feet in the air doing full pirouettes! The trick is to keep your knees open and your arms out with poles poised to balance. T-bars are easier, as long as you have an understanding travelling companion.

One of the reasons that mono-skiing has been so derided is that there is no set style. It is up to the individual to find the most effective and comfortable technique. It is a big advantage, if not an imperative, to know how to ski. But once you have adjusted to having your two legs almost glued together, it is actually easier and much less hard work off the pistes. As the ski surface is so broad it is much more buoyant in deep snow. In mono-skiing you only have two edges to worry about rather than four. This avoids the pain and embarrassment of two skis shooting off in opposite directions in deep snow. Whereas it can be difficult, and even dangerous, to ski off-piste in heavy crud or slush, on a mono-ski this is not a problem.

The first time you try mono-skiing you should start by just rocking your knees from side to side and experimenting with your position until you have a well-balanced mid-stance. Be prepared to have a lot of wipe-outs. An all-in-one ski suit is not just for posing—it stops you getting snow down your midriff. Do not worry about losing the ski as it has mini-brakes and is attached by a safety strap to one leg, but do be careful that the ski does not bounce back and whack you on the head. A mono-ski turn is initiated by the inside upper edge (the opposite of correct ski technique). When traversing, the upper body should be twisted even further round than in skiing. A common mistake for beginners is to chicken out of skiing into the fall line. This can result in a rather ungainly 360° pirouette! Mono-skiing can be done in all sorts of snow conditions, both on and off the piste, but like snowboarding it is at its best in powder when that sensation of 'floating' is pure heaven.

PARAGLIDING

One of the trendiest and most adventurous *nouvelles sensations* is paragliding, or *parapente* as it is called in France. In a ski resort this usually involves taking off into the air James-Bond style on skis and gliding down the mountain attached to a brightly coloured canopy. The equipment only weighs about 15-20lbs (a hang-glider weighs about 1,000lbs) so it can easily be packed away into the skier's ruck-sack. The paraglider is strapped into a harness, with straps around the chest and legs. Once in the air, the steering is simple. There are two brake lines attached to the rear corner of the canopy. The idea is that if you pull on the left, you will turn to the left, and vice versa. To slow down you just pull gently on both lines. The brake lines are normally at about ear-level. To land you hold the brake lines and draw your hands down beside your body—as if you were standing to attention. Once you have landed on the snow, the canopy should collapse in a heap behind you, so you can roll it up and start all over again.

Many ski resorts are now offering paragliding lessons or joy-rides with a pilot. The British company Mountains Dynamic organises special courses in France. In these courses, beginners start off just gliding 6-15 m above a gentle nursery slope and gradually progress onto longer and higher flights.

FURTHER INFORMATION

British Association of Parasending Clubs 18 Talbot Lane, Leicester, LE1 4LR (Tel: 0533 530318).

Mountains Dynamic Travel Ltd 28 Station Road, Beccles, Suffolk, NR34 9QJ (Tel: 0502 717768). Specialises in ski paragliding in the winter and paragliding holidays in the summer. All courses are held in the mountains.

SNOWBOARDING

Snowboarding is like skateboarding or surfing on the snow and was originally invented in the 1960s by American beach bums who wanted something to play around with in the winter. But it is only recently that the sport has really caught on and become the newest, coolest alternative to skiing. Snowboarding is more than just a sport—it is a modern cult that appeals to the young and daring. Manufacturers have cashed in on the youthful element of this sport and brought out all sorts of crazy, colourful clothing, face-paints and even 'après-surf' wear. There are now special snowboarding holidays and even an 'in'-crowd 'shredspeak' language.

Skiing and snowboarding are both done in the snow, but that is about all they have in common. Snowboarding is done on a wide board, about three times the width of a normal ski, and up to two metres in length. You stand diagonally on the board, in the position of a skateboarder or surfer, using your hands rather than poles to balance with. Good skiers are often put off trying snowboarding as they know they will have to make a fool of themselves for a few hours. Unfortunately, being able to ski is of no advantage—it is the skateboarders and surfers who will find it easier. Although at first it feels a very awkward sport, in the long run it is easier than skiing as both your legs are attached to the same surface—there are fewer edges to get caught. Novice snowboarders with just a few weeks of experience may well be able to tackle steeper terrain than skiers with years of experience. Snowboarding is at its best in powder snow, when you feel as though you are literally surfing on air. But modern design has enabled them also to be successfully used on the pistes, on mogul fields or even on ice.

Most resorts will now hire snowboards. It is best to learn on a short board, but do not buy one as you will quickly outgrow it. Soft bindings are the most common. These look like a shell of a ski boot and do not release. Ordinary ski boots can be used, although many snowboarders prefer to use a more lightweight, but warm and waterproof boot. 'Regular' riders are those who prefer to lead with their left foot, while those leading with the right are riding 'goofy'.

Do not be afraid to fall, or 'bail' as a snowboarder would say. Beginners will find they get very bruised knees and bottoms, although serious injuries are rare. Knee-pads are a good idea. The best place to learn is in light powder. Choose a nice, gentle slope with a long flat run-out at the end. Most of your weight should be on the front leg, with the back leg steering. A common mistake for beginners is to stiffen the back leg—try to keep both legs bent and your arms in front of you. It will feel a little bit as though you are moving like a crab. To begin with, just concentrate on tracing a simple, straight line, as first-time skiers do on the piste. A snowboard works like a pair of skis—edging will make it curve. Assuming that you are 'regular' rather than 'goofy', to turn to the left you rotate your upper body to the left and downhill. At the same time you need to unweight, as in skiing. The downhill arm should always be extended and open. As the board turns, transfer your weight from toes to heels to roll the board onto its back edge. At this point, you should be leaning slightly into the hill.

One of the main hurdles for the beginner is having the courage to head down the 'fall line' (ie straight down the mountain). At first, this makes you feel totally out of control, but with a little more speed, the turns actually become easier. Honest. Also if you avoid going down the fall line, you will end up stuck at one side of the piste, and unable to turn and looking very uncool. Nearly everyone is better at turning on one side than the other, although this should even out with practice.

At the beginning of 1989, there were already over 250,000 snowboarders. Not everyone is so enthusiastic. Some more old-fashioned ski resorts resent the young, loud, image of the sport and view the snowboarders as some sort of piste pests. Admittedly, it is both terrifying and hazardous for a skier to come face-to-face with an out-of-control novice snowboarder. It is safer and more considerate for the virgin snowboarder to take the first few tumbles off the pistes. Perhaps one day we will see special snowboarders' nursery slopes.

One of the biggest hurdles for the snowboarder is getting on and off the lifts. Most lift-men are considerate enough to slow down the chairs when they see a snowboarder trying to get on, although you will find the odd vindictive one who speeds everything up as soon as he sees you. The best way to get onto a chair-lift is to unclip the back boot so you can push with one foot like a skateboarder. It is very much harder to use a drag-lift.

At competitive level, snowboarders ride over 60 mph. One of the most exciting sides of snowboarding is 'riding the half-pipe'. This is a spin-off from skateboarding, where huge plywood semi-circular ramps are used. For the snowboard half-pipe, the snow is dug into a big curved bowl, 100 m or longer and up to 15 m wide. The walls are several metres high—the idea is to ride on them like frozen waves. Competitors are judged on how high they can fly off them. There are all sorts of special jumps you can do, such as the 'nuclear air'—a contortionist trick which involves grabbing the front of the heel edge cross-handed with your rear hand. Some resorts that are keen on snowboarding are building half-pipes (there is even one planned in Voss, Norway).

Most people who try snowboarding get hooked. The initial few days are hard, but if you persevere, the sensation of floating through the powder gives an unrivalled feeling of freedom.

FURTHER INFORMATION

The Scottish Association for Snowboarding (not just for Scotland!) c/o Marywell Gas, Stonehaven Road, Aberdeen, AB1 4LQ (Tel: 0224 780209 or 867528).

Snowboard Camps: The snowboard camp is an American concept. The British Ski company, Just Ski, are organising special weeks in Serre Chevalier and other resorts. All standards are welcome. Further details from Just Ski, Travel House, Suffolk Rd, Lowestoft, Suffolk NR32 1DZ (Tel: 0502 589187).

TELEMARKING

Telemarking is the most graceful and elegant form of skiing. It is a Nordic technique that developed in a Norwegian town called Telemark. It started off as a way that cross-country skiers could turn and control their speed when skiing downhill. It is now considered almost an art form and has become very popular in the United States where they even hold telemark slalom races.

Telemarking is a real test of balance and concentration. The telemark skier uses heavy-duty nordic equipment. The boots look like leather walking boots with an extended toe. These are connected to the ski with a small clip at the toes. The heels are free to lift. This gives the skier much more freedom of movement than conventional skis although it does require a bit of getting used to. It will at first feel very precarious. It is the telemark turn that gives this style of skiing its name. This used to be the only way skiers could turn, until ski bindings were invented to keep the heel glued to the ski and so give more stability and power. The telemark turn involves sliding the outside ski forward and dropping the knee gallantly to the snow. You need a more even weight distribution than in alpine skiing. The idea is that you edge both the skis and have at least 30-40 per cent of your weight on the inside (uphill) ski. Performed correctly, this gives a lot of stability as the skis are acting as one mega-ski about three metres in length.

Unless you have exceptionally good balance and co-ordination, expect to take a lot of nose-dives when learning this turn. Once accomplished, it is a wonderfully fluid and relaxing form of skiing. It should also help your alpine skiing by improving your balance.

Traditionally telemark skiing is used off-piste as a way of going downhill when touring. The idea is to escape from the hassle of lifts. In Nordic countries such as Norway, the terrain is not very steep, so a special wax is sufficient for going uphill. In the Alps, you will probably need to use skins. The new commercial trend of telemarking, as practised in the States, is on the pistes, with the use of ski lifts. The purists object to what they feel is a plagiarism of their sport. American telemarkers are reinforcing the heels of traditional boots with bits of heavier material chopped off from conventional downhill boots. This enables them to telemark at a faster speed. But it somehow destroys the point of this beautifully old-fashioned way of skiing.

FURTHER INFORMATION

Highland Guides Nordic Ski Centre Ski Road, Aviemore, Scotland PH22 1QH (Tel: 0479 810729). Organises special telemark courses in the Scottish Highlands.

TOURING

Also known as ski mountaineering, ski touring appeals to the intrepid adventurer. This is the oldest and purist form of alpine skiing, and has remained essentially unchanged since the beginning of the century—although the 'skins' fitted to skis for grip are no longer made from seal skins. Ski touring gives the skier a tremendous sense of freedom as it is not reliant on ski lifts. It enables the fit and hardy to trek up to the highest peaks and ski down all sorts of virgin slopes. At its most basic level, there are day tours, involving just a few hours' climbing. But to really escape off the beaten track, skiers set off on longer tours, staying overnight in rustic huts. Most people go touring in groups, which encourages a great sense of comradeship and mutual trust. The skiers usually set off at the crack of dawn or even earlier, to enable them to 'skin' up to the top and ski down again before lunchtime. The afternoons are much more dangerous for avalanches so they are usually spent in the huts, eating, sleeping, or discussing the morning's activity.

Ski touring need not be a very high altitude sport, and in resorts like Kitzbühel in Austria, it can safely be done below the treeline. But the skiers who really want to get away from it all tour up to the higher mountains. Mont Blanc in France is a very popular high-altitude destination for ski tourers. The Haute Route is a famous route between Chamonix in France and Saas Fee in Switzerland.

Touring skis are wider, shorter and lighter than alpine skis. The skiers can 'skin' up all but the steepest ascents, with skins that are made of fabric attached to the bottoms of the skis to grip the snow. The boots are a cross between normal alpine ski boots and mountaineering boots. They need to be strong enough to support you when skiing downhill, but light enough to make the climbing process bearable. The skis have a special binding that allows the foot to lift when walking uphill, but which can also lock the foot down for more stability when skiing downhill. Ski tourers usually wear old-fashioned safety straps around their ankles rather than relying on ski brakes, as it could be disastrous to lose a ski when touring.

Ski tourers need to be steady, reliable skiers, who can turn proficiently in all snow conditions (powder, spring snow, heavy crud, ice etc) and do kick turns on the steepest of slopes. They also need a good head for heights as they may find themselves climbing goatlike over narrow ridges with a sheer drop on either side. When it gets too steep or icy for the skis to grip, the tourer can take them off, attach them to the side of the rucksack, and start climbing by foot. Crampons are special spikes that are attached to the boots for ice-climbing. The ski tourer should also be taught how to use an ice-axe and a rope and harness. *Harscheisen* are snow blades that are attached to the side of the skis for traversing steep icy slopes. Tourers need to know how to use a map and compass, and learn about winter mountain weather, avalanche risks, emergency procedures, avalanche search and rescue, and severe weather navigation. It is a good idea to carry a first-aid kit.

Ski tourers must be very fit, as they often have to climb for several hours and then still be strong enough to cope with some potentially tricky descents. It also takes some time and muscle-power to get used to skiing with a heavy rucksack on your back. In high tours, altitude sickness can be a problem. Finally, as with any off-piste, you should *never* go touring without a mountain guide.

FURTHER INFORMATION

Ski Club of Great Britain 118 Eaton Square, London SW1W 9AF (Tel: 01 245 1033). Organises special tours for all standards. There are also day tours in selected European resorts.
Highland Guides, Aviemore, Inverness-shire, Scotland, PH22 1QH (Tel: 0479 810729). Organise one-day courses in the Scottish Highlands from mid-December to late May. Women only tours available.

Intermediate Plateau: Undiscovered Skills

There comes a time when most skiers stop improving. If you are quite content with how you ski, congratulations, and you'd better skip this chapter! This final chapter is for everyone who, like myself, has ever been stuck at a stage when they do not seem to be getting anywhere. A lot of people never get past the stem christie, or can only do parallels in perfect conditions. As you get older and less fit, your skiing will deteriorate. Even expert skiers and racers can get stuck on a plateau, with no signs of improvement. In theory, as long as you are enjoying yourself, it does not matter how you ski. But if skiing is, as I believe, about discovery, then it is important to get the most out of your ability. The better you are, the greater the distance and variety of terrain you can ski and the more you will be able to discover. Even if you are not a long-distance freak, a good technique will enable you to enjoy the skiing more and not feel so mentally and physically exhausted at the end of the day. I am the perfect example of someone who got stuck on this infuriating intermediate plateau. I was definitely a fair-weather skier. When it was a clear, sunny day, and the snow conditions were perfect, I could ski as well as any other holidaymaker down a well-pisted blue or red run. But as soon as the conditions changed, the visibility declined, the slopes became icy, or I was faced with an unusually tricky mogul field, and my skiing would regress to an embarrassing novice standard. It would even happen when I was not using my own skis—I just did not feel confident. Whenever I needed to ski my best, all technique seemed to disappear. So I would sit grumpily on the chair-lifts, watching the experts carve their way down the steepest slopes, and trying to drum that image into my mind. But as soon as I set off down the slopes pretending to be that blonde bombshell doing short swings down the fall line, I realised what a fool I was. I felt about as co-ordinated as an elephant on roller skates. I did not have the technique or expertise to carry it off.

I could not force my uninspired body to do what it did not know how to do. The more frustrated I got, the more my skiing declined.

To be fair to myself and other recreational skiers, we do not have much time to improve. Most of us only ski one or two weeks a year. It takes about three days before you are back to the way you were skiing on the previous holiday. Before you have had a chance to learn anything, it is time to go home again. As you are only there for such a short time, it can seem a waste of pleasurable skiing hours to take classes. But just a couple of mornings or afternoons at ski school can make a lot of difference. Make sure you do this at the beginning of the holiday, before you have had time to slip back in to your bad habits. If you do not like or understand the instructor, please do not feel embarrassed to ask the head of the school if you can change. As with any sport, it is important to be taught by somebody whom you like and can identify with. Private lessons are expensive but can be worthwhile. The cost can be minimized by sharing an instructor with a couple of like-standard friends. In theory, a good instructor should be able to teach you even if you do not speak the same language.

Some of the best skiers are the worst teachers. They can *show* you how beautifully they ski, but they cannot break this down and explain how they do it. It is no good a teacher just yelling 'Bend zee knees', 'Weight on zee downhill ski'. The body usually fails to execute what it is told to do unless it has had direct experience of why this works. Awareness is the key to improvement. You need to 'discover' how it feels to ski properly.

Although my skiing benefited from some good skiing lessons, it was only when I started reading up on the subject, got fit, took some courses, and began to understand how to ski that I started to improve. The first time I skied gracefully down a very steep, icy mogul field in foggy conditions, I felt as much elation as if I had just conquered Everest with bare hands. For the first time, I was aware of what I had been doing wrong, and my skiing went through quite a remarkable period of metamorphosis.

There were three different methods of teaching that I found particularly helpful. Ali Ross, Sarah Ferguson and Peter Lightfoot are all well-respected British instructors. You will probably find one method suits you more than the others—the trick is to choose the one that attracts you the most. These skiing gurus all run weekly courses in the Alps, and Sarah and Peter run day courses in this country on artificial slopes. If you do not want to commit yourself to a whole course, you can read up more on their techniques. *Ali Ross on Skiing* is an excellent book that really gave me the background theory that I was lacking. *Skiing Is Only a Game* by Peter Lightfoot is a fun book, full of learning games for you and your friends to play on holiday. Sarah Ferguson has just written a new book, *Skiing from the Inside*. Although these books are very useful, they are obviously not as effective as doing the courses themselves, and are best used as food for thought and inspiration.

Finally, I found that being fit really helped improve my skiing, so I have also included a section on this below. I hope you discover something new.

THE ALI ROSS CLINICS

Ali Ross only started skiing when he was 18, but is now one of the most respected ski teachers in the world. He runs special weekly clinics for intermediate and advanced skiers, in France and Switzerland in the winter and in Tignes in the summer.

'There are very few recreational skiers who ever improve', is Ali's rather dismal observation. His clinics are devised to help these people understand what creates good skiing and to leave the course with enough information to carry on improving. The students are videoed on the first day, so that they immediately have a clear idea of what they are (and are not) doing. There are two and a half hours of concentrated tuition each day, the rest of the time being designated for practice. Ali believes that his clinics only work for skiers who realise that they have a 'serious problem'. 'They are *not* for anyone who thinks they are a fantastic skier. They are for those skiers who recognise that they could do better.'

The courses are taken very seriously and will not appeal to everyone, particularly skiers with big egos. But Ali's courses are very popular and some people have been going to them for six or seven years consecutively. 90 per cent of the students are middle-aged intermediates who think that they have gone as far as they can. Ali explains that people often do not recognise they have reached a plateau until they get older, have children and their skiing starts to deteriorate. For years, they may have got away with using physical strength and mental aggression as a 'prop for poor technique'.

Ali Ross used to work for the Wengen Ski School in Switzerland, where he specialised in working with people who were afraid. 'People who were scared did not understand conventional skiing techniques.' He feels that there is very little advantage in using conventional tuition techniques, unless the student understands how the skis work and how the body operates in conjunction with them. People are usually scared because they do not know what they are doing.

Ali's clinics start by taking things right back to basics. This means learning how to stand on skis. Your feet should be hip-width apart and you should adopt an S-shaped posture. Although this feels awkward and 'hunched' at first, it is vital if your body is going to operate properly in conjunction with the skis. The next thing is to realise that the skis are not 'hostile planks' but are actually the 'tools' that will make you turn. If you examine the side of a ski you will notice that it is wider at the heel and tip and narrower in the middle. It has a natural curve. When it is moving, and pressure is applied to an edge, the ski will bend in an arc and take the skier round the corner as if he were travelling on rails. Ali advises his students to resist the urge to turn—the edged and pressured ski will turn them. The skis should carve rather than skid round the turns. Although many skiers can get away with not edging on soft easy pistes, if they are to progress, they *must* learn this basic edging principle. This induces a safe feeling of being in control and the body can then respond by angulating into a perfect skiing position.

One of the biggest hang-ups of holiday skiers is parallel turning. Ali calls this 'parallelitis'—when all the skier is interested in is looking stylish and skiing with the legs glued together. Parallel turns are actually just a natural evolution of skiing faster and effective technique. It is no use brutally trying to hoist your legs together as this is only a 'mime' of effective skiing. Ali advises his students to ski with their feet about hip-width apart. If the legs are too close together the skier will not be properly balanced. There is no way anyone (unless they were training for a job as a geisha girl!) would walk along with the feet crammed together, so why do it when skiing?

Part of the 'unlearning' process in Ali's clinics is to stop associating the words 'snow plough' or 'wedge' with beginners. These basic techniques are the foundations of good skiing, and Ali uses the wedge as a training technique for all standards of skier from beginners to competitive racers. Next time you are skiing, try going down a gentle slope in a narrow wedge position. Put one hand firmly on the side of each knee and then experiment with pressing one knee at a time progressively inwards. It should feel as though the ski is carrying you around in a curve. One side usually feels better than the other, as we are all slightly one-sided. When it is properly executed, this exercise is very effective as it makes you feel very secure and in control. This forms the basis of parallel turning. As your technique and speed increases the skis will naturally gravitate together.

FURTHER INFORMATION

Ali Ross's Clinics are bookable through **Supertravel** 22 Hans Place, London SW1 (Tel: 01 584 5060).

Ali Ross on Skiing by Ali Ross (Weidenfeld and Nicolson, £9.95)

THE COMPLETE COURSE IN BALANCE

'T he Complete Course in Balance' also aims to help the skier past that intermediate plateau. The courses are led by Sarah Ferguson, who was British Freestyle Champion in 1978 and coach to the English and British Freestyle Squads from 1981 to 1984. Sarah takes a holistic approach to skiing. 'We look at the whole person rather than just telling them what to do. Coping with emotions is very important when dealing with intermediates.' She prefers to call it 'coaching' rather than 'instruction'.

Sarah Ferguson believes that the main reason skiers get stuck on a plateau is that they have a 'lack of awareness'. There is not enough 'feedback'. 'Awareness is feeling more and thinking less.' She does not believe in the conventional method of just using verbal instructions, as this tends to make people think more. Like Ali Ross (see page 232), Sarah encourages her students to trust what the skis will do. They are also shown that their bodies can be trusted to learn and adapt.

The courses are held in Switzerland. 'Coaching' starts before the skiers even leave the country. Pre-ski audio cassettes are sent for preparation at home. The cassette includes stretching and strengthening exercises to improve posture and fitness (for the importance of fitness, see page 230). There is also an introduction to visualisation. Students are supposed to practise with the tape twice a week for the month prior to the course in order to 'reawaken the body and mind'. This visualisation is a form of pre-ski training. 'The body doesn't reallly know the difference between what is real and what is vividly imagined,' says Sarah. If you have not skied for eleven months, the mind is like 'a garden path blocked with weeds'. The visualisation exercises aim to clear this path and remind the brain what it is like to ski. 'If you are positive and use the exercises to reinforce what you already know, you will be getting free and safe ski practice.'

Sarah recommends the following mental exercise. Lie down or sit comfortably with your back straight and legs uncrossed. Imagine yourself in your ski gear. Feel comfortable and prepared to go skiing. Visualise your favourite resort. Think of the run which brings back the happiest memories. Allow yourself to feel positive and excited about going skiing. Imagine you are putting your skis on and listen to the click of the bindings. Have a look at the slope ahead and notice the texture of the snow under your feet. Push off down the mountain, listening to the sound of your skis and feeling the sun on your face and the crisp fresh air. Imagine that you are skiing fluidly down the run, breathing evenly and in rhythm with each turn. Try to sustain a positive image until you reach the bottom of the slope. If you fall, or something goes wrong, 're-edit' and start the visualisation again. The tape will talk you through the exercise. This visualisation can also be practised when you are sitting on a chair-lift or just before you are about to ski a run. Sarah calls it a 'guided daydream'. It will not be useful for beginners as it demands a recall of sensations.

The Complete Course in Balance comprises six half-days of instruction. Every evening there are stretching and relaxation exercises with the yoga teacher, Annie Sarson. In the warm-up and stretching exercises, Annie tries to get the skiers to utilise their physical strength and mobility to the best possibility advantage. By stretching out at the end of the day, post-ski stiffness is minimised. The relaxation and visualisation exercises from these classes can also be used in everyday life. The sessions with Annie aim to 'raise body awareness' and incorporate lots of breathing exercises. Sarah also teaches breathing exercises on the slopes. Breathing is of paramount importance when it comes to skiing. It is amazing how many skiers, even experts, hold their breath when they are tackling a challenging run. Sometimes I used to turn purple in the face when I reached the bottom because I had forgotten to breathe! But steady, even breathing is essential in order for the muscles to relax and the body to perform at its best. I was amazed how much my skiing started to improve once I remembered this simple point.

As well as videoing the students' skiing as a form of feedback, Sarah also uses an 'ideal image' video. This projects ideal images of skiing and uses Baroque music to penetrate the brain's alpha waves. The following day, the students ski while listening to the same music on a cassette. The music is supposed to trigger off the 'ideal images' from the video. Sarah says she has seen 'remarkable results' with this method which particularly encourages fluid, linked turns and rhythmical skiing.

FURTHER INFORMATION

Accommodation is in chalets or hotels, arranged through **Made to Measure Holidays Ltd** 43 East Street, Chichester, West Sussex, PO19 1HX (Tel: 0243 533333). Or contact **Sarah Ferguson** 4 Coombe Court, Langton Matravers, Swanage, Dorset, BH19 3DP (Tel: 0929 425054).

Skiing from the Inside by Sarah Ferguson (Simon & Schuster £4.95)

THE INNER GAME

'**T**he Inner Game is a fascinating psychological coaching-method devised by American Timothy Gallwey in the seventies. The principles can be applied to any sport but have been known to work particularly well with skiing, tennis and golf. Gallwey first became interested in the way we interfere with our own ability to achieve and learn when, at the age of fifteen, he missed an easy volley on match point in the National Junior Tennis Championships. He decided that we have a tendency to sabotage our own learning process.

The Inner Game is all about relearning how to learn. It is rather like playing at being children again. Children are natural learners. According to psychologists, you learn more in your first five years than you can absorb in the rest of your life. Children do not think they know anything to start with. They have no pre-conceived idea of what they should be doing. It is no good bombarding a child with technicalities. When it is learning to walk no-one says 'Put the left foot two inches in front of the right, in a parallel position with the knees bent to 63 degrees...' The toddler learns by experiment and sensory feedback. They have clear minds open to discovery. Adults, however, try to force the learning process by memorising a series of individualised actions. They know exactly 'what to do', they just cannot seem to do it. This is why conventional tuition can be so frustrating.

For example, look at the typical old-fashioned ski-school set-up. The teacher stands the class in line and then gives precise verbal instructions as to how a certain manoeuvre should be done. The students wait until it is their 'turn' and then frantically try to remember what is the 'right' way to do it. If they do not 'succeed' the teacher tells them everything they did 'wrong'. Half the class will probably go away feeling angry, stupid and humiliated but determined to 'try harder' the next time. In the Inner Game there is no 'failure' or 'success', 'right' or 'wrong'. In sports psychology terms, there is no 'ego' interfering.

Peter Lightfoot of Ski Skills, who bought the European rights for Inner Skiing in 1983, calls this ego 'the little voice'. According to Lightfoot, whenever we ski we hear this 'little voice'. It seems to always want to give a running commentary. This is the voice that tells you to 'smarten up' as your friend is watching from the chair-lift. It tells you to 'bend your left leg more', 'not to be scared', that 'you do not like the slope as there are icy patches', and 'to watch out because you nearly fell back there'. A couple of seconds later and you are face down in the snow, and the voice is still chattering away telling you how 'stupid' you are, and that 'you will never be a good skier'. One of the main aims of the Inner Game is to keep this 'ego' or 'little voice' occupied so that your body has a chance to rely on sensory feedback. It is a form of 'guided discovery learning' which uses all sorts of games and fun exercises in order to release that learning block.

It certainly worked for me. I tried a day's course with Peter on the dry slope in Chatham, Kent. Before the coaching started, Peter asked us all what we wanted from the day. Some said they wanted to 'ski faster', others that they wanted to be 'less scared', 'more efficient', 'to ski a mogul field with ease' or to 'ski gracefully with fluid, linked turns'. A few of us wanted to 'ski faster and more fluently' while one woman admitted that she just wanted to 'look better'. Peter reminded us that there was no 'fail' or 'succeed' in the course and that we were simply to 'commit' ourselves to the exercises. 'Commitment' is one of the key words in the Inner Game. It is not the same as 'trying', as this implies self-doubt. Commitment is being clear about what you want (eg to ski faster and more fluently) whilst trusting that you have the potential to achieve it.

Easier said than done. In the first half-hour, I thought it was a total waste of time and money. I could not see the 'point' of the exercises. Why should I ski down the slope pretending to be a Japanese tourist sightseeing? I later discovered that this was a warm-up exercise, designed to make me focus on the 'here and now' and encourage me to trust my body was capable of skiing while I looked around me. I must admit that this exercise did nothing for me, but Peter said that even this sort of negative feedback was important as it was a way of sifting out which exercises worked for me.

The Inner Game comprises all sorts of games—it is up to the individual to choose the most suitable ones. The exercises have been devised to increase sensory awareness, so you learn through sensory feedback rather than reasoning. Although the 'sightseeing' game did not work for me, I soon discovered a couple that did . One of the simplest was 'The Knee Chase Game'. At the beginning of each turn the outside knee starts making 'advances' to the inside knee. The inside knee is 'coy' and keeps moving away just out of reach. As soon as it is about to catch up, the inside knee becomes the outside, and the game starts all over again. By focusing on the knees, my legs loosened up and started absorbing all the bumps, pressures and stresses of skiing.

It was a sci-fi game that helped improve my balance. Peter told us to pretend that we had a laser beam in the forefinger of each hand. As I turned, I fired a beam with the forefinger of my outside hand. This was aimed at the snow from the beginning of the turn to the end and was accompanied with great Star Wars sound effects. I visualised the beam hitting the snow, sizzling and leaving a blackened scorch mark in its wake. Although at the time it just seemed a silly but fun thing to do, this exercise actually increased my awareness of the 'pull' from the outside of the turns.

By the afternoon, we were all so relaxed and enjoying ourselves so much that we had stopped analysing and asking 'Why?' The man who had wanted to 'ski a mogul field with ease' was particularly delighted with the coloured balloon exercise. He was told to imagine a mogul field with a fluorescent coloured balloon in the centre of each mogul. As he turned, he burst the balloons with his sticks, making the appropriate popping noises.

But my favourite was the 'motorbike' exercise. Peter told us to choose a bike, be it a piddly little 50 cc 'putt-putt' with a shopping basket on the front, or a massive 1,000 cc job. Feeling macho, I opted for a 1,000 cc Kawasaki. I sat astride, reached for the handlebars, turned on the headlights, kicked the starter and zoomed off. As I banked around the 'corners' I aggressively changed down gear and revved up, making the obligatory 'rrrmm rrrmm' noises. I was so absorbed in being a Kawasaki that I forgot I was on skis. I could not believe how fast and smoothly I had come down the slope. Those who were not such speed-freaks were happier on a 'bicycle', or pretending they were 'cats', 'eagles' or even 'willow trees'. The woman who had wanted to 'look better' was careering down the slope pretending to be a gorilla, with an imaginary bunch of bananas under one arm, and a lot of very realistic grunting noises. Funnily enough, she did look better! She was having such fun that she was relaxed, much more balanced, and looked in control.

FURTHER INFORMATION

Daily Mail National Ski Courses are held on dry slopes across the country. Peter Lightfoot also runs six-day **Ski Skills** courses in Villars, Switzerland. Further details from Peter Lightfoot, Ski Skills Limited, Ranelagh House, 52 Binswood Avenue, Leamington Spa, Warwickshire CV32 5RX (Tel: 0926 831251).

Skiing is Only a Game by Peter Lightfoot (Fernhurst £6.95).
The Inner Game of Skiing by Timothy Gallwey and Bob Kriegel (Pan £3.95).

FIT TO SKI

Skiers are an illogical lot. Most of them spend the whole year slumped behind a desk but still expect their bodies to perform like an athlete's for that couple of weeks on the slopes. If you are unfit or very overweight, you will never get the most out of your ski holiday. After a couple of days you will be too exhausted to enjoy yourself. It can also be dangerous. Most accidents happen on the last run of the day or when you are tired. The stronger and more flexible you are, the less likely you are to have an injury. Ideally, you should have been exercising for several months before the holiday, but just two months will make a difference. You must do a minimum of three sessions per week. Although there are many specific exercises designed for skiers, you should first of all spend at least a month developing general all-round fitness. By this, I mean you need to be aerobically fit and have strong and supple muscles. If you are over 35, very overweight or have not exercised for years, you should consult your doctor before starting this or any exercise plan.

Aerobic fitness will help you cope with the high altitude and lack of oxygen. Walking is a simple, safe exercise for anyone who is out of condition. Try to walk briskly for a minimum of 30 minutes, three times a week, without stopping off to look in shop windows! Fell-walking and mountain biking are both excellent exercises for aerobic fitness and in preparation for skiing. If you already have a reasonable level of fitness, running will condition your legs for the slopes. Running downhill is particularly good for simulating the stress that skiing puts upon the lower body. Although it is an aerobic exercise, swimming is not so good in preparation for skiing, as it does not put enough stress on the body.

Many skiers make the mistake of thinking that all they need are well-conditioned quadriceps (front of thighs). As the knees are so vulnerable, you also need the support of strong hamstrings (back of thighs), abductors (outer hips and thighs) and adductors (inner thighs). Most gyms will have special weight machines for this. You should also work on your back and stomach muscles as this will give you a solid trunk support. Although skiing is predominantly a lower-body activity, do not forget to exercise the arms, particularly the triceps, as they take a lot of strain when poling. Bench dips (see below) are a good exercise for working the triceps.

In preparation for skiing you need to work on flexibility as well as muscle strength. Injuries can be prevented if the joints are protected by strong *and* supple muscles. If you think about some of the awful contortionist positions that skiers end up in, you will understand how important flexibility is! I recommend investing in a good book such as Tony Lycholat's *Stretch into Shape* (Thorsons £1.99). Try to do at least 10-15 minutes' stretching every day for a couple of months prior to your holiday. Make sure you include a calf stretch, particularly for the lower part of the calf (achilles tendon) as this will help the ankle flexion. Women, in particular, who wear high-heel shoes, often suffer from a tightness in this area. Always stretch slowly and carefully—*never* bounce.

Warm muscles are much less prone to injury, so on holiday I always do some gentle stretching in the warmth of the hotel or even in the lift station before skiing off in the morning. Stretching at the end of the day helps reduce muscle soreness.

A wobble board improves balance and strengthens the ankles. There are also special machines that simulate the action of skiing. Many gyms and sports centres, such as the YMCA, now offer special pre-ski fitness classes. If you really want to get serious you can hire a personal trainer. This costs from £15-£60 per session, but if you find a good trainer, it is well worth the investment.

A couple of months before last season, I was put through my paces by Les Yerril, an experienced trainer from Executive Health Centres (79-89 Lots Road, London SW10. Tel: 01 352 1325). He devised an excellent ski programme. Although it was hard work, I have outlined it below as it really made a remarkable difference to how I tackled those slopes. I had much more power, a wider range of movement, and greater stamina than ever before. Deep powder skiing, which I usually find exhausting in the legs, was much easier and more enjoyable. I did not experience those third-day 'skiing blues' and covered many more kilometres than in the past.

Before we started training, Les explained how skiers need to be anaerobically as well as aerobically fit. This means that you need explosive power to cope with high-intensity bursts of energy as well as cardio-respiratory efficiency for dealing with the lack of oxygen at high altitude. We started each session with a 10-minute warm up on an exercise bike (a brisk walk will do instead). The circuit alternated 30 seconds of fast sprinting on a rebounder (mini-trampoline) with 30 seconds of specific exercises to work the muscles used in skiing. If you do not have a rebounder, you can run on the spot (make sure you are wearing proper running shoes) or use a skipping rope. The important point is to keep your heart rate high, at about 80 per cent of your maximum (to ascertain your maximum deduct your age from 220). For example, if you are 25, your maximum heart rate is 195 and you should work at 80 per cent of this which is 156 beats per minute. To start with just do 20 seconds of each exercise. Correct technique is very important so do the exercises slowly until you are familiar with them. Then try to do as many repetitions as possible in the 20-30 seconds. Start with two circuits, building up to five by the end of six weeks. Do the circuits three times a week on alternate days. The only apparatus you will need is a solid box, crate or even a telephone directory, a bench, and a stop-watch or clock with a second hand.

NB: Do not attempt these circuits without supervision until you have built up a good level of fitness from general training.

THE SERIOUS SKIER'S
FITNESS CIRCUIT

1a. SPRINT. 20-30 seconds.

1b. SPOTTED DOG. 20-30 seconds.
This is like a brisk marching movement. Stand in an upright position with your left leg in front of your right. Jump your right leg forward. At the same time, swing your right arm straight up in front of you. Quickly change legs and arms.

2a. SPRINT. 20-30 seconds.

2b. DIAGONAL SIT-UPS. 20-30 seconds.
Lie on the floor with knees bent. Try to touch your right knee with your left

hand or elbow. Curl up as far as you can *without* taking the lower back off the floor (you may only curl up a couple of inches). Do not strain. Change sides. Repeat.

3a. SPRINT. 20-30 seconds.

3b. SQUATS. 20-30 seconds.
Stand with your feet parallel, slightly wider than hip-width apart. Bend down as deep as you can, taking the pressure in the legs. Do not take the legs lower than parallel to the floor. Try to keep the back straight—do not arch. Repeat.

4a. SPRINT. 20-30 seconds.

4b. PRESS-UPS. 20-30 seconds.
Lie down, back straight, stomach pulled in. Weight over shoulders. Lower yourself down to the floor, as far as possible. Half-press-ups (from the knees) for the less macho.

5a. SPRINT. 20-30 seconds.

5b. STEP-UPS. 20-30 seconds.
Right foot first, step both feet onto a bench or stair. Step down. Do 15 seconds with right leg leading, 15 with left leading.

6a. SPRINT. 20-30 seconds.

6b. TORSO RAISE. 20-30 seconds.
Lie on your stomach on the floor, legs about hip-width apart. Rest the back of your hands on your bottom. Lift your head, shoulders and chest off the floor, using your back muscles. This need not be a big movement, but make sure you do not use the muscles in your legs or buttocks. Control the movement on the way down.

7a. SPRINT. 20-30 seconds.

7b. WEDEL JUMPS. 20-30 seconds.
Stand with feet parallel to one side of a slightly raised platform such as a telephone directory (minus the cover or you may trip up on it!) or large book. Jump sideways onto the platform with your feet together, knees bent. Be careful that you land square. Jump off to the other side and then back on to the platform. Repeat.

8a. SPRINT. 20-30 seconds.

8b. BENCH-DIPS. 20-30 seconds.
Sit on a bench or strong chair. Stretch your legs out in front of you, resting on your heels. Support yourself with your hands palm-down on the bench or chair about shoulder-width apart. Bend at the elbows and dip down. Stretch arms out until they are *almost* straight. Repeat.

Finally, always remember to stretch out at the end of the session. It sounds like an awful lot of hard work, but if you discipline yourself to three one-hour sessions per week, it is not so bad. The next time you are skiing down those powder fields, I am sure you will be glad you worked so hard.